D0609255

DATE DUE

DE 16 '94			
MY 7 '99			
OC 21 '99			
DE 19 0			

DEMCO 38-296

8/30/93
Ru

The nature of perception has long been a central question in philosophy. It is of central importance not just for the philosophy of mind, but also for epistemology, metaphysics, aesthetics and the philosophy of science. This volume represents the best of the latest research on perception, with contributions from some of the leading philosophers in the area, including Christopher Peacocke, Brian O'Shaughnessy and Michael Tye. As well as discussing traditional problems, the essays also approach the topic in the light of recent research on mental content and representation. The volume represents a major statement on one of the most debated areas of philosophy.

The contents of experience

THE CONTENTS OF EXPERIENCE

Essays on perception

edited by TIM CRANE

Lecturer in Philosophy, University College London

CAMBRIDGE UNIVERSITY PRESS

Cambridge
New York   Port Chester
Melbourne   Sydney

Published by the Press Syndicate of the University of Cambridge
The Pitt Building, Trumpington Street, Cambridge CB2 1RP
40 West 20th Street, New York, NY 10011–4211, USA
10 Stamford Road, Oakleigh, Victoria 3166, Australia

First published 1992

Printed in Great Britain at the University Press, Cambridge

A catalogue record for this book is available from the British Library

Library of Congress cataloguing in publication data

The contents of experience: essays on perception/ edited by Tim Crane.
xii+275 pp. 19x11.3 cm.
Includes bibliographical references and index.
ISBN 0-521-41727-9
1. Perception (Philosophy)   2. Experience   I. Crane, Tim.
B828.45.C66   1992
121'.3--dc20   91-34041 CIP

ISBN 0 521 41727 9   hardback

TC

Contents

Preface

This volume began its life at a conference on Perception and Perceptual Content at the Centre for Philosophical Studies, King's College London, in May 1990. The essays by Thomas Baldwin, E. J. Lowe, Christopher Peacocke and Michael Tye were first presented at that conference. (The other paper presented at the conference, Richard Sorabji's 'Perceptual Content in Ancient Greek Thought', will appear in print as 'Intentionality and the Physical' in Martha Nussbaum and Amelie Rorty (eds.), *Aristotle's de Anima*, forthcoming from Oxford University Press.) J. J. Valberg's essay is an extract from his book, *The Puzzle of Experience*, forthcoming from Oxford University Press; it is reproduced here with permission. The essays by Michael Martin, Brian O'Shaughnessy, Paul Snowdon and myself were written especially for this volume.

I am very grateful to Richard Sorabji for the original suggestion that I organise the conference, to King's College London for the financial assistance, and to the participants at the conference for making it such a worthwhile and enjoyable occasion.

A number of people have helped me in bringing this volume to publication. Judith Ayling has been an understanding and astute editor from the outset. Bill Brewer and Jonathan Dancy read the typescript for Cambridge University Press, and offered many useful suggestions for improvements. Hugh Mellor generously gave his time and expertise in the preparation of the camera-ready copy. And finally, many thanks to Tabitha Jackson for her patient assistance with the final stages.

University College London
July 1991

Notes on contributors

THOMAS BALDWIN is a Lecturer in Philosophy at the University of Cambridge and a Fellow of Clare College.

TIM CRANE is a Lecturer in Philosophy at University College London.

E. J. LOWE is a Senior Lecturer in Philosophy at the University of Durham.

MICHAEL MARTIN is a Research Fellow at Christ Church Oxford.

CHRISTOPHER PEACOCKE is the Waynflete Professor of Metaphysical Philosophy at the University of Oxford and a Fellow of Magdalen College.

BRIAN O'SHAUGHNESSY was a Lecturer in Philosophy at King's College London.

PAUL SNOWDON is a Lecturer in Philosophy at the University of Oxford and a Fellow of Exeter College.

MICHAEL TYE is a Professor of Philosophy at Temple University.

J. J. VALBERG is a Senior Lecturer in Philosophy at University College London.

1 Introduction

TIM CRANE

1 The problems of perception

Anyone who studies the philosophy of perception will soon realise that there is not just one problem of perception. One reason for this is the bearing theories of perception have on other areas of philosophy. The obvious example here is the role of theories of perception in traditional epistemology – traditional accounts of the foundations of knowledge often depend upon particular conceptions of perception. And theories of perception also have an impact on general philosophy of mind, philosophy of science and aesthetics. As Strawson observed, philosophers' views on perception can often be the key to the rest of their metaphysics (Strawson 1979).

But perception is a subject of interest in its own right. Any full understanding of the mind must give a central place to perception, since it is through perception that the world meets our minds. But the nature of perceptual states is perplexing: do they give us access to the world that is in any sense 'direct'? Or is perception mediated by the awareness of some mental or nonmental intermediary? Are perceptions essentially conscious? Do they essentially involve sensation? Do they represent the world – do they have *content* – in the way beliefs or judgements do, and if so, can they be reduced to beliefs? In any case, how do they get their contents? And how do perceptions and their contents relate to the structure of the rest of the mind, especially to belief, desire and action?

It is with these questions, and others, that the essays in this volume are concerned. My aim in this introduction is to locate the essays in a very schematic history of these debates, and briefly locate the debates within other general issues in the philosophy of mind.

1

2 *Sense-data*

Much discussion of perception in the first fifty years of this century was concerned with the idea of *sense-data*. It is natural to begin with this idea.

It would be difficult to give a complete account of the idea of sense-data, if only because of the very different purposes to which philosophers have put this notion. As Baldwin and Snowdon point out in their contributions to this volume, epistemological and metaphysical issues were often inextricably bound up with issues in the philosophy of mind in the traditional dispute between Direct Realism, Indirect Realism and Phenomenalism. This makes it hard to see which problems are specifically problems about perception, and which therefore need to be solved by theories of perception (as opposed to theories of knowledge or reference).

But it is possible I think to separate two straightforward questions, both of which are questions about perception, and both of which have been answered by employing the idea of sense-data. The first is: what is the immediate object of perception? What is it that we immediately perceive when we perceive something? The second question is a question about phenomenology – about what it is like to have an experience. Does an experience of an object essentially involve the awareness of something else, apart from the way it represents the world to be – perhaps a sensation, or (on some views) a feature of a 'visual field'?

A sense-data theory would answer the first question by saying that the immediate objects of perception are sense-data, and then offer an account of their nature – of whether they are mental or nonmental, inhabiting a 3D or 2D space and so on. The arguments for this could very well be epistemological – like the sceptical arguments used by Russell to argue for sense-data in the first chapters of *The Problems of Philosophy* (1912). The theory might then say that material objects are perceived 'indirectly' in addition to sense-data (Indirect Realism), or that material objects are 'constructions' out of sense-data (Phenomenalism). Here the idea of a sense-datum is just the idea of an 'internal' object – an object whose existence depends on being perceived.

A sense-data theory would answer the second question by saying that what we are aware of in experience is some kind of phenomenological stand-in for the external object perceived. It would aim to identify this stand-in by introspection – as Moore did in a famous passage from 'A Defence of Common Sense', when he asked the reader to 'look at his right hand' to find out what he meant by 'sense-data'. Here the idea of a sense-datum is the idea of what is phenomenologically 'given' in experience – and it may be an open question whether it is an 'internal' object.[1]

Though these questions can be linked – and often are – they are logically distinct. One could hold, with Russell, that sceptical arguments require that the immediate object of perception is internal, but deny that it is necessarily phenomenologically detectable. And one could hold that there is a phenomenological 'given' in perception without holding that it is the immediate object of perception. (The 'sensational properties' of Peacocke 1983 could be seen this way.)

The distinctness of these questions helps to explain the extreme and conflicting reactions that many people have to the very idea of sense-data. The situation was well expressed by G. A. Paul:

> Some people have claimed that they are unable to find such an object, and others have claimed that they do not understand how the existence of such an object can be doubted. (Paul 1936, p. 103)

This situation can be diagnosed as follows. Those who claim they cannot find sense-data are thinking of sense-data as phenomenologically discoverable entities. They introspect – perhaps following Moore's laborious instructions – and find nothing that fits the description of sense-data. They look for the sense-data, but (in J. J. Valberg's words) 'all [they] find is the world'.[2]

But those who have arrived at sense-data through (as it may be) epistemological considerations, as Russell did in *The Problems of Philosophy*, will find these phenomenological considerations irrelevant. What drives them to sense-data is the Cartesian intuition underlying the arguments from illusion and hallucination. These arguments are supposed to show that the direct object of an experience cannot be an ordinary material object, since any experience could have just the character it has without that

---

[1]For more on 'internal objects' see J. J. Valberg's 'The puzzle of experience' (this volume), to which I am indebted.

[2]'The puzzle of experience' (this volume); see also the discussion of introspection in Michael Tye's 'Visual qualia and visual content' (this volume). It is possible to see some of J. J. Gibson's objections to sensation-based theories of perception this way. In *The Senses Considered as Perceptual Systems*, he claims that 'the theory of sensations as the basis of perception presumes that the infant at birth must see the world ... as a flat picture'. He thought that (something like) sense-data only figure in experience when we take the 'pictorial attitude' to what is seen: 'if it were possible to detect pure sensations' he writes, 'we could all be representational painters without trying' (Gibson 1968, p. 237).

object existing. So the direct object of experience can never be a material object, but must always be something else – an internal object or sense-datum. Given the power of the argument from illusion, how could anyone possibly deny that sense-data exist?[3]

In 'The puzzle of experience', J. J. Valberg argues that the simple but powerful thought underlying the argument from illusion forms the first half of a very general antinomy about the object of experience. There is a natural way of reasoning about experience that goes like this: things could be exactly as they are in my experience without the external object of the experience existing. God could have interfered with the causal chain leading to my experience by eliminating the external object, and yet he could have left my experience intact. So the external object is inessential to my experience: the object of experience must always be internal (in the sense mentioned above).

But when we actually examine our experience as it strikes us – when we are, as Valberg says, 'open' to our experience – it is simply impossible to believe that the object of experience is always internal. When we are open to our experience, we find nothing but the world itself. But this is not a *refutation* of the natural reasoning – and this is why there is an antinomy. Valberg argues that we may avoid the antinomy by denying that experience is the product of a causal process. But, as he says, this is surely wrong.

Paul Snowdon starts a stage further on in the debate, and tries to explicate what exactly it is to perceive something 'directly'. If we disentangle this task from the epistemological considerations that have motivated it in the past, it becomes rather harder than one might think to say clearly what is involved in direct perception. After rejecting various definitions, Snowdon offers his own – roughly, a subject, x, perceives an object, y, if and only if x can *demonstratively* identify y (if x were capable of thinking demonstratively at all). The direct object of perception is therefore identified as the direct object of demonstrative thought.

Notice that this definition does not prohibit Snowdon from saying that the direct object of perception is an internal object – a sense-datum, in the first sense of that term suggested above. For if we can demonstratively identify such objects – '*that* after-image is orange' – then on Snowdon's account we can directly perceive them. But Snowdon's point is not so much

---

[3] I do not deny that phenomenology is appealed to in the argument from illusion; but the phenomenology need not be that of 2D patches of colour, as Gibson and other critics of sense-data have supposed.

to rule out internal objects, but to let in external objects as the direct objects of perception. And to forge a link here with demonstrative thought surely must be on the right lines.

Valberg and Snowdon are largely concerned with the first question – what is the object of perception? – and not so much with the second – what is the phenomenological 'given'? In 'Experience and its objects' E. J. Lowe tries to answer both, and in this respect he comes closest of all our contributors to advocating a traditional sense-data theory.[4]

Lowe presents an account of what it is to see an object in terms of a relation of causal dependency between an experience and the properties of the seen object, in such a way that one is thereby enabled to form judgements about what those properties are. The definition is not circular, since the notion of experience is independently characterised, in terms of its 'qualitative' or 'sensational' features (for more on these features, see section 4 of this introduction). Lowe then argues that perception in his sense – perception that necessarily involves sensation – is necessary for belief.

The role assigned to sensation on this picture is crucial. Seeing is defined in terms of having a visual experience, and having a visual experience is defined in terms of its 'intrinsic phenomenal or qualitative character'. To put it in terms of my two original questions: Lowe answers the question about the object of perception by means of his answer to the question about phenomenology. One directly sees an object when it is appropriately related to one's visual experiences, which are defined in terms of sensations. So on Lowe's view, one cannot see without a phenomenological 'given' – that is, without sense-data, in the second sense of the term mentioned above.

It may seem odd to be paying so much attention to sense-data. After the attacks on the various conceptions of sense-data by Austin (1962), Ryle (1949) and Wittgenstein (1958), it became orthodox to mock sense-data and their kin. The sense-data theory became the archetype of the sort of gross philosophical illusion. Sense-data were supposed to be a 'myth' (Barnes 1944) and believing in them involved a 'fallacy' – so much so that in a set of essays devoted to perception published twenty years ago, F. Sibley's *Perception: a Symposium* (1971), there was hardly a mention of sense-data.

I hope some of the essays in this volume show that there is much that is worth recovering from the sense-data tradition.

---

[4]Though unlike some traditional empiricists, and unlike modern sense-datum theorists like Brian O'Shaughnessy (1980) and Frank Jackson (1977), Lowe favours a treatment of sensations as properties of visual experiences, rather than objects.

3 *Representational content and experience*

But the critics of sense-data had many powerful objections. Particularly significant is the point – raised above in connection with the phenomenology of perception – that normal experience yields information about how things are in the world, not just about 'how it is with you', considered independently of the world.

This leads to what we can call (following Baldwin[5]) the 'Informational Theory of Perception'. Given the division of labour mentioned between the epistemology and the metaphysics of perception, the role to be played by an informational theory could be conceived as follows. Perception gives us information about our environment – it enables us to form beliefs (make judgements) about how things are in our immediate surroundings. This truism is enshrined in ordinary usage: we normally believe what we see. But what we believe is *that* things are so and so – our beliefs have propositional, or intentional, or representational *content*. So if we believe *what* we see, must not our experiences have some sort of content too? Indeed, we often see that it is raining, hear that the bus is coming, and so on. Don't these idioms give support to the idea that the chief function of perception is to represent the world?

The introduction of the notion of *content* is part of a wider movement in the philosophy of mind. Since the 1970s this area of philosophy has undergone important changes, and the most significant of these is the increased interest in the notions of *mental representation* and *content*. This interest has two main sources.

First, the question of meaning in the philosophy of language – the focus of research in much 1960s and 1970s philosophy – has been seen by many as requiring answers from the philosophy of mind. To understand how language represents, we have to understand how linguistic items gain their representational powers from the states of mind of those who use them.

Second, the growth of the cognitive sciences has provided a fruitful framework in which to study the notion of representation generally. In particular, computational or information-processing models of the mental have suggested ways to approach the traditional questions of the philosophy

---

[5]'The projective theory of sensory content' (this volume). 'Representational' would be a good name for this theory, but there is then a danger of confusing the term with another name for the sense-datum theory: the Representative Theory. As Baldwin says, calling it the informational theory leaves it open whether these 'informational states' are genuinely beliefs – as in Armstrong 1968 – or some other kind of state with content – as in Millar 1991.

of mind: how does the mind get 'outside' itself and represent external objects? What is the relation between mental states and states of the brain? What is reasoning, and how can it lead to action? The computational theory of mind, as defended by philosophers such as Fodor (1987), suggests ways of answering these questions: mental processes are, literally, computations: causal sequences of token representations, processed algorithmically.

This shift of interest in the philosophy of mind generally has, as one might expect, had its effects on the philosophy of perception. One obvious effect is the now generally accepted assumption that perceptions have content (whether or not they have other features too). Moreover, recent empirical studies of vision have thrown light on the mechanisms by which this content is produced. In particular, computational theories of vision attempt to specify the computational processes that result in visual representations of the objective world.[6] These theories employ the notion of representation, and hence (implicitly) content, and one would thus expect that they might shed some light on the philosophical debates surrounding these notions. The following questions, in particular, arise: how are the specifications of content employed by computational theories related to those which the common-sense psychological vocabulary employs? And how is the upshot of these putative computations – the '3D description' – related to the phenomenology of experience – descriptions of which could be offered by any articulate perceiver? The first question is a general one in the philosophy of psychology and cognitive science; the second is specific to the philosophy of perception.

But whatever such psychological theories achieve, we still need to give an account of the phenomenology itself. And this is where the phenomena of perception once again raise their own distinctive problems. For although it is right to say, with the informational theory, that experiences have contents, this is not yet to say very much. The notion of *content* is a philosophical term of art – so without an account of perceptual content, the informational theory is a mere promise. The essays by Peacocke, Tye, Baldwin and myself offer, in very different ways, some elements of such an account. It will be useful to locate them relative to a landmark of recent philosophy of perception – chapter 1 of Christopher Peacocke's *Sense and Content* (1983). This will also help to introduce the idea of sensation.

---

[6]One psychological theory that has had an enormous impact on recent philosophy of mind is that of David Marr and his associates – see Marr 1982. For a good survey and discussion of the issues involved here, see Boden 1988, chapters 1-3.

In this chapter, Peacocke aims to clarify the distinction between the representational and sensational properties of an experience, and to argue that 'concepts of sensation are indispensable to the description of the nature of any experience' (Peacocke 1983, p. 4). Peacocke here is setting himself against the claim that the subjective character of any experience may be *completely* characterised by a description of its sensory channel (sight, touch) and its representational content. I shall call this theory – that the subjective character of any experience may be completely so characterised – a *'Pure* Informational Theory' (PIT).

Peacocke argues that any PIT is inadequate, since experiences have essentially sensational properties too. These are 'other aspect[s] – other than representational content – of what it is like to have that experience' (Peacocke 1983, p. 5). He illustrates what these other aspects are by using examples like the following. Suppose you are standing on a road, and in the distance there are two trees, one a hundred yards away, the other two hundred yards. Your experience represents them as being both the same size, but one takes up more 'space' in your visual field. Although there is a sense in which one 'seems' bigger than the other, it does not seem to *be* bigger than the other; it is not *represented* as being bigger. The PIT cannot account for this aspect of the experience, since it takes an experience to be exhausted by how it represents the world to be.

The natural way for the PIT to respond is to try and show that the features of experience that Peacocke is calling sensational are really representational. For example, it could be said that the content of the experience includes the angle subtended in the visual field by the perceived object.[7] So the nearer tree, though represented as the same size by the experience, subtends a larger visual angle, and this explains the phenomenological effect without invoking any nonrepresentational, sensational properties.

Peacocke responds to this suggestion by observing that a perceiver can have the experience of the two trees without possessing the concept of subtended angle. And he argues that this cannot be part of the representational content of an experience, because

---

[7]See Rock 1975, pp. 39, 47, 56. Michael Tye takes this line against Peacocke in 'Visual qualia and visual content' (this volume).

it is a conceptual truth that no-one can have an experience with a given representational content unless he possesses the concepts from which the content is built up. (Peacocke 1983, p. 19)

So the concept of *subtended angle* cannot be part of the representational content of the experience (of the two trees) if a perceiver can have that experience without having that concept.

Whether this is right depends on how we understand the crucial terms 'concept' and 'representational content'. But at least on the face of it, the claim seems too strong. Consider, for example, the experience of colours. As I look out of my window, I see an old brick wall and a shabby brown fence. Their surfaces have many different colours – shades of brown, grey and red. I can, at this moment, distinguish all these colours that my experience offers me, and they are *presented* or *represented* to me as different. But is it right to say that I must have *concepts* of them all in order for my experience to be like this? It is not obvious that I am able to classify all these colours – for instance, I am not confident that my experience gives me anything that will enable me to identify them if I saw them again. Whatever 'concept' means, it just seems too much to ask that I have concepts of all these shades of colour in order to perceive them.[8]

Soon after *Sense and Content* was published, Peacocke changed his mind on this issue. In 'Analogue Content' (Peacocke 1986a, p. 15) he remarks that

When we enter a room, even a room full of abstract sculptures, we perceive things in it as having particular shapes: and there is no question of this requiring that we had in advance concepts of these particular shapes.

Thus an experience can represent the world as being a certain way – it can have a representational content – without the subject having a *concept* of that way. We can call the contents of such experiences, '*nonconceptual* contents'.

In 'Analogue Content' and 'Perceptual Content' (Peacocke 1989a), Peacocke argued that experiences have nonconceptual contents, but not simply on the basis of intuitions about phenomenology, such as that

---

[8] I should mention that some philosophers would say that I must have a *demonstrative* concept – *that shade* – for each shade I perceive. Whether this is right, of course, depends on the correct theory of demonstrative content: a contentious subject.

mentioned. He argues that the contents of experience should not be individuated in terms of the Fregean criterion of difference for senses, or 'modes of presentation': if two senses, s and s^*, are identical, then the thought that *the thing presented by s = the thing presented by s^** is uninformative. It follows that if you can rationally wonder whether s^* is s, then s and s^* are different senses or modes of presentation.

But it is quite possible, Peacocke claims, for a perceiver to perceive two distinct lengths – say the lengths of a column and a window – as the same, yet to rationally wonder whether in fact they are the same length. In this case, to learn that the length of the column is identical with the length of the window would be informative. Yet *ex hypothesi*, the lengths are perceived as the same. So the ways in which the lengths are perceived are not Fregean senses or modes of presentation (Peacocke 1986a, p. 14). Since, in standard terminology, concepts are individuated (at least in part) by the Fregean criterion, then this is one route to the thesis that perceptions have nonconceptual contents (see Crane 1988a).

It is very plausible then that the representational content of experience is not individuated by the principles that individuate the contents of beliefs and other propositional attitudes. And this, in part, is what makes them nonconceptual (though as we shall see, the term is not yet wholly clear). But what more can be said about these nonconceptual contents?

In his contribution to this volume, 'Scenarios, concepts and perception', Peacocke develops a more detailed account of the nonconceptual content of perception than he gave in his earlier treatments. He argues that the content of a perceptual state is what he calls a 'scenario': roughly, a set of ways of filling out the space around a perceiver with properties, relative to an origin (e.g. the centre of the chest of a human body) and a set of axes (typically up/down, left/right, forward/back). A scenario is thus not a proposition (in any of the traditional senses) nor a Fregean Thought, but a 'spatial type', composed of properties and a notional 'volume of the real world'.

But why are these types *contents*? Peacocke's answer is that it is because they have 'correctness conditions' – conditions under which they represent the world correctly. The scenario is the type which includes all and only those ways of filling out the space around the perceiver that are consistent with the correctness of the experience. What it is for the content to be correct, in the case of a scenario, is for the properties that make it up to be *instantiated*; for the type to be tokened.

This might be put more precisely as follows. Consider the actual space around the perceiver, and assume an origin and axes (as in the scenario), and call this a *scene*. The experience is then correct if this scene is a token of the spatial type that makes up the scenario.

Peacocke's conception of the correctness condition for scenarios may be usefully compared with the idea of truth conditions for propositions, conceived of as sets of possible worlds. (This is an analogy only: Peacocke's theory should not be seen as a version of possible worlds semantics for perceptual content.) Consider the set of worlds S that is the proposition expressed by the sentence 'Pigs fly'. S contains all those worlds in which pigs fly. For the belief that pigs fly to be correct, the actual world must be in that set. The correctness of the belief's content therefore amounts to the actual world's membership of S. Similarly, the correctness of an experience's scenario content amounts to the scene's membership of the set of ways of filling out the space around the perceiver that constitutes the scenario.

The notion of a scenario content should be seen as a development of, rather than an alternative to, the proposals of the earlier papers mentioned. For example, Peacocke had earlier used the idea of a 'matching profile' to capture part of the fine-grained content of an experience. A matching profile for a perception of an object is 'a set of directions: a given direction is in the set if and only if it is not discriminably outside the apparent direction of the [object]' (Peacocke 1986a, p. 4). This notion has clear affinities with one aspect of a scenario (though the scenario, of course, includes more than just directions). Also, the idea that the content of experience is 'analogue' – i.e. capable of having any value on a given dimension of variation, such as hue, shape, size etc. – is preserved in the scenario account.[9]

The main point of continuity, however, is that scenario content is *nonconceptual* content: it is specified in terms of concepts that the perceiver need not possess. One question that immediately arises is what precisely is meant by 'nonconceptual content'. This notion is not altogether clear. What is it, for instance, about the notion of a *concept* that permits me to have an experience which represents some property without my needing to have a concept of that property? Although different accounts of the nonconceptual content of perception have been offered, no one has satisfactorily said what

---

[9]For this, and for the sense in which scenarios capture the 'unit-free' character of perceptual content, see Peacocke, 'Scenarios, concepts and perception' (this volume) section 2(b).

it is about these contents which makes them nonconceptual. In my contribution to this collection I sketch my own answer to this question.

The problem of defining nonconceptual content partly derives from the fact that the notion of a concept is often taken for granted without being clearly defined. I focus on the inferential role of concepts, and argue that the sort of inferential structure that imposes conceptual structure in the case of belief is missing in the case of perception. (There is a sense, for instance, in which perceptions are not *revisable* in the way that conceptual states such as beliefs are.) We can thus give a clear definition of, and make a plausible case for, the claim that perceptions have nonconceptual contents, independently of swapping intuitions about what 'concept' means.

However, if there are nonconceptual contents, then the example of size in the visual field will not turn out to be an example of a sensational property *simply because* the subject needn't possess the concept *subtended angle*. This alone doesn't mean that it isn't a case of a sensational property; but it does mean that Peacocke's 1983 response to the PIT's claim (that the property is covertly representational) will not do. If we are still convinced that there is an important distinction between representational and sensational properties of experiences, we will need some other way of dividing the one from the other.

4   Sensations and 'qualia'

So what are the sensational features of experience? Many philosophers accept that in addition to their representational features, perceptions have sensational features too. An experience of a red thing does not simply represent red, but has sensational properties, or 'qualia', distinctive of such experiences. They may differ as to how this is to be understood, but they all would at least agree with Peacocke's remark in *Sense and Content* that 'concepts of sensation are indispensable to the description of the nature of any experience' (Peacocke 1983, p. 4). And as we saw in section 2, this is one of the guiding insights behind the sense-data theory.

In 'Visual qualia and visual content', Michael Tye disputes this consensus. He thus aligns himself with those philosophers who hold a PIT (see, e.g., Harman 1989). Though such a radical PIT is certainly controversial, one of the benefits of Tye's paper is to show how weak many arguments for qualia are – and, indeed, to force those who believe in them to say exactly why they do.

Tye's strategy is to argue that, in the case of vision at least, everything that we want to explain by using the notion of qualia can be explained in terms of representational content. He shows this by scrutinising the standard arguments for qualia – from introspection, hallucination, after-images, the irreducibility of 'what it's like', blindsight (see below), the inverted spectrum, Twin Earth and examples like Peacocke's – and he argues that they can all be accounted for in terms of content. The burden of argument, he claims, now lies with the defender of qualia.

One motivation for Tye's thesis is that qualia are supposed to be a problem for a general functionalist philosophy of mind – a theory that treats mental states as defined by their characteristic causal roles. Since it seems obvious that the characteristic causal roles of qualia-involving states can stay constant over imagined changes in qualia (the 'inverted spectrum'), it is generally felt that functionalism cannot account for qualia. And since the orthodoxy has it that functionalism is the main hope for a physicalist or 'naturalist' reduction of mentality, the existence and nature of qualia is a question that affects the most general issues in the philosophy of mind.

But even if the friends of qualia can show, against Tye and Harman, that there are such features of experience, they should not rest content there. For maybe qualia – or sensational features generally – are not *essential* to experience. Maybe even if they exist, they play no role in experience.

The task for the friends of qualia is made more pressing by the discovery of some extraordinary pathological cases: the 'blindsight' phenomena studied by L. Weiskrantz and his colleagues (Weiskrantz et al. 1974). They investigated the abilities of certain people who had a lesion in part of their striate (visual) cortex and who had previously been considered totally blind in that part of the visual field corresponding to the damaged part of the cortex. With some of these patients, Weiskrantz could

> demonstrate that they have a very good capacity to discriminate, to detect visual events in this 'blind' area, to locate them in space, to make judgements about the orientation of lines and gratings, to detect the onset and termination of movement and even to do simple pattern discriminations.

But the patients claimed not to be seeing anything:

> there is no acknowledgement of any such capacity at all: subjects say when questioned that they are just guessing and playing the experimenter's game when he insists on their saying 'yes' or 'no'

when a light is flashed briefly on their 'blind' field, or insists on their saying whether a grating is horizontally oriented or non-horizontally oriented ... none of which they can actually see. (Weiskrantz 1987, p. 314)

What this case suggests, on the face of it, is that a perceiver can make certain behavioural responses to information received without having (in the relevant part of the visual field) any sensations. Does this demonstrate that sensations are not essential to perception? If it did, then many theories of perception would be doomed.[10]

This is not an easy question to answer, since the interpretation of blindsight cases is still controversial.[11] But there seem to be at least three options. (1) Blindsighters are perceiving unconsciously – in the sense of 'receiving information' – but without genuinely believing anything. (2) They are perceiving *and* believing, without consciousness of either. (3) They are not perceiving at all.[12] To accept the first or second of these options requires us to drop the claim that perception essentially involves sensation. To accept the third requires us to deny that receiving information through the eyes, that is eventually acted upon, is perception. None of these seem particularly happy solutions.

We could, of course, deny that sensations have any crucial role to play in perception. We could instead take the notion of *delivering information* as more fundamental to perception than that of *sensation*. Lowe (this volume) criticises current computational theories of vision for this emphasis. In the final section of his paper he argues that such theories are guilty of treating experience, with all its sensational features, as 'effectively just epiphenomenal' – in Pinker's words, experience is a mere 'correlate of ... processing' (Pinker 1985 p. 38).

Here Lowe is in opposition to some of our other contributors: Peacocke for instance claims that his account of the nonconceptual content of perception gives 'a natural framework' in which to give the contents of the $2\frac{1}{2}$D sketches of Marr's theory; and he suggests that states with such

---

[10]This is why Lowe (this volume) recognises that blindsight is one of the biggest threats to his position, and deals with it in the radical way he does.

[11]It is, for instance, important to pay attention to the subject's own reports: 'under some conditions the patient will say that he does not see but has a "feeling" that something is there, and sometimes he may even achieve a strange kind of visual experience' (Weiskrantz 1987, p. 314).

[12]For the first option, see Evans 1982; for the second, see Mellor 1977, p. 98; and for the third, see E. J. Lowe, 'Experience and its objects' (this volume).

contents 'seem particularly well-suited to receive a realisation in a connectionist network'. And we have already seen how Tye's theory is designed to provide a framework for the objective scientific investigation of vision, once free of troublesome 'subjective' qualia. (Tye's only objection to Pinker's phrase would be that it supposes that these 'correlates' *exist*.)

But suppose we acknowledge that there are visual sensations, and that they have not been properly accounted for by *any* theory of perception: the whole story about vision has yet to be told. Then perhaps some of Lowe's views are not so far away from some of the claims of contemporary cognitive science. In particular, consider his useful discussion of the part played by projective geometry in forming representations of 3D objects. Lowe speaks here of a 'working knowledge' or an 'implicit grasp' of this geometry, which manifests itself in our dispositions to make reliable judgements of how things would look from various angles and in various orientations. This working knowledge does not have to be consciously articulated, and it is not represented in us in 'the form in which [it] would be expressed in textbooks of analytic geometry'. On this characterisation, then, the working knowledge bears some resemblance to the sort of unconscious or 'tacit' knowledge to which some theories in cognitive science appeal.

But this still doesn't answer our original question about sensations: what are they doing in perception? In most traditional accounts of perception, visual sensations were construed as inhabiting a 'visual field' – a (normally) two-dimensional array of sensations with an intrinsically spatial articulation.[13] It was supposed by many that once the sense-datum theory went, the visual field went too (see Hamlyn 1957). That this is not so is argued forcefully in Michael Martin's and Thomas Baldwin's contributions to this volume. But if they are right, then how should a theory of perception understand the visual field, and (in particular) how should it understand the visual field's relation to the representational or informational role of perception?

The traditional sense-datum theory held that the construction of experience of the objective world out of the visual field is performed by cognition. (This is explicit in Lowe's account too – it is 'working *knowledge*' of the laws of perspective that constructs experience from the

---

[13]Not all philosophers who believe in a visual field think of it as 2D. See e.g. Price 1932; Jackson 1977; Peacocke 1983, chapter 1; Martin, 'Sight and touch' (this volume) and Baldwin, 'The projective theory of sensory content' (this volume).

retinal image.) All that perception delivers is a visual field, which although spatially articulated, *underdetermines* the spatial articulation of the visual world. Thought is needed to bridge the gap.

For those unhappy with this picture, as we have seen, an informational theory seemed the natural response – perception delivers information directly about the world, about how things are, not just about how it is (initially, in any case) with you. But this can lead to the denial of the original datum that there does seem to be a visual field, with conscious sensory properties, and these do seem to have *something* to do with perception. So how is the spatial articulation of the visual field related to the spatial structure of the perceived world?

Baldwin offers an answer to this in his ambitious paper, 'The projective theory of sensory content'. He sees his projective theory as a synthesis of the three currently dominant theories of perception: the informational, representative and adverbial theories. Baldwin finds deficiencies in each of these theories, and attempts to salvage the attractive aspects of each theory in his synthesis. In particular, he intends his theory both to answer our question about the visual field and to explain the role of sensory qualia in perception. The latter task is done by showing how, in fact, they have 'primitive intentionality' – they form a more basic level of representation than the full propositional content of perception. The idea is, essentially, that in vision, the qualitative properties of the sensory field are 'projected' out into actual physical space, and do not inhabit a private mental space. Qualia thus, in effect, constitute a primitive kind of representation of physical space.

Baldwin points out that something like a projective theory of *touch* was put forward by Brian O'Shaughnessy in *The Will* (1980). The relations between sight and touch are taken up in Michael Martin's paper. What are the differences and similarities between these senses? Both senses give us information about the spatial properties of our environment, but what makes them different senses? Martin claims that the difference lies in the *spatial* structure of visual and tactile experience. In vision, we experience objects as having spatial locations, but also as having apparent spatial *relations* to other experienced objects. And these relations are perceived simultaneously with the locations. That, according to Martin, is what underpins the concept of the visual field.

But touch is different: in touch, we do not experience the spatial locations and relations of objects simultaneously. Rather, touch is dependent on body-sense and proprioception in a way that prohibits the postulation of a 'tactile field' of the same kind as that which occurs in vision. In touch, Martin claims, we employ our body-sense to investigate the spatial properties of objects around us. In bringing my body into contact with other things, I use it as a sort of 'template' to figure out its (egocentric) location, size and shape – and this is the basis of touch.

In addition to this account of touch, Martin also has a more general, methodological point to make. The differences between the senses have not been widely discussed by philosophers, who often just discuss the case of vision and assume that their conclusions can be generalised across the other senses. In the final part of his paper, Martin provides reasons for thinking that this traditional approach is mistaken. The considerations about the radically different spatial structure of visual and spatial perception – and the consequent differences in sensory 'fields' involved – lead him to question whether there can be a *general* philosophical account of perception for all the senses, or whether each sense has to be given a separate account.

Martin, Baldwin and Peacocke all acknowledge the influence of Brian O'Shaughnessy on their essays. It is appropriate, therefore, that this collection should end with a major new contribution by O'Shaughnessy, 'The diversity and unity of action and perception'. In this wide-ranging paper, O'Shaughnessy investigates the reasons for believing in the 'intuition' that while action comes from 'within', perception comes from 'without'. If this is so, how can such antithetical mental phenomena be so closely entwined? O'Shaughnessy claims that while we do not perceive our own actions – or, better, our own 'willings' – we do, in a very important sense, will our own perceivings. So there is actually something wrong with the initial intuition. In a detailed discussion of the mental action of *listening* (nicely complementary to Martin's discussion of touch) O'Shaughnessy shows how perception can be both brought from within – as a result of the will to listen – and constituted from without – by the heard sound. Perception and action are not as antithetical as it might initially be supposed.[14]

[14]I am grateful to Bill Brewer and Christopher Peacocke for very useful comments on an earlier version of this introduction. Special thanks are due to Mike Martin for detailed comments on this introduction, and for many valuable discussions about perception.

2 The puzzle of experience

J. J. VALBERG

I – REASONING ABOUT OUR EXPERIENCE[1]

The puzzle I shall discuss in this paper is a puzzle about the object of experience – or perhaps I should say, about the object of visual experience, since that is what I shall exclusively consider.

1

The puzzle takes the form of a conflict, or antinomy. Roughly, there are two ways we can reflect on our experience. We can reason about our experience, or we can be (as I shall say) *open* to it – to how things are within our experience. If we follow a certain line of reasoning about our experience, we are led to the conclusion that the object of experience is not part of the world, an external object. However, if we are open to our experience, all we find is the world. So, if we reflect in the right ways, we get pulled first in one direction and then another. This, very simply, is the puzzle. And indeed, it is a simple puzzle.

I shall call the reasoning which enters into the puzzle, the reasoning whose conclusion is one half of the antinomy, 'the problematic reasoning'. In the first half of the paper I shall set out the problematic reasoning. In the second half I shall complete the puzzle by presenting the other half of the antinomy.[2]

---

[1] © J. J. Valberg 1992. This paper is an extract, with some alterations, from the first two chapters of a book, *The Puzzle of Experience*, by the same author, to be published by Oxford University Press (referred to below as 'Valberg forthcoming'). It is reproduced here with permission. Places where material has been cut from the original are indicated thus: '{...}'.

[2] In Valberg forthcoming I consider ways we might try to escape from the antinomy.

It always helps to think in terms of a specific case. Consider the book lying on the table in front of me. The problematic reasoning purports to show that the book is not, and could not be, the object of my experience. More generally, it purports to show that no external object, no part of the world, could ever be an object of experience. The object of experience is, rather, always an internal object.

What do I mean by the 'object of my experience'? And what is an 'external object (part of the world)' versus an 'internal object'? Let me attempt to give a preliminary account of these ideas – so that I can use them in the reasoning. I'll begin with the idea of an 'object of experience'.

2

One way to explain an idea in philosophy is by reference to examples. It would therefore be helpful if we could give a clear-cut example of an object of experience. It would be particularly helpful if we could say what the object of my experience is right now. The trouble, of course, is that in the present context, where we are about to consider and evaluate an argument to the effect that the object of experience is never an external object, what counts as the object of my experience is up for grabs. Thus we cannot say, by way of explaining the idea, that the object of my experience right now is the book in front of me, or the table on which the book is sitting, since if the problematic reasoning is correct such things are not the objects of my experience. What we need, obviously, is an explanation of 'object of experience' in general terms, terms which leave open whether the book and the table are, or could be, objects of my experience.

By an 'object of experience' we shall mean something *present* in experience. Thus one might express the conclusion of the problematic reasoning by saying that what is present in experience (present to us, present) is always an internal object; that external objects are never actually present to us. For example, the book and the table are not present in my experience. But we may now be asked to explain what we mean by 'present in experience', 'present to us', etc.

Presence (in experience) connotes a kind of direct or immediate availability. An object which is present is right *there*, available to us. This makes it tempting to view presence as the reciprocal of Russell's idea of acquaintance (Russell 1912). That is, an object with which we are (in Russell's sense) acquainted is present in experience; and an object which is present in experience is one with which we are acquainted.

But in fact this is only partly correct, since whereas both ideas imply immediate availability, Russell's idea is meant to be more general. Objects of acquaintance, for Russell, may be either 'particulars' or 'universals'. However, as we shall understand this, experiential presence is limited to the category of particulars. What is present, directly available, is always a particular. In the tradition, particulars are temporal (but not, necessarily, spatial) objects. That is, they are objects of which it makes sense to ask how long they have existed or lasted, when they began to exist, and so on. (Such questions cannot be asked of universals.) Hence, the second point to make about presence in experience is that an object present in experience is always a temporal object. This leads directly to a third point, viz. the intimate connection between experiential and temporal presence. We have a strong inclination to view objects that are present in experience as being, at that very time, existent: if something is *now* present, it *now* exists. This inclination to encompass the object within the temporal present does not extend to reference, or thought in general. There is no problem about referring to, or thinking of, objects which no longer exist. But our inclination is to say that such things cannot be present in experience, that they cannot *now be* objects of experience. {...}

3

But what is the 'direct availability' that objects have in virtue of being present? I do not know how to define it. Perhaps we can catch hold of the idea indirectly, by relating the idea of presence to ideas wherein we can discern a requirement for the kind of availability that we are trying to catch hold of. (What this involves will become clear as we proceed.) We shall mention two such ideas: that of 'focusing on' or 'fixing on' or 'picking out' an object; and that of 'demonstrative reference' to an object.

Consider first the idea of focusing on (fixing on, picking out) an object. It should be clear that focusing on an object is not the same thing as the object's being present to us. For, unlike the latter, it is something we can be said to 'do'. Thus it may take effort, and we may tire of it. And we may choose, or decide, to focus on a particular object, or intend to focus on it. And in certain circumstances we may be said to try and fail. In short, focusing, in contrast to presence, is subject to the will. We can do things (turn our heads, remove obstacles, etc.) which bring it about that a certain object is present to us. But in itself, the presence of an object is just a fact, not something we 'do'. Moreover, given the presence of an object, it may or may not be the case that we focus on it. This is a basic experiential possibility: objects can be present to us without our actually focusing on them.

But (here is the important point) we cannot focus on something *unless* it is present in our experience: the fact of an object's presence is what makes the object available for us to focus on. Thus an object which is present in experience is, in virtue of that fact, available (then and there) for us to focus on or pick out. Suppose, e.g., we allow that the book on the table is something that might be present in my experience. If it is present, it may or may not be the case that I am focusing on the book. If however I am focusing on the book, it must be present to me. Its presence in my experience is what makes the book available for me to focus on (pick out).

The other idea we mentioned above was that of demonstrative reference. Perhaps in this case we can proceed by means of examples. Think of the distinctive kind of singular reference that we would make by the expression 'this', were we to use that expression in an assertive utterance of a sentence like 'this feels hot' or 'this looks blue'. Here we have, I assume, uncontroversial examples of demonstrative reference. Taking our cue from such examples, it should be evident that demonstrative reference is closely connected with focusing on, or picking out, an object. But it also seems evident that, despite both being things we can be said to 'do', making a demonstrative reference and focusing on something are not one and the same. Like all reference, and in contrast to focusing, demonstrative reference involves the use of symbols. Hence, to focus on an object is not thereby to make a demonstrative reference to it.

The connection is the other way around: when we make a demonstrative reference to something we thereby focus on (pick out) the object to which we refer. So (this is the point that interests us) just as we can think of the fact of an object's presence as what makes the object available for us to focus on, or pick out, we can think of this fact as what makes the object available for demonstrative reference (what makes the object demonstratively available). A fact of presence, we might say, is what creates the possibility of focusing, and what creates the possibility of focusing creates the possibility of demonstrative reference.

4

To sum things up, by an 'object of experience' we shall mean something present in experience: something which is right *there*, available for us to pick out or focus on, and refer to demonstratively. Further, we shall understand that the 'something' which is thus available falls in the philosophical category of 'particulars', and is hence a temporal object; and that we are inclined to suppose that it exists at the time when it is available (present).{...}

This is what we shall mean by 'object of experience' in stating the problematic reasoning, the reasoning which purports to show that the object of experience is always an internal object. The explanation leaves open (I hope) whether the object of experience is external or internal. I realise, of course, that it relies on ideas – presence, demonstrative reference, focusing (picking out), and so on – which raise difficulties of their own, ideas which philosophers have spent a great deal of time worrying about and trying to clarify. But I think that when we actually state the problematic reasoning (§§5-8), and actually use these ideas, the attendant difficulties will just not matter. That is, they will not prevent us from following the reasoning, and getting involved in the puzzle.

We also mentioned, as requiring preliminary explanation, the idea of an 'external object (part of the world)', and the contrasting idea of an 'internal object'.

The first point to make is that 'object' in 'external (internal) object' does not mean what it means in 'object of experience'. Thus for 'object' in 'external object' we may substitute 'thing'. The same substitution in 'object of experience' not only fails to preserve meaning; it fails to make sense. As far I can see, there is in this case no expression which can be substituted for 'object' so as to preserve the meaning of the whole expression. To provide an expression with (roughly) the same meaning as 'object of experience' we must replace the complex phrase 'object of' (e.g., by 'something present in').

An 'external object (thing)' or 'part of the world' is an object which has an existence that is independent of presence in experience. Let us assume that the book is now present in my experience. Clearly, the existence of the book is independent of this fact. The fact of its existence and the fact of its presence are distinct facts. Thus although the book is present to me, it need not have been. (It might have been in the drawer right now.) The book, then, is (as we say) part of the world.

An 'internal object' is an object whose existence is not independent of its presence in experience. In this case, existence and presence collapse into one. The fact of existence and the fact of presence are the same fact.

Examples of internal objects are after-images and hallucinatory objects (Macbeth's dagger). Thus we do not regard such objects as part of the world.

The book on my table is an example of what philosophers call a 'material (physical) object'. It fills out space. Material objects are external, part of the world. What about immaterial objects (if there are any)? These too (if there are any) will be part of the world. The world will contain, as Descartes thought, two radically different categories of objects and phenomena. Some will consist of matter, others of spirit. Whether Descartes was right in this view is not relevant here. What is relevant is simply that internal objects are *not im*material objects. (An after-image is not like a ghost.) Internal objects are neither material nor immaterial. They do not consist of anything. They are not part of the world.

It will be useful to introduce the convention of emphasising the demonstrative 'this' to show that what we thereby refer to is something present in experience (demonstratively available). If I assert, '*this* is a book', the use of the emphatic 'this' shows that it is of something present in my experience that I assert that it is a book. Suppose that I am hallucinating. Then, since what is present in my experience is not a book but an internal object, my assertion is false (or at least not true). Or suppose I am uncertain whether I am hallucinating or not. Then (in the manner of Macbeth) I might ask, 'Is *this* a book?' Here the use of the emphatic demonstrative shows that my uncertainty is uncertainty about the status of what is present in my experience. I am uncertain whether what is present in my experience is or is not a book, an external thing. I am uncertain, i.e., whether the object present to me is part of the world or an internal object.

We said that in the case of internal objects, there is no distinction between existence and presence. There are places in Berkeley's philosophy where he seems to say that this is true with respect to everything (apart from God, and individual minds). To exist is to be present (or as Berkeley puts it, 'to be is to be perceived'). I mention Berkeley's view not because we are going to take it seriously, but simply to place the contrast we are trying to explain in a familiar historical perspective. In Berkeley's kind of Idealism, we might say, there are no external objects; all objects are internal.

Perhaps we should point out, finally, that the conclusion of the problematic reasoning is not Berkeley's Idealism. It is not that whatever exists exists only in so far as it is present, but that whatever is present exists only in so far as it is present.

5

We shall turn now to the problematic reasoning. Most moderately well-educated people in our culture are acquainted, in an outline way, with the basic facts about the transmission and reflection of light, the nature of the eye, and the process in the nervous system and brain which results or culminates in visual experience. We know (roughly) that light is reflected from physical objects and travels in straight lines; that it impinges on the eye and produces an image on the retina; that this excites the optic nerve; that a 'message' travels from the optic nerve to the visual cortex of the brain; and that finally, as the upshot of this chain of events, visual experience occurs. Such facts are part of everyday knowledge. Some people may not have heard about the visual cortex, but everyone (unless there is something wrong with him) knows he has eyes and a brain, and that light is reflected from objects and then travels to his eyes, and that because of what happens after that – because, i.e., of what happens in the nervous system and brain – he then has the kind of experience he has, that his experience is the way it is.

I shall call this 'the causal picture of experience'. The causal picture of experience is not what philosophers sometimes call 'the causal theory of perception'. The latter attempts to state the conditions which are logically (conceptually) necessary and sufficient for its being true of an external thing X that X is, for a subject S, an object of experience. With this aim, the causal theory asserts about the broad fact that there is a causal connection between X and S's experience, that that fact is a logically necessary condition of X being an object of experience for S. The causal picture, on the other hand, does not make any assertion *about* the broad fact of the causal connection. It simply *asserts* the fact, or rather, a set of more or less detailed facts (drawn from physics and physiology etc.) which make up the broad fact.

The causal picture of experience is not in any sense a 'philosophical' view or theory. Someone might be very interested in the causal picture of experience, perhaps spend his whole working life doing research and experiments on this or that aspect of it, and never raise a philosophical question about it. Yet the causal picture of experience is the starting point of the problematic reasoning, and the problematic reasoning is most certainly philosophical.

Simply contemplating (or learning about, or adding to) the causal picture of experience is not philosophical. Things get philosophical when we begin to reflect on certain possibilities implicit in the picture. The present activity in my brain, I remind myself, is the causal outcome of a chain of events involving light rays being reflected from a certain object – the book on the table, say. In turn, the activity in my brain is causally responsible for my experience being as it now is. But, I reflect, in that case (here is where philosophy begins to creep in) if the activity in my brain could somehow be held constant, the earlier parts of the causal chain might be eliminated without this having any effect on my experience. If the activity in my brain were to continue as it is, my experience would continue as it is. It would continue as it is even if, say, something interfered with the light rays being reflected to my eyes; or even if the object reflecting the light rays were miraculously annihilated. God (it is handy to bring God in here) might arrange such a situation. God might eliminate the object while maintaining the activity in my visual cortex. Isn't that a coherent state of affairs, something God might bring about? And if the activity in my brain were to continue on as it is, my experience would also continue on as it is. It would continue to run along perfectly smoothly despite the fact that the external object would no longer be there.

This possibility, which is implicit in our everyday knowledge about the causal dependence of experience on objects and processes in the world (implicit, i.e., in the causal picture of experience), might be summed up by saying that the external thing, the object in the world, is 'potentially irrelevant' to experience.

Now once we grasp this possibility, this idea about the potential irrelevance of the external object, we are squarely in the realm of philosophy. We didn't begin there (we began outside philosophy, in the realm of everyday knowledge) – but that is where we are now. Thus we might think of the problematic reasoning, so far, as divided into two stages: an extra-philosophical stage, where we simply contemplate the causal picture of experience (the facts of physics and physiology, plus the fact that the process culminates in experience); and a transitional stage (transitional into philosophy), where we bring to light a possibility implicit in this picture. Of course, we have not yet reached the conclusion of the reasoning. To say that God might maintain the activity in my brain as it is while eliminating the book, and thus that my experience might continue as it is in the absence of the book, is not yet to say that, as things are, the book is not the object of my experience. (To say that, potentially, the book is irrelevant to my experience is not to say that, actually, it is not present in my experience.) This requires a further argument, a third stage in our reasoning. But before getting into that, I think we should pause to reflect on the second stage.

6

Suppose I now assert:

> (G) Were God to eliminate the book but ensure that the activity in (the visual part of) my brain remains the same, my experience would remain the same.

There are two points I wish to make in regard to (G). First, what I assert in asserting (G) is *true*. Or rather, it is *in some sense* true. For (and this is the second point) it is not entirely clear what I am asserting. In particular, it is not clear what exactly it is that I assert would remain the same were the activity in my brain to remain the same; i.e., what I mean when I assert that *my experience* would remain the same.

The activity in my brain is something which is going on now, up here in my head. Is that the sort of thing I mean in (G) by 'my experience' – something which is going on in my head (or if not in my head, somewhere else)? We must put this question aside for the time being.[3]

Instead, let us approach our question by remarking that if 'my experience' remains the same, I would not be able to *tell* that the book has been eliminated. But this needs to be qualified, since, as we have described it, the situation does not preclude my reaching out and discovering that the book is not there. Perhaps we should say that I would not be able to tell the book is not there 'by using my eyes'. Imagine my eyes are wired up in such a manner that, if I keep them open and look at the book, when the book is removed I get a distinctive sensation in my finger tips (like an alarm going off when jewellery is removed from a case). But in that event I would not be using my eyes 'in the normal way'. What is the 'normal way'? One has his eyes open and looks in the appropriate direction. But that is what I do when my eyes are wired up and I get the sensation in my fingers.

---

[3]See section VI of Valberg forthcoming.

We could play around with this for a while yet, but sooner or later it must be clear that the qualification we are looking for involves a restriction not on my *means* of telling, but on my *basis* for telling whether the book is there or not. And the necessary restriction would seem to be this, that, in so far as I rely on how things are *in my (visual) experience*, I would not be able to tell whether the book is there or not. That is, were God to intervene in the manner described, then, in so far as my basis for telling is restricted to how things are in my experience, I would not be able to tell that the book is no longer there.

This suggests that the first step toward understanding what it is in (G) that I assert would remain the same, is to recognise that 'my experience' in (G) is elliptical for something like 'how things are in (within) my experience'. Experience is a subject-matter about which we can say how things are *within* it, a subject-matter which can be described 'internally'. It is, in this respect, something like a story. We can say what happens *in* a story. (A story can be described 'internally'.) If someone did not appreciate this, he would not know what we mean by a 'story'. Similarly, if someone did not appreciate that experience can be described internally, he would not know what we mean in this context by 'experience'. By the same token, it must be evident that in the sense in which this is true of my experience, or a story, the activity in my brain cannot be described internally. Yet, it seems, the activity in my brain stands back-to-back in a causal chain with my experience. That is to say, the activity in my brain is causally responsible for how things are within my experience. (The activity in my brain has effects which reach, so to speak, right inside my experience.)

To make our meaning explicit, then, let us replace (G) by

(G*) Were God to eliminate the book but ensure that the activity in (the visual part of) my brain remains the same, how things are in my experience would remain the same.

But of course this is still unclear, or vague. What is it that is supposed to remain the same when, as we say, 'things would remain the same in my experience'? What do we include here under the vague word 'things'? For *what*, exactly, is the activity in my brain supposed to be causally responsible?

This brings us to a delicate point in our reflections. When we say of something that it is present in my experience, that it is the object of my experience, surely this is relevant to how things are within my experience.

Are we then to include such facts among the 'things' that, were God to intervene in the manner described, would remain the same in my experience? Are we (in other words) to say that if God intervened in this way the object of my experience would remain the same? It may seem that, under the guise of clarification, we are being asked to settle the outcome of the problematic reasoning. For if the answer to the question is 'Yes', if we say that the object of my experience would remain the same, then, since by hypothesis God eliminates the book, it follows immediately that the book is not the object of my experience. And this would be held to beg the issue which the reasoning is supposed to decide.

I think the best way to proceed is without, just yet, giving any further clarifications. Let us simply acknowledge the vagueness in (G*) and carry on with the third stage of the reasoning. All we are now committed to, then, is that were God to intervene etc. it would *in some sense* be true that 'how things are in my experience would remain the same'. In what sense? This will emerge in the course of the reasoning – by things that we assert, or imply, along the way. Of course, such a procedure carries no guarantee against mistakes: an unwarranted assumption may slip in, there may be an equivocation, and so on. But we can worry about that later on, once we have before us the completed reasoning and the consequent puzzle.

It should be emphasized that we are not claiming to have identified an innocent or neutral sense in which it is true that, were God to ensure that the activity in my brain remains the same, 'things would remain the same in my experience'. On the contrary, we are explicitly leaving open the sense in which this is true. But it is in some sense true; this much we are not leaving open.

7

The third stage of the problematic reasoning is, like Descartes' First Meditation, essentially first-person singular. I will reason for my own case, and the reader is invited to do the same – substituting his 'I' for mine.

The first step is simply to pick out or focus on something present in my experience. So I will do that. I will focus on *this*. This what? At any other time I would have said 'this book', but I am not allowed to say that now. I can say that my eyes are directed toward the book, or that I am looking at the book; but I cannot say (or imply) that the book is present in my experience. Let us say simply that I am focused on whatever it is that is present now in my experience while I am looking at the book. Certainly there is, right now, *something* present in my experience.

It seems equally certain that, whatever this 'something' is, I can remain focused on it for a little while. That is the next step. Having focused on something, I remain focused on it for a little while (about five seconds should be enough). I do this very closely, never letting my attention waver, always staying right with the object on which I am focused.

All this goes smoothly. There are no breaks, no gaps. I focus on something, on *this* object (whatever it is that is present when I look at the book), and stay with it, with *this* object, for a brief period of time. Now, in so far as focusing is something I 'do', it would seem that I have just given a description of what I have done in the last five seconds of my history. I focused on whatever object it was that was present in my experience when I looked at the book, and I remained carefully focused on that object for five seconds.

Let us now reflect on this bit of my history in light of the potential irrelevance of the book. Consider the hypothesis that half way through the last five seconds God intervened in the manner we have described: God eliminated the book but maintained the activity in my brain just as it was when the book was there. When the book was there, it reflected light to my eyes; this process eventuated in the activity in my visual cortex. The hypothesis is that half way through the last five seconds, God (as it were) took over from the book, having eliminated it, and directly maintained the activity in my brain.

The point about the hypothesis is that it seems to be compatible with how things have been in my experience during the last five seconds. Well, how have 'things' been within my experience? Think back to the beginning of the five second interval. I contemplate the spread of objects within my experience. I focus on one – *this* one, the one which if I weren't playing this little game I would say is the book. I stay carefully focused on the object. (Five seconds pass.) So (looking back now) here is how 'things' have been within my experience for the last five seconds: *this* object has been present. Thus, the hypothesis of God's intervention is compatible with the fact that *this* object, the object on which I have been focused, has been present in my experience for the last five seconds. Had God intervened, the book would have ceased to exist two and a half seconds ago (this is part of the hypothesis). Had God intervened, the activity in my brain for the whole of the last five seconds would have continued just as it has (this is also part of the hypothesis). Had the activity in my brain continued as it has, within my experience things would have been as they have been (this follows from the causal picture of experience). How have 'things' been? Once again, *this* object has remained present to me. So, *this* object is such that had God eliminated the book, it would have remained (just as it has remained) present to me.

I am pedantically labouring things here because it will make it easier to spot a mistake (if there is one) when we come to examine the reasoning.[4] At this stage, I will simply enter the following observation. The crux of the matter is the assertion that had God intervened, *this* object would have remained (just as it has remained) present within my experience. What is my basis for such an assertion? The thing to bear in mind is that my basis is not anything I discern in or about the object that I mentally latch on to. I cannot, by inspecting the object, discern that it has the property of being able to survive the elimination of the book. My basis for the assertion has nothing at all to do, really, with what I can *discern* in my experience. It lies entirely in what I *know* about the relation between what I can discern and the activity of my brain. My basis, you might say, is entirely indirect: it lies not in what is available 'out front' but in what I know about the relation between what is thus available and the things that are happening 'back here'.

To repeat, had God intervened, *this* object would have remained (just as it has remained) present in my experience. There would have been a rupture in the world; a certain external object, a book, would have suddenly ceased to exist. This would have been evident to an onlooker, but for *me*, within *my* experience, things would have flowed smoothly on, without a ripple or a flicker – just as they have done. That is to say, *this* object would have been (just as it has been) present to me for the whole of the last five seconds.

What follows? It follows (plainly) that *this* object, the object on which I have actually been focused for the last five seconds, is not the book. For my having been focused on *this* object is compatible with the supposition of God's intervention, and it is part of the supposition that, half way through the last five seconds, God eliminated the book. So the object on which I have actually been focused, *this* object, is such that it might have survived the elimination of the book. So it cannot be the book.

---

[4]See sections IV-VIII of Valberg forthcoming.

Once we have settled on the appropriate internal description of my experience, the logic of the argument is simple (whether it is legitimate to apply such an argument in the present context remains to be seen). Suppose I pick up a book and hold it in my hand for five seconds. I now consider a certain Book X of which it is true that, had God eliminated Book X in the last five seconds I would still be holding on to the book I actually have in my hand. Would it not follow that the book in my hand is not Book X? Of course, the two cases are in some respects very different. Thus, whereas arguing in this way for the non-identity of Book X and the book now in my hand seems like a pointless rigmarole, precisely some such roundabout argument seems necessary if we are to accept the non-identity of the book on the table and the object now present in my experience. Formally, though, the reasoning is in both cases the same.

Now clearly (thinking again just about the experiential case), the reasoning is not restricted to the object on which I am now focused and the book in front of me on the table. It works for *any* object in the world and *any* object on which I might focus. Any object in the world, any external thing (apart from my brain), is such that God could eliminate it compatibly with keeping the activity in my brain the same. Hence, for any object on which I choose to focus and any external object (apart from my brain), I can, it seems, show by such reasoning that the object on which I am focused cannot be identified with the external object, since I can show by the reasoning that the object on which I am focused could survive the elimination of the external object.

We might put this in the form of a reductio – a reductio of the assumption that the object present in my experience is an object in the world. I focus on the something (anything) now present in my experience, and assume that it is an external object, part of the world. On this assumption, I can (by our reasoning) prove that the following two propositions might both be true of the object on which I am focused: (i) that for the whole of a certain interval of time *t* I remain focused on this object; (ii) that part of the way through *t* the object in question ceases to exist. Since anything present in my experience is available for me to focus on, such a reductio can be constructed for anything present in my experience. With respect to anything present in my experience, then, I can reduce to absurdity the assumption that it is part of the world.

8

If the object present in my experience is never part of the world, never an object whose existence is independent of the fact of its presence, what is it? What else could it be but an object whose existence is *not* independent of its presence in my experience, an internal object? For example, *this* object, the object present in my experience right now when I look at the book, is not an external object (part of the world). It is not a book, but an internal object. Generally, what is present in my experience, what is available for me to focus on and refer to demonstratively, is never part of the world but always an internal object; it is always (in the traditional jargon) a 'sense-datum'.

Some comments are in order here. On Russell's use of the term 'sense-data', which has become pretty much standard, sense-data are by definition internal objects. Russell's procedure is first to argue that the objects of experience are internal, and then (in effect) to dub these internal objects 'sense-data' (see Russell 1912, chapter 1). But Russell's usage is not universal. Moore, unlike Russell, seems to define the term 'sense-data' ('sensibles') in such a way as to leave it open whether sense-data are external or internal. In effect, 'sense-datum' for Moore means: that which is present in experience (object of experience). The question for Moore, about which he can never quite make up his mind, is whether sense-data (thus defined) are or are not external things (or parts of external things).[5] Thus, if we express the conclusion of the problematic reasoning by saying that the object of experience is always a 'sense-datum', this would accord better with Russell's use of the term than Moore's.

The world itself, then, although I can talk and think about it, is never demonstratively available to me. Something (an internal object, a sense-datum) always 'gets in the way'.

We have now reached the conclusion of the problematic reasoning. There are (as the reader will no doubt have judged for himself) aspects of the reasoning which might be questioned, and which in any case need to be examined very carefully. {...} But I believe that the more carefully we examine the reasoning, the more powerful it will seem. However that may be, for the remainder of this paper, we shall assume that the reasoning is correct, and hence that its conclusion has been established.

---

[5]See, e.g., Moore 1962, chapter 2; Moore 1905; Moore 1913; and Moore 1918. The last three are reprinted in Moore 1922.

9

The puzzle, as we said, is an antinomy. Half of the antinomy is a piece of reasoning (the problematic reasoning). Let me try now to complete the antinomy, to evoke a sense of the conflict. I will present the conflict in the same way it presents itself to me.

I start by going through the problematic reasoning. I conclude that *this* object, the object present to me when I look at the book, cannot be the book. It cannot be the book because, by the reasoning, it could survive the elimination of the book. So it, *this* object, is an internal object, something which exists only in so far as it is present in my experience. But wait, *this* object is a *book*. The object present to me when I look at the book on the table *is* the book on the table. There is nothing else there. Now I realise that, as a contribution to philosophy, thoughts of this sort may appear a trifle quick and simple-minded; yet it is precisely such thoughts that come over me when I reach the conclusion of the problematic reasoning. And when they come over me, they totally overcome the conclusion. The reasoning establishes that *this* is an internal object. But it isn't. It, *this* object, is a book.

What gives me the right to say this? Where is the argument? There is no argument. The arguments are all on the other side. I do not *conclude* that the object present to me is a book, but that is all I find – the book. That is to say, the book is all I find when I am *open* to how things are in my experience. If I reflect on the fact that how things are now in my experience is the causal product of what is happening now in my brain, I seem driven to the conclusion that the object present in my experience when I look at the book, *this* object, is not the book. Yet if I am then open to (how things are in) my experience, all I find is the book (see Bouwsma 1942, p. 218).

Thus the antinomy is a function of the fact that my experience is a subject-matter on which I can reflect in two very different ways. There is the indirect way: reasoning, in terms of the causal picture of experience, to a conclusion about how things are in my experience. And the direct way: simply being open to how things are in my experience.

10

{...} But what is it to be 'open' to our experience? We remarked in §5 that the problematic reasoning becomes philosophical at the point where we begin to discern, and reflect on, a certain possibility implicit in the causal picture of experience. Being open to our experience is totally unlike this kind of reflection; but in its own way it is philosophical.

At least this is true. We do not *go around in life* being open to our experience. (In fact, we could go through life without ever being open to our experience.) Imagine I am in a cigar store. I pick up what looks like a box of cigars on the counter. To my surprise, it is not a box of cigars. 'This is a book.' We can agree, I take it, that this thought would not be philosophical. In particular, it would not involve my being open to my experience. But the content of the thought seems to be the same as that of the thought which I have when, in our example, I am open to my experience. What then is the difference? What is the difference between my cigar store thought and that with which I overthrow my belief in the conclusion of the problematic reasoning?

The cigar store thought, it may be said, involves a different implicit contrast. Thus while both thoughts have the same manifest content, they have different implicit contents. In the philosophical case, my thought is 'this is a book (not an internal object)'. In the cigar store case, my thought is 'this is a book (not a cigar box)'. The implicit contrast in the philosophical case is that between external and internal (I implicitly use the concept *internal object*); in the everyday case the implicit contrast is between two everyday kinds of external objects.

But surely in everyday life we sometimes bring to bear the external/internal contrast. This happens (implicitly) when, e.g., we discover that we have suffered an illusion, or have been hallucinating. Suppose someone has set up for my benefit an elaborate trick. He first gives me a substance which causes me to have incredibly vivid hallucinations of isolated objects. For example, under the influence of the substance there is in my experience something which, if I did not know better, I would say is a book in front of me on the table; knowing what I know, I judge the object of my experience to be internal. The substance wears off. I am given what I assume to be more of the substance but is in fact a placebo. Once again, within my experience there is something which in normal circumstances I would automatically have taken to be a book, but which in present circumstances I take to be an internal object. I am confounded. 'This is a book (not an internal object).' Here again, in thinking this thought I am not being philosophical. More specifically, I am not being open to my experience. Yet the thought has the same implicit content as the thought that I have when, in the philosophical case, I am open to my experience.

The difference would seem to lie not in the content of the thoughts but in the basis or grounds of the thought, or belief, which they overthrow ('this is an internal object'). In the everyday case, the overthrown thought is based on certain beliefs I have about my condition or situation on a particular occasion. In the philosophical case, the overthrown thought is based on a piece of philosophical reasoning which applies *no matter what* my condition or situation is.

We might say that although the content is the same, the antecedents of the thoughts are different in the two cases. We can be open to our experience only *in the face of* philosophical reasoning (such as the problematic reasoning). It turns out, then, that being 'philosophical' in one sense (that of being open to our experience) presupposes being 'philosophical' in the other (that of discerning and reflecting on possibilities implicit in everyday facts).

There is a further point. When the thought '*this* is a book (not an internal object)' is philosophical, it is not just the antecedents that are different; the consequents are different as well. Thus when (in the everyday case) I have been convinced that I am hallucinating, I am genuinely surprised to discover that the object present to me is a book (not an internal object). Am I surprised in the philosophical case – i.e., when I am open to my experience? Having reasoned to the conclusion that this is an internal object, am I (when I open up to my experience) surprised that this is a book? No, nothing like surprise comes into it. It does not matter how convinced I am of the reasoning, I am still not surprised.

I am not surprised because, in becoming open to how things are in my experience, I learn nothing new – I gain no new information. But this seems to entail that when I become open etc. I *already know* that the object present to me is a book. (I already know that all I shall 'find' is the book.) It may not be clear how we are to make sense of this. If I already know the object present to me is a book, what is it that gets *overthrown* when I open up to my experience? To put it another way, if I already know that what is present to me is the book, how can it be true that I am convinced by the reasoning? If I already know the object present to me is a book, I believe the object present to me is a book. But to be convinced by the reasoning is to believe that the object present to me is not a book, that it is an internal object.

11

Perhaps it will be said, in order to account for the fact that in becoming open to (how things are in) my experience I learn nothing new, we do not have to suppose that I already know the object present in my experience is a book. We may simply note that when I become open etc., within my experience things look exactly as they looked before, when I was convinced by the reasoning. Now it is true (or so we may assume) that when I become open to my experience nothing looks any different. But there is something else we must take into account, viz., that when I become open to my experience, what I find is the *book*. If what I find is the book, and if in finding the book I learn nothing new, it follows (doesn't it?) that I already know it is the book that is present in my experience. In that case, once again, how can it be true that I am convinced by the problematic reasoning?

It occurs to me that there is a way in which both of these propositions can be true: that I am convinced by the reasoning, and thus believe that the object present to me is not the book but an internal object; and that (at the same time) I know that the object present in my experience is the book, part of the world. When I am convinced by the reasoning I believe the conclusion despite the fact that it conflicts with what I know. I know that the conclusion cannot be accepted, but the reasoning sets up a barrier. That is, I am not open to what I know. When I become open to (how things are in) my experience, I become open to what I already know. In fact, it is a condition of 'becoming open' in this way that we already have knowledge of that to which we become open.

The basic possibility here is familiar to everyone. It is a possibility whose reality we experience, first-hand, in bad faith or self-deception. Thus we live with it all the time. In bad faith we are not open to (we are closed off from) something we know: we are 'not open' in the way of being not open which requires our knowing that to which we are not open. In so far as we are not open to what we know, we can believe something that is inconsistent with what we know. Bad faith is a possibility for everyday consciousness. My idea (for what it is worth) is that there is a corresponding possibility for philosophical consciousness.[6] We can – this is

---

[6]The problem philosophers usually discuss in connection with bad faith is whether, and how, we might characterise bad faith in a way that both does justice to what it is and yet

a possibility – reason ourselves into a state of being closed off from what we know. A belief held in bad faith is overthrown by our becoming open to what we know. Something like this happens (I think) when, having reached the conclusion of the problematic reasoning, I open up to my experience. I become open to what I know (that the object present to me is a book) and thus my belief in the conclusion of the reasoning is overthrown.

The idea, it must be stressed, is not that the philosophical case is a case of bad faith. (Bad faith may indeed enter into philosophising, just as philosophy may be seized upon for purposes of bad faith; but these are further complications.) The idea is that both cases contain the same core phenomenon of being closed off from what we know; hence both contain the same possibility of becoming open to what we know. But surrounding this common core, there are differences.

First, there is a difference in *why* we become closed off from what we know. In bad faith it is because what we know bothers or disturbs us; it is something we want not to be true. In the philosophical case, what gets in the way is not wanting but reasoning, thinking. (It is not that I want the object present in my experience not to be a book, but that I have an argument which forces me to the conclusion that it is not a book.)

In both cases, notice, it is essential to the possibility of becoming open that there is something to overcome (the difference lies in what it is that must be overcome). Thus, as we remarked in §10, we can be open to our experience only *in the face of* philosophical reasoning. Similarly, we can be honest with ourselves only *in the face of* there being something which we want not to be true. (This is why it is not 'easy' to be honest with ourselves.) The point is not, of course, that if we know something to be true but do not want it not to be true, we are therefore dishonest with ourselves (in bad faith); rather, we are neither honest nor dishonest with ourselves. The same sort of point holds in the philosophical case. Where there is nothing (no reasoning, no arguments) to overcome, we can be neither open to, nor closed off from, how things are in our experience. We simply move through life, dealing with the world. In a real sense, only a philosopher can

---

avoids the appearance of paradox. I know of no such characterisation, but this is not a topic I shall pursue. My thoughts on bad faith, such as they are, were influenced by reading (several years ago) an unpublished manuscript on self-deception and rationality by Eugene Valberg.

be 'open' to his experience. (Only someone who has a motive for being dishonest with himself, can be honest with himself.)

The second difference is this. If what we must overcome in the case of bad faith is wanting something not to be true, it follows directly (and trivially) that bad faith reflects back on the subject in a way that potentially distinguishes him from other subjects: there is something that *he* (but not necessarily others) wants not to be true. The philosophical case does not, in any comparable way, reflect back on the subject. We have, to be sure, often conducted our discussion in terms of how things are in *my* experience. But the 'my' here is impersonal. Thus it is of no interest or importance that what I find when I am open to my experience is a particular book, or a book at all, or that it is on a table in front of me, JV. I take the things present to me to be representative objects of experience. And when I speak of how things are in 'my' experience, I put myself forward as a representative subject of experience. I view myself, you might say, as speaking on behalf of all such subjects.

The last two differences we shall mention are the most important. When I am honest with myself, when I become open to what I know, the belief which thereby gets overthrown is seen for what it is – a false belief. This characterisation does not seem quite strong enough for the way I view the conclusion of the problematic reasoning, when I become open to how things are in my experience. That *this* is not a book (but an internal object) strikes me not just as false but absurd. On the other hand, it has a kind of support which a belief overthrown by self-honesty does not have. In bad faith I close myself off from what I know because I want what I know to be true *not* to be true. In the philosophical case, however, I close myself off because of an argument, the problematic reasoning. What happens to this reasoning, when I become open to my experience? Nothing. The reasoning stands. I need only work through it once again to become, once again, convinced of the conclusion. (Remember, being open to my experience does nothing to refute the reasoning.) Of course, in the case of bad faith, I may still want the relevant truth not to be a truth, and this may tempt me back into bad faith; but there are no arguments here (except those which themselves rest on bad faith). Thus while I may slide back into bad faith, there is no antinomy.

12

When having reached the conclusion of the problematic reasoning I become open to my experience, everything looks as before. And in a real sense, everything *is* as before. I already knew the object present to me was a book. Nothing has changed, yet things are different: I am open to what I already knew. The conclusion of the reasoning is overthrown.

It might be of interest to compare this transition with what Hume says concerning the results of his philosophical reasoning about experience. Hume too speaks of a transition in which the conclusion of his reasoning gets overthrown; but it is a different kind of transition.[7] He says the reasoning loses its hold on him, when he leaves off philosophising and re-enters the stream of everyday life. He does not see how to refute the reasoning but,

> nature herself suffices to that purpose, and cures me of this philosophical melancholy and delirium, either by relaxing this bent of mind, or by some avocation, and lively impression of my senses, which obliterate all these chimeras. I dine, I play a game of backgammon. (Hume 1739, book I, part IV, section VII)

Thus it seems that even while he has the reasoning clearly in view, Hume knows that it will not be long before nature and everyday life reassert their hold over him, and the deliverances of his philosophical reflections fall by the wayside.

This is certainly the fate of a lot of philosophising. We return to everyday life and our best philosophical conclusions drop out of sight. But this is not the kind of transition that occurs when, having reached the conclusion of the problematic reasoning, I am open to my experience. Here the transition is not something which occurs when I cease philosophising; it is *part of* the philosophical exercise. It occurs not when I have forgotten about the problematic reasoning but (as we said) in the face of the reasoning. What happens? My attitude toward the conclusion of the reasoning undergoes a radical reversal. Before, the conclusion seemed true; now it seems absurd. It is like a change of aspect, except for one thing – there is no surprise.

---

[7]See Valberg forthcoming, section VIII.

We may draw some further comparisons. Consider plain old-fashioned Naive Realism. When I become open to my experience I think, '*this* is a book (not an internal object)'. But that is just what the Naive Realist thinks. Where is the difference?

The Naive Realist thinks just what I think; but the Naive Realist (we are, admittedly, in the land of philosophical mythology now) does not see the force of, and hence is not convinced by, the problematic reasoning (or any other philosophical argument with the same conclusion). In his case there is lacking, then, something essential for the possibility of being open to his experience. There is nothing for him to overcome. Thus he cannot be open to (how things are in) his experience. The point is not that he is closed off from his experience. He is, and can be, neither one nor the other: neither open to, nor closed off from, his experience. (Recall the case of self-honesty. It is only with respect to something we know to be true but do not want to be true that we can be honest or dishonest with ourselves.)

But (on second thoughts) this is not quite right. It gives us no way of distinguishing the Naive Realist from the Man In The Street (ourselves when we are not being philosophical, when we are just moving through life). Perhaps we might think of the Naive Realist as someone who pits the view, or the attitude, of the Man In The Street against the conclusion of the problematic reasoning, but without seeing the force of the reasoning. In so far as he concerns himself with the reasoning, he distinguishes himself from the Man In The Street. He is a philosopher. In so far as he fails to see the force of the reasoning (which is not the same as seeing a mistake in the reasoning), he is not in a position to be open to his experience, in which respect he resembles the Man In The Street. There is something of each in the Naive Realist, of the philosopher and the Man In The Street.

To round things out, let us bring on stage a philosopher who claims to accept unequivocally the conclusion of the problematic reasoning (an Indirect Realist, or a Representationalist). This person does not question the existence of external objects, but (since he accepts the conclusion of the reasoning) maintains that such objects are never present to us. And that's that. In contrast to the Naive Realist (and The Man In The Street), a philosopher who holds such a view has the possibility of being open to his experience. But he simply isn't. Like the man who remains in bad faith, he could be open to what he knows – but he isn't.

13

In one of Heidegger's lectures published under the title *What is Called Thinking* (Heidegger 1968) there is a place where he seems to point to the same funny kind of transition that we have been trying to convey, the transition that occurs when in the face of philosophical argument we become open to how things are in our experience. In the present and following three sub-sections, I shall quote and comment on certain bits of the lecture in question. This will provide us with the occasion to restate, and solidify our grasp of, the antinomy.

The passage which chiefly concerns us occurs in the fourth lecture of Part I. For our purposes, the lecture starts to get interesting when Heidegger takes up the question of 'what it is to form an idea'.[8] Philosophers, he says, disagree about how to answer the question. So he turns to science: in the first instance, psychology. From the standpoint of science, 'ideas' are the product of what goes on in the organisms that we are (in our nervous systems and brains). The trouble, according to Heidegger, is that science never makes clear 'what it is to which ideas are attributed and referred'; what or who the 'subject' is supposed to be. Is it the living organism, the soul, consciousness? Science does not tell us, Heidegger says, even though in themselves 'the scientific findings are correct' (Heidegger 1968, p. 41). So he tries a different standpoint, a different kind of reflection:

> We stand outside of science. Instead we stand before a tree in bloom, for example – and the tree stands before us. The tree faces us. The tree and we meet one another, as the tree stands there and we stand face to face with it ... This face-to-face meeting is not, then, one of these 'ideas' buzzing about in our heads. Let us stop here for a moment, as we would to catch our breath before and after a leap. For that is what we *are* now, men who have leapt, out of the familiar realm of science and even, as we shall see, out of the realm of philosophy. And where have we leapt? Perhaps into an abyss? No! Rather, onto some firm soil. Some? No! But on that soil upon which we live and die, if we are honest with ourselves. A curious, indeed

[8]This question keeps recurring in the lectures as part of a developing theme. I am, for my own ends, focusing on a central but nonetheless fairly narrow cross-section of this development, which cannot purport to represent Heidegger's thought in these lectures as a whole.

unearthly thing that we must first leap onto the soil on which we really stand. (Heidegger 1968, p. 41)

Now we don't have to take all of this on board; but it should not be hard to see a similarity between our transition and the 'leap' which Heidegger describes.

Let us first observe the direction of the 'leap', viz., away from science, and from the kind of philosophical reflection that is based on 'scientific findings'. It is, Heidegger thinks, on the basis of such 'findings' that we are led in philosophy to conclude that what is presented within experience are 'ideas buzzing about in our heads'. The problematic reasoning would seem to be a prime example of this kind of philosophical reflection (an example of what Heidegger at one point refers to as 'scientific philosophy' – Heidegger 1968, p. 43), although the conclusion of the reasoning is not that the objects of experience are 'in our heads' but that they exist only within experience, that they are internal objects. Perhaps we may regard the talk of 'ideas buzzing about in our heads' as a metaphor or image for internal objects. Thus you could say that this is where we end up when we reason about experience on the basis of science: we end up 'inside our heads', cut off from the world. How (if I may continue in this vein) are we to get 'outside our heads' again, back in touch with the world?

This is where the business of the 'leap' comes in – because it is *not* going to be further 'scientific findings', or further reasoning on the basis of such 'findings', that enables us to break through the veil of 'ideas'. We have to 'leap', Heidegger says, 'out of the familiar realm of science and even ... philosophy'. We make the 'leap' and then we are 'face-to-face' with the tree, with a part of the world.

Notice how Heidegger characterizes the 'leap'. It is not onto new ground, but 'onto the soil on which we really stand'. In other words, we 'leap' and arrive where we *already are*. He's right. The transition from scientifically based reflection on our experience (like the problematic reasoning) to the attitude in which we simply open up to our experience, this is like a 'leap'. A 'leap' that brings us back out in the world: back to where we are and were all along. It is, as he observes, a 'curious' thing. We have to 'leap' to get to where we are.

14

With all this 'leaping' around, however, we are in danger of forgetting something: the problematic reasoning. It hasn't gone away. When I open up to my experience I 'stand outside science', hence 'outside' the purview of the problematic reasoning. I make the 'leap' and meet the world 'face-to-face'. Very well. But what about the reasoning? We have said nothing which undermines or threatens it in any way. If I now return to the reasoning, each of the steps seems to be in order. The conclusion seems inevitable, and for a moment I am actually convinced. When I make the 'leap', I leave the reasoning behind. But I leave it untouched, intact – even though I now dismiss the conclusion. By itself, the 'leap' cannot solve our puzzle. Just the opposite. The more impressed we are by the simple yet radical way in which it turns things around, the more puzzling the puzzle will seem.

Bear in mind, Heidegger does not wish to question 'the scientific findings'. And who would (except, of course, within science)? Yet it is implicit in 'the scientific findings' that how things are within my experience is the upshot of a chain of events in the world, ultimately events in my brain. Imagine I have just made the 'leap' – '*this* is the book (not an internal object)'. What should stop me from having the thought that the book, *this* object, is now reflecting light to my eyes, that the light is stimulating the optic nerve, that signals are being sent from my optic nerve to the visual part of my brain? All this (I remind myself) is happening right now, as I look at the book. Moreover, what is happening right now in my brain is responsible for how things are in my experience.

You see of course what is going on. When in the face of the reasoning I open up to my experience (when I make the 'leap'), what confronts me is the book: *this* object is the book. But I can now use the same object, the book, to illustrate the reasoning, and thus reach the conclusion that *this* object is *not* the book. It is as if I had entered an impossible space. I move in a perfect circle, but somehow end up at a point other than where I began. I ought to end up where I started, out in the world; but I end up stopping short of the world, with an internal object. And obviously, the process can continue. Thus if I once again open up to my experience, the same sort of radical displacement occurs. Once again, I am faced by the book. But once again, I am free to use the book to illustrate the reasoning.[9] For what are we supposed to do, place a *ban* on the reasoning?

---

[9] {...} We find an expression of our puzzle in some of Moore's writings. At one point in 'A Reply to my Critics', after rehearsing an argument to the effect that the object of experience is never an external thing, he admits that the conclusion he has reached is incompatible with the view which, in the previous section of the 'Reply', he had said he was 'strongly inclined' to accept (that the object of experience generally is an external thing). He continues: 'And this is the truth. I am strongly inclined to take both of these incompatible

15

Actually, this seems to be Heidegger's position. At a later point in the lecture quoted above, he says:

> When we think through what this is, that a tree in bloom presents itself to us so that we can come and stand face-to-face with it, the thing that matters first and foremost, and finally, is not to drop the tree in bloom, but for once let it stand where it stands. Why do we say 'finally'? Because to this day, thought has never let the tree stand where it stands. (Heidegger 1968, p. 44)

So this is what I should do with the book: I should let it 'stand where it stands'. Heidegger's point would be that after I make the 'leap' and am 'face-to-face' with the book, that is where I should stop. My mistake is in not stopping, in letting myself get seduced back into the reasoning.

The question is why we should consider this a mistake. The reasoning begins 'outside philosophy', with the causal picture of experience – the 'scientific findings'. Is this a mistake? (Is there something wrong with the thought that the book, *this* object, is currently reflecting light to my eyes? Or that my optic nerve is being stimulated, etc.?) But implicit in the causal picture of experience is the possibility that enables us to prove the world is not what is present in experience.

Perhaps we are passing over the mistake without realizing it. Perhaps the mistake lies, after all, in the causal picture of experience. This (I suspect; what follows is to a large extent guesswork) is Heidegger's view. Of course he would not say that all of the picture is mistaken (the pure physics and physiology are safe); just the last part, where we represent the activity in the brain as causally responsible for how things are in our experience. Let us reflect on this suggestion.

The mistake, we might say, occurs not in science itself but where we attempt to draw within science the subject-matter each of us calls 'my experience'. If someone put forward the hypothesis that it is not the activity of the brain but the esophagus that determines how things are in experience, we would say he is mistaken. This is not the kind of mistake that interests

---

views. I am completely puzzled about the matter, and only wish I could see any way of settling it' (Moore 1942, pp. 658–659). The last sentence quoted expresses my own situation in this regard.

Heidegger. What Heidegger would say is mistaken is the idea that experience, i.e., how things are in experience, can in the first place be viewed as causally determined. The point, really, is about the concept of causation. Heidegger (I am guessing) sees a certain limit to the legitimate use of this concept. Roughly, we may apply it to how things are in the world but not to how things are in our experience.

This needs to be understood in the right way. Suppose acid is spilled on the book in front of me, causing it to change colour. If the book is present in my experience, to cause such a change might be described as 'causing a change in how things are in my experience'. We may assume that Heidegger would not object to this way of speaking. Here our use of the expression 'how things are in my experience' is not primary but derivative. Let me try to explain this.

In the acid case, the change in (as we put it) 'how things are in my experience' is caused by causing a change in an object, the book, which happens to be present in my experience. Strictly speaking, it is the change in the *book* which is caused by the earlier events; it is only because the book happens to be present in my experience that we are entitled to speak of a change in 'how things are in my experience'. In such a case, our use of this expression is derivative. If however we say that the activity in my brain causes a change in 'how things are in my experience', here our use of the expression is primary. For in this case, clearly, it is not because a change is caused *in an object* which happens to be present in my experience that we are entitled to speak of a change being caused in 'how things are in my experience'. In what is the change caused? The only way to answer this, it seems, is to say that the change is caused in 'my experience', i.e., in 'how things are in my experience'. Henceforth, when we speak of an illegitimate application of the concept of causation to experience, this is what we shall mean: we shall mean an application of the concept which requires us to use the expression 'how things are in my experience' in a primary (versus derivative) way.

At the end of §9 we remarked that the antinomy is a function of the fact that experience is a subject-matter on which we can reflect in two very different ways. We can reason about it in terms of the causal picture of experience; and we can be open to it. But what if the causal picture of experience involves an illegitimate use of the concept of causation? What if we therefore reject the idea of a *causal* picture of *experience*? Then the problematic reasoning will barely get off the ground. It will get cut off before it reaches the second stage, i.e., before it has a chance to become philosophical (see §5). Thus we will not be able to 'reason' ourselves into a state of being closed off from what we know; we will not get drawn into the impossible circle.

16

To give it a name (and without too much regard for historical accuracy), I shall call this 'Heidegger's solution' of the puzzle. Let me try to characterize the general conception of things which underlies the solution.

The starting point is that we find the world present in experience (we find ourselves 'face-to-face' with the world). There are many ways we deal with, and think about, the world. One of these is the 'scientific' way. When we think about the world scientifically, the aim is to understand why things happen as they do. The use of the concept of causation is essential to this aim. To think scientifically is to think in causal terms, and we can think scientifically about anything in the world. Now we ourselves, we human beings, are included in the world. Thus we can think scientifically about ourselves, and about how we are related to other things in the world. This scientific study of ourselves in the world will include the study of our sense organs and nervous systems and brains; it will include the ways these things are affected by things outside our bodies, and the ways they affect each other. But there is one thing our scientific study of ourselves cannot (legitimately) include, viz., our experience – that from 'within' which we are faced by the world, the object of our scientific studies. Here we have a subject-matter that stands outside science, outside the scope of the concept of causation. If we do not heed this limit, if (in particular) we try to think of how things are in our experience as the causal product of what is happening in our brains, we shall be driven to a conclusion that conflicts with our starting point: the fact that we find ourselves faced by the world.

With one exception, I adhere to all of this. The exception is, I cannot persuade myself that it is illegitimate to extend the concept of causation to how things are in my experience. So I see no way of avoiding the conflict. What reason (apart from the conflict, the puzzle) is there for setting this limit on our use of the concept?

True, we cannot raise causal questions everywhere. In mathematics and logic, e.g., such questions are generally conceded to be out of place. The traditional explanation (this will be good enough) is that in these cases our subject-matter is abstract, hence atemporal. Hence the concept of causation cannot get a foothold. But it seems obvious that, whatever exactly we are talking about, when we talk about 'how things are in experience' we are not talking about something atemporal. On the contrary, it seems obvious that we are talking about something which can change (which is in fact changing all the time) and is thus temporal. If there is a reason for placing experience outside the scope of causation, it does not lie with considerations of temporality.

What may incline us to embrace Heidegger's solution is the very real sense of difficulty, and obscurity, that we may feel (or ought to feel) with the thought that the activity of the brain is causally responsible for 'how things are in experience'. This thought touches a sensitive area at the heart of the puzzle. It would be a kind of relief to discover a limit which the thought transgresses, and on this basis to dismiss the thought as illegitimate.

But, to repeat, I cannot persuade myself that there is such a limit. What is happening right now in my brain (I tell myself) is causally responsible for things being as they are right now in my experience. Is this not a meaningful proposition? Don't we all, each for himself, believe such propositions to be (in some sense) true? Don't we all *know them* to be true? Don't I (we) know that if I were to take certain drugs, or if someone were to tinker in the right way with my brain, things would be different in my experience? More radically, don't I (we) know that if the activity of my brain were to cease, there would be nothing in my experience (there would be NOTHING, no such thing as 'my experience')? These seem to be legitimate causal propositions – causal propositions about experience. They must be legitimate, because they are *true*. Everyone (including Heidegger) believes, everyone knows, they are true. Here, as I see it, is where all the argument comes to rest. However difficult and philosophically troublesome causal propositions about experience may be, the (hard, undeniable) fact is that certain propositions of this kind are true. It is true that how things are now in my experience is the result of what is happening now in my brain. If this proposition is true, we cannot solve the antinomy by excluding it as illegitimate.

3 *How to interpret 'direct perception'*

PAUL SNOWDON

1 *Introduction*

Perception, or what we think of as perception, is studied by both science and philosophy. That there are significant theoretical questions about perception which scientific study of it leaves unanswered is something which needs both a justification to be accepted and an explanation as to how it is possible. I shall not attempt to provide either justification or explanation here, but it is to be expected, surely, that the existence of philosophical questions (if they do exist) derives, in part at least, from the existence of intelligible and interesting categories, in terms of which we wish to frame questions about perception, which questions, because of some feature of those categories, do not belong to science in the ordinary sense.[1]

This is one reason why it has an importance which cannot be exaggerated to ensure that the categories in terms of which philosophers incline to discuss perception are in good conceptual order. One sort of philosophical question can be called *compositional*: what are the ingredients in, what elements compose, the perceptual relation?[2] The sound categories that are needed here are those for candidate ingredients. However, a second sort of traditional question has been, or appears to have been, *functional*. Do our perceptual experiences enable us to *directly perceive external objects*? How should we interpret that question? Is *it* in good conceptual order?

---

[1] If this vague suggestion has any plausibility, it will apply only to *some* of the categories which philosophers employ in thinking about perception. Other categories, such as those of sensation and inference, have been shared by both disciplines. With these a different account of the relation between science and philosophy must be given.

[2] Candidates for assessment as ingredients are beliefs, sensations, sense-data, causal links, inferences, concepts, behavioural dispositions, content-bearing quasi-judgements, and so on.

In the present paper I wish to develop an interpretation of this second question which, as I see it, is one of the issues that have been at the heart of the traditional debate. My concern here is, primarily, to state and clarify the interpretation, and I cannot say as much as needs to be said to make a persuasive case for thinking the interpretation is faithful to a significant amount of traditional discussion. I also wish to present and partially assess some traditional arguments, on the assumption that they are supposed to support a certain answer to the question (when it is interpreted in the way I am recommending) as to what we directly perceive.

I begin with three quotations selected more or less at random from the philosophical tradition.

All philosophers, from Plato to Mr Hume, agree in this, that the immediate object of perception must be some image present in the mind.

This is Thomas Reid (1785, essay II, chapter 7, p. 124).

Thus it becomes evident that the real table, if there is one, is not the same as what we immediately experience ... The real table ... is not immediately known to us at all, but must be an inference from what is immediately known.

This is Russell (1912, p. 11). Finally, here is Ayer:

What ... is immediately given in perception is an evanescent object called an idea. (1956, p. 89)

In these remarks a basic traditional philosophical claim about perception is being described or expressed. It is not the purpose of all these authors to endorse the theory, but they mean, at least, to *identify* a crucial thesis (or thought). The tendency, then, has clearly been to express a disputed and supposedly important thesis in sentences in which the verb 'perceives' (or related verbs such as 'experiences', 'knows' and 'sees') is coupled with the adverb 'immediately' or 'directly'. I shall use the expression 'directly perceives', which I shall sometimes abbreviate to 'd-perceives'. So, following this tradition, we can express a fundamental question as: do we directly perceive external objects? About the notion of an external object it is enough, for present purposes, to explain it as that of a space-occupying (or spatially locatable) object which could, in principle, exist independently of being perceived.

Clearly, then, philosophers have intended to use the words 'directly perceives' to stand for a certain *relation*, a relation which, they think, it is important to be told is (or is not) one in which we stand to external objects. What relation, if any, is it?

2   *Three Approaches*

We can distinguish three ways of answering this question. The first is to be found in J. L. Austin's famous discussion of these terms in *Sense and Sensibilia* (1962). Austin's radical view seems to be that the words do not stand for any relation at all.

> We have here, in effect, a typical case of a word, which already has a very special use, being gradually stretched, without caution or definition or any limit, until it becomes, first perhaps obscurely metaphorical, but ultimately meaningless. One can't abuse ordinary language without paying for it. (Austin 1962, p. 159)

This attitude is, I believe, not plausible. It is *prima facie* most unlikely that, to modify Reid's description, all philosophers from Plato to Ayer have agreed in assenting to a meaningless sentence. This simply lacks the ring of truth.[3] We can also remove the support Austin provides for his claim by remarking that a failure to use 'directly perceives' in accordance with its usage in ordinary language (and, hence, its normal interpretation, if it has one) does not license talk of an abuse; it licenses, rather, talk of a technical use. It in no way, therefore, supports Austin's conclusion to point out how, in various ways, the standard philosophical usage does not conform to normal use.

Now, it is undeniable that this technical use has often been made without anything in the way of a definition or elucidation.[4] (Indeed, it is worth pointing out that the tendency to use the term 'direct perception' without an explicit introductory definition can still be found. We encounter it in a book as recent and as good as Pitcher's *A Theory of Perception* (1971, p. 4). The expression simply insinuates itself at the beginning and thereafter remains in

---

[3] I do not think that it is a *decisive* refutation of Austin's position that it has the consequence that a large number of manifestly intelligent and reflective people have endorsed nonsense. There is plenty of evidence from earlier times, but also, alas, from the present that that is *not* impossible. We ought to be very reluctant, though, to accept a view with such a consequence.

[4] Austin is right, in the quotation, to talk of lack of definition. He is not, though, entitled to talk of no limits, or of no caution, in the use of 'direct perception'. That is manifestly unfair.

the discussion.) But this merely means that a definition (or elucidation) needs to be constructed by us on the basis of the use to which the term has been put. In particular, the construction of an elucidation needs to be sensitive to the considerations or arguments that have been thought to be relevant to the questions expressed using the term.

The second attitude I want to mention is more sympathetic to the possibility of a coherent interpretation than Austin's. It maintains that we can fit standard discussions on to a number of rather different interpretations of 'direct perception', but once we become explicit about these various interpretations we realise that none of them specifies a relation which makes the question as to whether we directly perceive external objects interesting. None of these questions is interesting because, once they are properly articulated, it becomes more or less obvious what the answers are. The thought is that the impression of an interesting question is sustained solely by not keeping separate the separate questions. An exposition of this point of view is provided by Dretske in *Seeing and Knowing* (see Dretske 1969, chapter 2, §6).

Now, there is, I think, much truth in this attitude; there has been, as I shall argue, a lot of confusion in the thinking about perception which has issued in remarks containing the words 'direct perception'. However, and this is the third attitude, we can hold that, once the confusions are set aside, there remains an interpretation of 'direct perception' which leaves a difficult and interesting question as to whether we do directly perceive external objects. I shall argue for that attitude. The choice between the second and third approaches, though, cannot be settled by any points that can sensibly be made about them when they are understood in such a general way. To make a case for the superiority of the third over the second approach it is necessary to give and develop an interesting interpretation.

3 *Some constraints*

There are different ways to present an interpretation of a tradition of discussion, and it is a strategic issue which is best. One is to take certain philosophers as representatives, to scrutinise and to criticise their discussions, and display the interpretations as emerging from those considerations. A second is to specify the interpretation and to display its merits in a general way. The first strategy has the possible disadvantage of requiring the reader to be pitched straight into criticism of writings which might be unfamiliar or unappealing. The second has the possible disadvantage of allowing the interpretation to appear arbitrary and strange. I prefer, in this exposition, to adopt what is basically the second strategy and so to run the second risk.

In outline, then, I want to advance two main suggestions.

(1) There are, fundamentally, two ways of understanding talk about direct perception. The first is epistemological. However, the epistemological interpretation does not exhaust what has been understood, and it does not give a good account of the core of the traditional issue. What is needed, therefore, is a non-epistemological interpretation.

(2) The best way to elucidate the issue non-epistemologically is to take it as dealing with the correctness (that is with the *truth*) of a certain class of demonstrative judgements we are all inclined to make (or accept) on the basis of our perceptual experience and which is expressive of our normal view of the relation to the external world which perception gives us. The question whether we d-perceive external objects is the question whether these judgements are correct (that is, *true*).

In arguing for this I am guided by two constraints.

(a) It is desirable to give an interpretation of 'x directly perceives y' which has the consequence that it can be said that we all, prior to critical philosophical reflection, hold that we d-perceive external objects. This is desirable because it is clearly normally assumed by philosophers who say that we do *not* d-perceive external objects that if we accept their claim then we need to revise our beliefs. A revision in our beliefs, in my sense, requires that a previously held belief be abandoned. They obviously take themselves to be revisionary theorists of this sort. So, to make sense of their views it would be best if this conviction could be validated.

(b) The second constraint is harder both to explain and to justify. It is, I think, assumed by traditional theorists that the revision they are endorsing amounts to placing a certain kind of object (external independent particulars) outside the range of objects, if any, which can be d-perceived. We want, therefore, an interpretation of 'directly perceives' which makes it a relation you could *in principle* stand in to that sort of object. The issue is: *do* we stand in that relation to external objects? This means, I think, that we want our interpretation of 'x d-perceives y' to make it an extensional, two-place, relation; the question, then, is whether we can, saving truth, fill the y-place by an expression designating an external object, and the x-place by an expression designating ourselves.

With these guidelines in mind, what account can we give of 'd-perceives'?

On anyone's account, and on the different accounts I shall be considering, 'd-perceive' is taken as inheriting as part of its meaning one feature of the modified verb 'perceive', namely, that if it is true that x d-perceives y then it follows that y exists or has existed. But what is the relation of d-perceiving?

4 *Epistemological interpretations of 'direct perception'*

In the quotation from Russell we can discern one sort of interpretation. Russell opposes the claim that we directly perceive the table with the claim that the table must be an inference from what is immediately known. I want, to begin with, to follow through the task of interpreting the issue so that this contrast or opposition is made sense of. We should, though, view Russell's remark primarily as a representative for a group of approaches, between members of which there will be differences, but which can all be said to be, in some sense, epistemological. The basic points I wish to make about the account that emerges from consideration of Russell will apply, I think, to all epistemological accounts – that is, to the general class of which I am taking a certain remark of Russell's as representative.

The most direct attempt to sustain the contrast between what is directly perceived and what is merely inferred, would be the following definition:

(3) x directly perceives y iff x perceives y without inference.

Now, we can surely dismiss as absurd the thought that what is meant here is: our visual powers vary depending on whether we are engaging in inference or not. No-one would hold that when we are inferring we can see certain objects which we cannot see when we are not inferring. Inference does not affect our visual acuity. So, the issue cannot be: when we are not inferring what in the way of objects can we perceive? What is needed, therefore, is a more sensible understanding of the link between what we can perceive and inference, such that it might make sense to be told that what we thought we could see without inference, we are only aware of on the basis of inference.

In order to make sense of this we have to ask: what sort of thing can we tell (or perceive, or become aware of) by inference? The answer is, of course, that by inference we can tell (or arrive at the conviction) that something is the case. That is, there is a perfectly sensible contrast between:

(4) the things you can tell to be the case straight off, without needing to engage in inference

and

(5) the things you can tell (or detect) only by inferring them from other (supposed) facts.

But this means that if 'direct' is explained as 'uninferred' (in order to sustain Russell's contrast) the only sort of objects for which d-perception is appropriately understood are, as we might put it, propositional-style objects. Thus, it might be said, I can tell immediately that there is something green (or green-looking), but I cannot perceive (or tell) directly that there is something which is an apple. Once we acknowledge this, we can agree that we have an intelligible issue: what, in perception, is the perceiver able to tell is the case without inference? If it was our purpose to pursue this epistemological question we would need to fix, in some way, a procedure for determining what is detectable without inference.[5] However, we do not need to do this, because this interpretation does not give us an account of 'directly perceives' which satisfies the second of the criteria I earlier gave. It gives no account of a relation in which I can stand to (or fail to stand to) a particular external object; it gives us, rather, and so to speak, a 'relation' in which I can stand to some facts concerning certain objects, and, maybe, not to some other facts concerning the self-same objects.

Here is a simple illustration. It might be that I can d-perceive that that is green-looking, but that I cannot d-perceive that it is an apple. But, suppose that that is a green-looking apple. The question – 'do I directly perceive *that thing* or not?' – is evidently, I suggest, without significance, given the present interpretation of 'direct perception'.

Now, the argument I have just advanced in favour of a part of claim (1) can be set out in a simple way. It amounts to this:

(6) If we interpret 'directly perceives' epistemologically it yields an intensional context.

---

[5] I am not implying that this would be easy. We would need to have a proper account of inference, but would also need to have some ground to think that there is a type of data available without inference as a general feature of perception, rather than that being something which varies from context to context, depending on the varying skills and acquired sensitivities of perceivers.

(7) We do not want 'directly perceives' to create intensional contexts. We want an extensional notion.

There is, to be sure, an element of over-simplification in this argument, but I wish to let it remain in such an extreme form, because I also think that when the complexities are worked through we arrive at the same conclusion.[6] (I try to work through some of the complications in the following footnote.[7])

5 A non-epistemological interpretation of 'direct perception'
It would be fair to say that this argument establishes at most part of (1). It makes a case for saying that an epistemological understanding is not adequate given one of our desiderata. This does not show that there is an

---

[6]A frequently encountered syndrome in philosophical writings is that of, in parts of the discussion, using 'd-perceives', and presenting arguments, in such a way that it cannot bear an epistemological sense (for basically the reason presented), but at other times both explaining it in epistemological terms and endorsing arguments which require such a reading. Berkeley exhibits this syndrome in an impressive way.

[7]The oversimplification in this argument concerns premise (6). Let us suppose that 'EP' expresses an epistemologically distinctive relation between a perceiver and a proposition (such as being able to tell that it is true without inference). Then we can define a relation 'x d-perceives y' as (something like): there is a proposition P such that x EP's P and P concerns (is about) y. Now, this is defined in epistemological terms, and is therefore in an extended sense epistemological, but there is no reason to deny that it is extensional. (6) is not, then, as it stands, accurate.

There are, further, no grounds, at least none of a kind that the restricted considerations my argument is appealing to could yield, for doubting the well-definedness of such a notion.

The major reason for doubting that such an epistemological notion could fulfil the role of suitable elucidation of 'd-perception' is as follows. The traditional debate is whether we d-perceive physical objects. A satisfactory elucidation of the notion must assign to the expression a relation which there is at least some chance could be shown not to hold between us and such common-or-garden items as tables, by the arguments which revisionary theorists can be supposed to have according to our account of the debate. If, then, we adopt an extended epistemological definition it is presumably because it is thought that epistemological considerations fulfil this condition. That is, it must be thought that epistemological arguments *might* determine an answer. However, epistemological arguments essentially rely on considerations about the distinctive epistemological status of propositions as determined, supposedly, by the kinds of concepts which those propositions contain. Thus, it might be argued that no proposition which contains the concept of an external physical object, can be non-inferentially determined as true. But no principles of this sort can be used to show that there are not propositions which, while not containing physical object concepts, are still, in the relevant sense (that is, the sense invoked in the extended definition) *about* what are in fact physical objects. If this claim of mine is true then no *epistemological* argument could show that the extended epistemological relation does not hold between us and physical objects.

There is, then, a case, without relying on (6), for holding that an epistemological elucidation of 'd-perception' will yield an unsatisfactory account of the debate.

interesting non-epistemological account. Is there one? I want to answer by suggesting one.

Our lead comes from Hume (1777, p. 152). He says:

> no man, who reflects, ever doubted, that the existences, which we consider, when we say this house, and that tree, are nothing but perceptions in the mind.

Hume himself does not, at this point, use the expression 'directly perceives', but he does state his view by saying that there is no '*immediate* intercourse between the mind and the object' (italics mine), and 'immediate' is, of course, the other term traditionally used. So, what can we say in elucidation of 'direct' if we take Hume's 'immediate' to mean the same?

Hume directs our attention to the objects we can single out in a demonstrative way in virtue of our experience. His claim is that the existences, that is the objects, we are actually 'considering', which is to say, are framing our thoughts about, when we think thoughts which we would express using such demonstrative expressions as 'this house', are perceptions in the mind, and, of course, are *not* external, space-occupying, bodies. We are thinking about, are fixing on, something, when we think 'that house', even though it is *not*, on Hume's considered view, a house at all. So we can say that he is concerned with the question: what are the objects which we can actually demonstratively single out in judgements made on the basis of perceptual experience? They, whatever they are, are the immediate objects of awareness. His answer is that they are 'perceptions in the mind'. Developing this, we can suggest that what we directly perceive is what we can, in the course of and in virtue of our perceptual experience, demonstratively pick out. What we can d-perceive is what we can fix on as objects of demonstrative thought in virtue of our experiences.[8] So the question what we directly perceive becomes: what is the character of those objects? An initial elucidation of d-perception, then, is:

> (8) x d-perceives y iff x stands, in virtue of x's perceptual experience, in such a relation to y that, if x could make demonstrative judgements, then it would be possible for x to make the *true* demonstrative judgement 'That is y'.

---

[8] I mean what you can think thoughts about in that distinctive way which would receive expression in spoken language in (certain) sentences containing demonstratives. How to unpack the 'certain' is a problem the proposal faces.

To get an understanding of what is intended here, consider the demonstrative judgements you think you can make now in virtue of your current visual experience. Let us assume that you are inclined to think 'That is a page'. (I am assuming that you think you can see the page on which these words are written.) You hold, that is, as we might put it, that amongst the items which your current visual experience puts in your demonstrative range, is a page (one external space-occupying object). On the other hand, your current visual experience does not put the machine which printed this page in your demonstrative range. Your visual experience (almost certainly) does not place you in such a relation to any object as would entitle you now to think with truth 'That is the printer'. Hume's claim, and this is what I am interpreting as the general content of revisionary claims about perception, is that, contrary to what you think, your visual experience does not actually put you in a position to demonstratively pick out the actual, external, space-occupying page either. In fact, according to Hume, the page is no more within your demonstrative range than is the printer.

6 *Clarifications and objections*

How satisfactory is this as an interpretation? I want to make a sequence of remarks about it, some expressing things which are, as I see it, in its favour, others expressing difficulties.

(a) The first desideratum that was proposed was that we confer upon the expression '*x* d-perceives *y*' a sense such that it would be correct to express our pre-philosophical opinion as being that we do d-perceive external objects. Now, that requirement is, surely, fulfilled, in the only sense that it is reasonable to demand it. It may be that we would not all pre-reflectively make the meta-judgement that we are, in perceptual experience, placed in such a relation to external objects that we can demonstratively pick them out, but we all do make and accept the demonstrative judgements themselves, and so could not reject, and are committed to, the meta-judgement.

(b) The second desideratum was that we confer an interpretation on '*x* d-perceives *y*' which makes it an extensional two-place relation. I take it that it is obvious that the analysis does achieve this.

(c) Another objection might be expressed this way: 'Surely, we do not want to say that only creatures capable of demonstrative judgements can d-perceive objects. If there is a properly defined notion it must, presumably, specify a relation which all perceivers can stand in to external objects, even if they are not thinkers.' This objection may not, perhaps, be strongly felt, but in reply we can point out that it is a misunderstanding to suppose that the analysis faces this problem. The relation which d-perception expresses is one that creatures not cognitively capable of demonstrative thought can stand in to external objects. It represents that subject–object relation which, when allied with a capacity for demonstrative judgement, guarantees the possibility of a *true* demonstrative thought.

(d) The chief clarificatory problem that the proposal faces is that of limiting in some way the sort of demonstrative contact with which d-perception should be equated. For there are cases where we do not need to do anything which would be intuitively regarded as d-perceiving an object in order to be placed by perceptual experience in a position to demonstratively single that object out. This means that the present elucidation has not quite captured the relation of d-perception. This problem is raised by the following kind of case. I look at a picture of a cat, and think 'That is my cat'. For that judgement to be true I must be able to demonstratively single out my cat in virtue of my perceptual circumstances. But it is clear that my contact with my cat is fairly *indirect*. It is certainly not direct. So, it is not quite right to equate the assertion of the directness of perception of external objects with its being the case that our perceptual experience enables us to be in demonstrative contact with them.

The response to this problem which seems to me to be on the right lines is to point out that in the picture case the demonstrative picking out is a *dependent* picking out. That is, there is another item I am in a position to pick out, namely, the picture, and in the circumstances I can pick out my cat as *that* cat only because I am in such a position. My ability to demonstratively single out my cat depends on the truth of a more basic, and in itself nondependent demonstrative judgement. If this point is sound then we need to say that the notion of direct perception is to be explained as the relation yielded by perception which enables *nondependent* demonstrative thought-contact to be made. So the thesis that we do not directly perceive external objects amounts to the claim that we are not placed by our perceptual experiences in a relation to external objects which enables us to do that.

This clarification relies on a fairly intuitive notion of dependence. Can we provide more of an explanation of the notion? This becomes pressing in virtue of the following possibility. It may be that a single perceptual experience puts us in a position to nondependently demonstrate two, non-identical objects of a rather different type. Now, if these objects are, in some way, tied together, there is a sense in which our demonstration of one depends on that of the other, namely, that we would not be in a position to demonstrate one if we were not also in a position to demonstrate the other. However, we surely do not want to conclude that it follows from this that each demonstration is, in our sense, dependent on the other.

To pursue this issue, I want to take a slightly different example. Suppose that I am looking at a television screen depicting Gary Kasparov, and I think 'That is Kasparov'. I think that this should be classified as a dependent demonstration. Why? It need not be that as I watch I think 'That is a television picture of Kasparov'. I can lose my sense of the screen. However, unless I would acknowledge under questioning the truth of 'That is a television picture of Kasparov' then we should say that I am making a mistake; I am mistaking a screen for a man. So the demonstration of Kasparov is dependent in that it actually homes in on Kasparov only if there is a relational property which I, as thinker, would acknowledge as applying to some distinct item which I can demonstrate. The suggestion, then, is that your perceptual experiences put you in a position to nondependently demonstrate x just in case they put you in a position to demonstrate x where that does not depend on there being a y (not identical to x) such that you can count as demonstrating x only if you acknowledge that y bears a certain relation to x.

The most this does is to expand to some extent our understanding of the notion of nondependence. The task, of course, remains of saying, in a general way, under what conditions someone does count as demonstrating x only if he or she acknowledges that it bears a certain relation to another (demonstrable) item. That task I cannot, at the moment, carry out.[9]

(e) The elucidation of 'x d-perceives y' defines a relation which holds, if it holds, between a subject of experience and certain objects. (Indeed, I regarded that as something which we wanted our account to sustain.) However, in a lot of discussion in philosophy in which the terminology of

---

[9] I have concentrated on distinguishing the sort of demonstrative contact I am interested in from demonstrative judgements such as 'That is my cat' said when facing a picture of the cat. But there are, of course, other demonstrative utterances which we are entitled to make where the item demonstrated is in no sense 'directly perceived'. Thus, someone might say 'A cat got stuck up the tree in my garden' and I can reply, 'That cat is stupid'. This kind of demonstrative thought-contact is also *dependent*, but on a certain *narrative* context. The claim that we d-perceive y is the claim that our perceptual experiences place us in such a relation to y that we could make a true and non-dependent (in either way) demonstrative judgement 'That is y'.

'direct perception' is employed the question that is raised is whether certain features, aspects or properties are d-perceived. This way of speaking is *not* explained along the present lines, and requires a different treatment.

(f) Having gradually clarified the content of the interpretation I think that there will be the following objection, which is, perhaps, the most direct and basic which the proposal faces. 'The present interpretation cannot be right, because no-one could, or does, seriously entertain the claim that our perceptual experiences do not put us in a position to demonstratively think about external objects, but plenty of philosophers are seriously prepared to doubt that we directly perceive them.'

Part of the reply to this objection is that it is mistaken to deny that philosophers have doubted whether our perceptual experiences put us in a position to demonstratively think about external objects. It certainly looks correct to me to interpret Hume as maintaining that. But let us consider very briefly also Russell. Russell held that 'this' and 'that' are the only names 'in a logical sense'; that we can only use such 'names' of items with which we are at the time of use acquainted; and that our experiences do not acquaint us with physical objects. So Russell also held what on the present account someone who says that we do not d-perceive external objects holds.[10]

Another part of the reply is that when we recommend an interpretation we are doing so because it *makes most sense* of someone's arguments. Unless we interpret him as arguing for this the debate is opaque to us. It is then, surely, quite possible that the best interpretation might come as a surprise, and indeed, be quite unwelcome, to the thinker being interpreted.

This completes what I feel able to say in a general way in favour of, and in elucidation of, the interpretation I am proposing.[11] There is, of course, a viewpoint which has not been addressed seriously; that is the viewpoint of people who agree that 'direct perception' is an important non-epistemological notion, but who would disagree with the present account

---

[10] I am thinking of Russell's well-known views in the decade leading up to the First World War. Russell, it seems to me, fits the account well. Of considerable relevance to the objection I am considering, and rather less straightforward in relation to it, are Moore 1918, pp. 220–252, and Price 1932.

[11] It is because Locke, unlike Berkeley and Hume, does not really anchor his understanding of 'direct perception' (or related expressions) in a context of a consideration of various arguments about perception, or of a consideration of what he saw as the difficulties faced by his own view, that his account of perceptual experience is especially hard to interpret. In particular he seems not to have considered the implications of his theory for demonstrative thought. That Locke is a difficult case fits nicely with the present proposal.

and offer an alternative one. Such a viewpoint would be held by John Foster and Frank Jackson (see Foster 1985, pp. 159–163, and Jackson 1977, chapter 1). In the present paper I cannot consider such alternative views. Instead, I want to develop the proposal by incorporating more of the traditional discussion into it, partly in an effort to extend the case for thinking that the account captures the debate, partly in order to assess the arguments themselves.

7 The options

If my account of the question is acceptable, then there are two further claims between which we must choose. The first is that in ordinary perception we are so related to external objects that we can (nondependently) demonstratively pick them out. That is how I interpret the thesis of Direct Realism. The second is simply that we are not so related to external objects. Call that Indirect Realism. There are three remarks about these options that I wish to make.

(a) Indirect Realism is a negative and not a positive claim. It can be accepted by people who disagree about the correct characterisation of experience for which Direct Realism has been rejected. In particular, there is no need for the Indirect Realist to hold that our experiences put us in a position to pick out such objects as sense-data, or indeed, put us in a position to demonstrate anything. To deny that our perceptual experiences enable us to demonstrate external objects strictly does not imply that there is anything else we do d-perceive. Thus it is possible to hold that our experiences do not enable us to d-perceive external objects, not because, on reflection, we can discover an intruding sort of object which acts as a screen between the subject and external objects, but because, on reflection, we form the view that experience does not quite *reach far enough into the world* to enable us to do so. It follows that a proponent of sense-data as d-perceivable objects must provide more support for his thesis than is provided by whatever arguments he has against Direct Realism. This also means that arguments against the cogency of sense-datum theories are not as such arguments *for* Direct Realism.

(b) On this understanding of Direct Realism, it is not obviously correct to equate a defence of Direct Realism with the assertion that a proper description of our perceptual experiences must employ physical object concepts, that there is no totally adequate description of experiences in neutral terms. I call this the Description Thesis. (For a defence of this thesis see Strawson 1979, pp. 41–60.) This is not obviously adequate because there are experiences, for example, very realistic hallucinations, for which, arguably, a proper description must employ physical object concepts, but which do not, according to our ordinary understanding of them, sustain d-perception of such objects. The Description Thesis bears on our issue only if we can also support the claim that the Description Thesis itself would not be true unless we do d-perceive external objects.[12] Further, the thesis that we d-perceive external objects, interpreted in the present way, does not obviously entail the Description Thesis. It seems clear that there could be individual experiences in which an external object was d-perceived but which would not strike the subject that way. It would also need an argument to show that it is impossible for an (indefinitely) extended stretch of experience to fulfil such a condition. There is, then, no simple connection between what we d-perceive and what is (in a currently fashionable way of speaking) the manifest content of our perceptual experience.

(c) We can distinguish two attacks on Direct Realism. One consists in arguing that we do not directly perceive external objects because there are no such objects. Possibly this thesis is backed by the claim that the notion of an external object is incoherent. We can view Berkeley as arguing for this. More usually, however, the arguments do not challenge the existence of external things, but try to show that they are not amongst the things we can, in perceptual experience, demonstratively pick out. It is this second kind of argument that I shall consider, and relate to the proposed interpretation.

8 *Direct perception and epistemology*
Before I discuss these arguments I want to say a little about the relations between the issue as I have characterised it and epistemology. There is first a worry that needs voicing. I said that there is a non-epistemological question about perception, and I offered my elucidation as an interpretation of it. In what sense, it might be asked, is the present interpretation *non-epistemological*? It explains the relation of direct perception in terms of a certain kind of judgement which would be true if the relation holds; it might seem, therefore, that since it defines the relation in terms of the truth of a certain kind of judgement, the issue of whether the relation obtains

---

[12]This is a different point from the criticism sometimes voiced, in discussions of transcendental arguments, that the Description Thesis does not imply that there actually are physical objects. If this criticism is correct then the doubt expressed in the text is sound, but the doubt in the text might be sound without the present one being correct.

turns out to be an epistemological one. However, what needs emphasising is that the property of the judgement that the issue turns on is simply its *truth*, which is not, in the relevant sense, an epistemological property. (I hope that I do not have to argue for that last point.) For the relation to obtain which sustains the possibility of a true demonstrative thought it is not required that the subject has any justification for believing that the judgement is true, nor that he knows that it is true. The dispute solely concerns the truth of such demonstrative claims (should they be framed) and so is not an epistemological issue.

We have, then, two questions:

(9) How do we know, or, what justification do we have for believing, that there are material objects?

That is an epistemological question. (A related epistemological question is: how do we know, or what justification do we have for believing, that there are the particular objects we think there are?)

(10) Are the demonstrative judgements true?

That is a non-epistemological issue in the sense that its topic is not justification or knowledge. I would say that (9) belongs to the theory of knowledge, whereas (10) belongs to the theory of *perception*, properly so-called.

Now, saying that there are two questions or topics does not determine what relation, if any, exists between them. Rather than consider the issue in that general form, I want to argue for a view of the relation by providing an assessment of a claim about it advanced by Frank Jackson.[13] Jackson, in the course of discussing a certain argument, says:

> What lies behind this objection is the very common assumption that Direct Realism is epistemologically superior to Representationalism. I think that this assumption is mistaken and that the two theories are on a par regarding our knowledge of the external world. (Jackson 1977, p. 147)

---

[13]There is something unfair to Jackson in taking a remark of his as stalking horse in the discussion, for I need to interpret his remark in line with my reading of the notion of d-perception, whereas he endorses it on the basis of his interpretation, which is certainly different. It cannot, therefore, be said that he has, or would have, endorsed the statement when it is treated my way.

The assessment of this remark that I wish to argue for is that it is partly right but also partly, and seriously, wrong.

Note, as a preliminary, that I am interpreting Direct Realism in my sense; Representationalism, not so far defined, can, for present purposes, be defined as the conjunction of Indirect Realism and external world Realism. The truth in Jackson's remark is that Direct Realism *provides no solution to* epistemological questions; so, by counter-asserting Direct Realism as against Representationalism, one is not asserting something which avoids the problem of scepticism. The simple reason for saying this is that what Direct Realism asserts is that certain (sorts of demonstrative) judgements are true, and that simply does not *say* how or why we know that they are true. It does not *say* how we are justified in believing they are true. So, a worry about knowledge (or justified belief) receives no answer in Direct Realism. (An answer to an epistemological worry must, I take it, *say* something about justification or knowledge.)

It may be objected: since Direct Realism involves the assumption that there are material objects, to defend Direct Realism will involve providing arguments for that claim, arguments which will give or constitute such a reason. Surely, therefore, Direct Realism does answer the sceptic. But the answer to that objection can be seen by considering how the debate goes. The Indirect Realist has a set of arguments in support of his view. The Direct Realist must try to show that they do not support a denial of his view. At that point there are two, non-necessitated, theories: Direct Realism and its denial. If at that stage the Direct Realist wants to provide further reasons he will need to construct arguments justifying the distinctive claims in his theory, with which the opponent he is taking seriously disagrees. Now, the present opponent does not raise questions about the existence of physical objects, so there is, as yet, no reason to provide a justification to believe in them. Suppose, however, an opponent comes on the scene who queries Direct Realism because of its commitment to physical objects, and the Direct Realist wishes to engage seriously with this point of view, then he will need to provide a justification for his belief in physical objects. But this amounts to there being available to the Direct Realist epistemological arguments which do not rest on, but rather *on which rests*, his Direct Realism. This means, then, that the Direct Realist, in my sense, does not, in what his Direct Realism accepts, have a claim which is an answer to the sceptic's problem. He needs such an answer prior to justifiably asserting his

Direct Realism (if, that is, he becomes worried about its justification in that respect).

It is, therefore, a mistake to suppose Direct Realism is an answer to, or is in some sense a position which avoids, scepticism. In saying this, I am proposing that we agree with Jackson. However, it would be a mistake to infer from this that Direct Realism is 'on a par' epistemologically with Representationalism. The reason this does not follow is that someone who is trying to justify Direct Realism is trying to justify a view which is significantly different from Representational Realism; although there is some overlap in the general claims they assent to (e.g. that there are tables, etc.), there is also a significant difference, in that Direct Realism accepts as true certain demonstrative judgements not accepted as true by Representational Realism. This means that the epistemological task of justifying them need not be the same.

This argument, I think, gives a sound reason for saying that there *may* be epistemological differences, and hence, for not assenting to Jackson's claim, but it does not show that they *are* different when considered in relation to epistemology. Since I have not provided a full interpretation of the epistemological question, I cannot argue this question in a thorough way. However, I do wish to make a case (or at least the start of a case) for the more limited claim that Direct Realism is required by, and Indirect Realism (including Representationalism) is inconsistent with, any defence of the claim that our current belief-acquisition practices give us knowledge of the physical world. (On some conceptions of epistemology, of course, such a claim would not be of any interest.) The reason is that perceptual demonstrative judgements are, arguably, fundamental to the belief-formation mechanisms we actually employ, and which we take to provide us with knowledge of our environment.

I shall sketch an initial argument for this by considering cases which are of the sort Gettier famously described. Now, although philosophers, in order to explain why Gettier cases are not cases of knowledge, have been tempted to construct complex theories about the conditions for knowledge, it seems to me that Harman's simple proposal that inferentially formed beliefs cannot constitute knowledge if, roughly, they are based in some crucial way on falsehoods, is both enough to deal with them and an intuitively plausible requirement for knowledge by inference. Anyway, I shall assume, in the present argument, that it is on the right lines. This is of interest to us because there are cases very like Gettier's original ones which are more perceptual; for example, I am looking in the direction of $p1$ where there is a flower. Between me and the actual flower there is a cunning flower-picture which is what I am actually seeing. I do not realise that the picture is there and so form the obvious belief. Allowing that there is nothing else to be added, we do want to say that I do not know that there is a flower at $p1$, although I justifiably and correctly believe that there is. Why not? Again, the obvious suggestion is that the existential belief (there is a flower at $p1$) is an inference from a demonstrative belief (that is a flower at $p1$), where the demonstrative judgement is false. The correct demonstrative judgement is: that is a flower-picture at $p2$. Thinking of the example this way, we can use Harman's suggestion to explain why these cases are not cases of knowledge. But the consequence of doing so is that we treat our perceptual demonstrative beliefs as fundamental to the acquisition of our existential beliefs about our immediate environment. Therefore, any position which denies the truth of such judgements cannot be consistent with a defence of the claim that the way we currently acquire such beliefs is knowledge-yielding.

The conclusion of this argument is, surely, very plausible – indeed, there is something artificial about arguing for it in such an indirect and contentious way. But the support provided is by no means conclusive. In the first place it rests on the adoption, which I do not wish here to defend further, of a certain treatment of Gettier cases. For present purposes the more interesting doubt is one which an opponent of the conclusion who accepts the treatment of Gettier cases would express. He would need to suggest an alternative *false* belief from which the existential proposition could count as being inferred. There is an obvious candidate, namely:

(S) I can see a flower at $p1$.

Now (S) differs from the demonstrative candidate in two ways. It is explicitly about perception, and it is non-demonstrative. Both features should be discussed in candidates for expression of the basic information we perceptually receive, but it is the second aspect which is of interest here.

I cannot give a full consideration to the suggestion, but shall restrict myself to two remarks, one clarificatory, the other critical.

(a) To claim that the issue between Direct Realism and Representational Realism is epistemologically neutral (on the recommended interpretation of these positions) requires that the demonstrative judgements, the truth value of which is in dispute, are irrelevant to what is understood as the concern of epistemology. Let us call this idea 'neutralism'. In the above argument the concern of epistemology was taken to be that of explaining or defending the conviction that our normal cognitive procedures can yield knowledge of our environment. Neutralism then requires that our demonstrative judgements be, as we might say, 'side-lined', that is, regarded as not fundamental to our cognitive procedures. Instead, judgements as to what kind of object is currently being perceived are regarded as central. If, however, the epistemological enterprise is viewed according to a more classical vision of it as the task of providing a justification of our major convictions then neutralism requires merely that a justification for our convictions about our environment can be provided which does not rely on those demonstrative judgements. I would recommend that we think of the debate between Hume and certain neo-Lockeans (such as Mackie) as being over whether this is possible. Hume denies it, while Mackie affirms it.[14]

(b) The difficulty with regarding a proposition like (S) as fundamental, rather than the demonstrative ones, can be brought out by envisaging a situation where I can see exactly two things, which are manifestly an apple and a tomato. Now, I shall, no doubt, believe that I can see an apple and I can see a tomato, but this conjunctive belief is a completely general one and is logically neutral as to which object is which. Why, though, would I believe such a general proposition in the usual case? The reason is that one particular object presents itself as a tomato, and the other as an apple. This is cognitively more fundamental than the general belief. But, it seems to me, to express this more basic fact of manifestation I need to say (or think) that *that* (the particular presenting item) is a tomato, and *that* (the other item) is an apple. I need, that is, such demonstrative propositions.

So although 'd-perception' is not an epistemological concept, it is arguable that at least part of the importance of issues expressible using it is epistemological.

9 *The argument from illusion: the Humean paradigm*

I have tried to present a certain interpretation of the question whether we directly perceive external objects, an interpretation which both fits the way some philosophers have spoken and, at least, gives us certain things which, I have claimed, are desirable in an interpretation. However, the fruitfulness

---

[14]In his first *Enquiry*, Hume (1777, p. 153) presents what he thinks is the decisive point. It has to be conceded to the neo-Lockeans that Hume's argument is not as strong as Hume thought. But this concession does not settle the *issue* in their favour.

of the way of presenting the question may be revealed also in the way it allows us to state the arguments brought to bear on the issue. So the next stage of the discussion has two purposes. I want to state (some of) the arguments in order to assess them, but I also want to state them in a way which conforms to the present characterisation of the issues, thereby giving some support to it.

The traditional arguments have names: the argument from illusion, from hallucination, from the finite speed of light, and so on.[15] However, they all share a common structure. They all, in effect, take a central sort of case, and either claim or argue that in that type of case we do not d-perceive an external object. I shall call that part of any argument its *Base Case*. Since, however, the arguments are designed to support a completely general conclusion, they incorporate a *spreading step*, which amounts, supposedly, to a justification for thinking that the negative conclusion about the Base Case holds generally of what we, prior to these arguments, take to be perceptual experiences. In the standard presentation these distinct aspects are not always explicitly separated. But it is important to separate them because in some of the arguments it is the spreading step that might be questioned, whereas in others it is the treatment of the Base Case itself.

I shall start with the so-called argument from illusion.[16]

We need not worry, as some have done, about the name. It is true that, when giving examples to illustrate the argument, philosophers have cited cases to which the ordinary term 'illusion' does not apply. For example, we would not call a sighting of a tilted circular coin a case of illusion, though that is an example often given (see Ayer 1956, p. 87). The mismatch between title and example is, however, unimportant, for it grounds nothing more than a criticism of the *name* commonly given to the argument. There is a substantial question about the cases which are often suggested to sustain the argument and that is whether they all actually display the feature which the theorist needs to appeal to in order to ground his conclusion. It is by no means clear, for instance, that the coin case does contain any such feature.

---

[15]The phenomena to which these arguments appeal can also be appealed to in arguments which are of relevance to the epistemological debate. There is not, then, *one* argument from illusion, but, at least, two, and they need to be stated in different ways. This is one explanation of the failure to separate issues.

[16]Of the argument from illusion Professor Dummett has written: 'If this is regarded as an argument, properly so-called, with premises and a conclusion, it is difficult to make out what are the premises and what the conclusion. Rather, it is a starting point' (Dummett 1979, p. 2). My aim is to provide just such an account of the structure of the argument of which Dummett despairs. But see also footnote 19.

However, I want to avoid that sort of issue by considering an example which is fairly clearly appropriate for the argument.

The simplest exposition, as I think of it, of the argument from illusion is that given by Hume, in section 12 of the *Enquiry Concerning Human Understanding.* He says:

> The table, which we see, seems to diminish, as we remove farther from it: but the real table, which exists independent of us, suffers no alteration: it was, therefore, nothing but its image, which was present to the mind ... the existences, which we consider, when we say, *this house* and *that tree*, are nothing but perceptions in the mind. (Hume 1777, p. 152)

Now, Hume in his exposition pays absolutely no attention to the spreading step; he argues his conclusion in connection with the case of the table we move away from, but immediately draws a completely general conclusion, that is, a conclusion about *any* 'this...' and 'that...'. Since Hume's argument is restricted to it, I want to look at his argument for the Base Case.

There is, however, another issue to raise before I start considering that, an issue which was mentioned earlier. Hume concludes, in effect, that the judgement

'That is a representation'

is true (in respect of the Base Case). But we need to separate two moves. The first is the move away from what we ordinarily think; call that the *negative revision.* What we ordinarily think is: that is an external object. The negative move away is taken in conceding that that is not actually true. The second move is that which asserts a positive characterisation of what *that* is – say, a representation or a sense-datum or a percept. Call that the *positive revision.* This again is a distinction quite neglected by Hume in his exposition. But it is clear that there are separate issues here; and that one could make the negative revision, without endorsing any particular positive claim. Moreover, the negative revision is prior. We do not need a positive claim unless the negative revision is accepted. So I shall restrict consideration of Hume's argument, and indeed all the other arguments hereabouts, as arguments simply for the *negative*, rather than the subsequent, positive, claim.

Hume's strategy is to argue that 'the table, which we see' has a property which 'the real, independent table' lacks. If that is so, then it follows that 'the table we see' is not the real table. Further, Hume clearly implies that it is 'the table we see' which we are designating or talking about when we talk of 'that table'. Putting this together, we come out with the following, very simple, representation of Hume's argument:

(11) That ('the table we see', the visually presented item, whatever it is) seems to diminish.

(12) The real table suffers no alteration, i.e. does *not* diminish.

Therefore:

(13) That is not identical with the real table (that ≠ the real table).

Now, unfortunately, this is not a valid argument. The property ascribed to the item designated by 'that' is not the property denied to the real table. We have to ascribe to Hume the following argument:

(14) That (whatever it is) is getting smaller, diminishing in size, during period p.

(15) The real table is not diminishing in size during period p.

Therefore:

(16) That is not the real table.

This is surely a valid argument. We could, if we wished, think about the argument in that form. But there is a reason to modify our exposition a little. Hume is not (and proponents of the argument are not) interested simply in establishing a non-identity between that (the seen 'table') and the external table. He wants, rather, the conclusion that that (whatever it is) is not *any* external object. We should, therefore, make explicit an assumption which was, in effect, contained in (15). The assumption is that the object mentioned in (15) is the external object which the seen 'table' would be if it were an external object. As we might say, the external table is the appropriately placed ('AP') external object. So, we might read the argument as this:

(14) That (whatever it is) is getting smaller, diminishing in size, during period p.

(17) The AP external object (which is the table) is not getting smaller during *p*.

Therefore:

(18) That is not identical with any external object.

Taking that as a complete statement of this argument, the argument, that is, for the Base Case, how should we react to it?

Now, I think we can see that one sort of reaction which is often given to the argument from illusion is not really relevant. The argument is sometimes met by the reply: 'Nothing follows because we can easily *explain* what is going on in the case. There is nothing mysterious about that being the way things appear in such circumstances.' This comment, probably true though it is, quite fails to engage with the options that any critical assessment of the argument must choose between. A critical reply is restricted to saying either it is invalid, or that one of the premises is false. The present reply does not take any of these forms and so does not contribute to its assessment.

We can limit our critical options further, as in effect we already have done, by so interpreting the argument that it is valid. We simply stipulate that it is the same predicate negated in (17) that is affirmed in (14). Our assessment must then deal with the premises.

It is hard to deny (17). We do all believe that our moving away from the table in no way affects its size; and we also believe that the table is the appropriately placed external object. What I have just said, which is obviously intended to focus critical attention on (14), is sometimes objected to with the question: 'How do you know? How do you know that the table's size is constant?' That is a frivolous question. (a) Anyone invoking this desperate question should be asked whether they seriously think that undermining (17) represents the best way to counter the argument. It is worrying if it does. (b) This challenge is, I believe, issued under the impression that the problem is an epistemological one; but it is not. So, any serious enquirer, at this stage, cannot but accept (17).[17]

---

[17] I am suggesting that behind the use of this sort of reply lies a failure to distinguish the issue under discussion from an epistemological one. We should note that Hume himself seems to have accepted such a distinction. One of the puzzles about his discussion in the *Enquiry* is that Hume mentions, in one paragraph, examples, such as double vision, apparently crooked oars in water (and so on), but describes them as 'trite', and lacking in real importance. But, the example he chooses to use in his own argument seems no less

This leaves (14). But, plainly, (14) *is* suspect. Why should we accept it? The only answer that Hume seems in a position to provide is that *that* 'seems to diminish'. But at this point, and allowing that it is actually true that *that* seems to diminish, we have to say that it is illegitimate to get from:

(19) That (whatever it is) seems to be diminishing.

To

(20) That is actually diminishing.

Maybe, after all, that seems to be diminishing without actually diminishing.

Note that the move from (19) to (20) is essential, for if the argument is presented with the 'seems to be diminishing' predicate in both premises, it fails, because, although still valid, we have no reason at all to deny that the actual external table *seems* to be diminishing.

So, if Hume's argument is understood so as to be valid, we have the option of rejecting one of the premises.

10 *Some general remarks*
I have presented an interpretation and criticism of Hume's version of the argument from illusion. We can use that treatment as a basis for a general characterisation of that sort of argument.

To construct an argument from illusion the Base Case needs to be an apparently perceptual experience in which there is some mismatch between how, in that experience, it appears to be (say, that there is an *F* thing), and how the apparently perceived object actually is (say not-*F*). The argument must then claim that the visually presented item (the d-perceivable thing) is *F*, but that the AP external object is not-*F*. This establishes a non-identity between them.

The defender of Direct Realism must, it seems, answer by denying that the properties of *that* (the d-perceivable thing) and the AP external object diverge. He must, of course, to that end, rely on a fundamental distinction within ordinary thought, namely, that between how an object appears to be

---

trite. The sensible reading of these passages, it seems to me, is that Hume is not contrasting cases but rather *uses* of cases. The trite employment is to support sceptical epistemological conclusions, whereas the profound employment is to refute our commonsensical identifications of what experience presents us with. This reading requires that Hume accepted something like the distinction in question.

and how it actually is. It is, I would say, a manifest conviction of ordinary thought that we can apply that distinction to items which are d-perceivable.

Now, although this gives a recipe for responding to the argument, it does not establish that the response will *always* be plausible. The best cases to consider are those where the chosen property F would be agreed by everyone not to belong to the AP external object. In that case it would represent an unthinkable inconvenience to avoid the argument by altering that opinion. Then the critical claim is that *that* (the d-perceivable thing, whatever it is) is F. The argument will be persuasive to the extent we are persuaded of the truth of that proposition. It cannot be said in advance of a consideration of particular examples whether that will be so or not. So I shall call that sort of proposition the *critical claim*.

The critical claim can be recommended in two ways for acceptance. The standard way is to say that it is simply obviously true. H. H. Price can be our representative for that viewpoint. He said:

> When I say 'this table appears brown to me' it is quite plain that I am acquainted with an actual instance of brownness ... This cannot indeed be proved, but it is absolutely evident and indubitable. (Price 1932, p. 62)[18]

The critical claim is treated as just manifestly true. The standpoint of the opponent has to be that it is not absolutely evident. However, the critical claim can also be presented as acceptable because it is involved in what is argued to be the best theory of appearances. The opponent has to deny that the best theory does involve the critical claim.[19]

The *structure* of the debate is clear, but its content and outcome cannot be determined in advance.

I have three further observations about the argument from illusion.

(i) A standard criticism of the argument is that its proponents simply assume the truth of some such principle as – 'if x appears F, then something is F' – but that we have no reason to accept it. It seems to me that to say this is to fail to capture the psychological source of the appeal of the argument. For most people, the general principle, if accepted, is itself an implication of, or a generalisation from, a more fundamental conviction that, for a

---

[18]Note that Price is not at this point presenting an argument from illusion.

[19]The existence of this sort of argument represents the truth in the remark by Dummett quoted earlier with which I disagreed. Illusions do raise the question as to how they are possible. A theory is needed to answer that. So, in one sense, they are 'a starting point'.

particular value of an apparent F (say, apparent colour, or shape), it is just obvious to inspection that there is something which is F. The more fundamental conviction is that to which a critic must speak.

(ii) We can distinguish between static values for F (say, having a certain colour or shape) and dynamic values, such as the alteration to which Hume's argument appeals. Dynamic versions of the argument face a problem not faced by static versions. To apply a dynamic predicate presupposes that there is a persisting object which satisfies the predicate. But it is not clear that someone whose considered view is that a persisting external item is not d-perceivable is entitled to suppose that that assumption is true. The thought that there is a persisting but changing d-perceivable item, to which a critical dynamic claim is committed, seems parasitic on the identification of d-perceivable items which the argument is designed to overturn.

(iii) There is a very important assumption which has been made so far, and which is usually made, but which needs spelling out. If the Base Case argument is sound it shows, as we might put it, that *that* (a d-perceivable item, whatever it is) is not an external object. But this conclusion only implies that the external object is not d-perceivable (that is, that the Direct Realist account is false for the case) on the assumption that it, the external item, would have to be identical to *that* in order to be d-perceivable. We can label this the Uniqueness Assumption, because it amounts, in effect, to the claim that there is, in a particular direction of attention, as it were, a unique, single, d-perceivable thing. It is acceptance of that Assumption which dictates that a defender of Direct Realism has to deny any truth to the critical claim. Now, it has to be admitted that it is extremely natural to accept the Uniqueness Assumption, but since the task of constructing a theory of perception which satisfactorily accommodates all evidence and pressures is so difficult, it should at least be considered whether abandoning it may not be the correct policy.[20]

11   *The spreading step*

The discussion has so far been concerned with the Base Case. What, though, of the second step in the argument? If the first step (the Base Case) had been sound, would the spreading step have been objectionable? The answer, it seems to me, is that it would be very hard to object to the argument at this point. For the general conclusion of the Base Case would have been: in cases

---

[20]Some of the ideas in Brian O'Shaughnessy's fascinating article 'Seeing the Light' (1985) might, as I read it, be relevant to the investigation of this proposal.

where the seen object (the *that*) seems *F*, but the external object is not-*F*, the d-seen object is not the external object. Now, given the normally chosen values for *F*, these cases would be so common that it would be hard to claim with any plausibility that despite experiences of this sort not giving us a d-perception of external objects, others still manage to. The principle at work here is *not* that it would be impossible for a limited number of (perceptual) experiences (or parts of them) to be importantly different from what has been agreed to be the status of the rest. That is not in itself impossible, as far as I can tell. Nor is it that there could be no justification for holding that a limited set of experiences belong to a distinctive category. It is rather that, given the ubiquity of the illusory (in the weak sense) base cases, there is nothing about the rest which could constitute them as enabling us to d-perceive external objects.

Arguments of this species (arguments from illusions) need to be resisted (if they are to be resisted) over their treatment of the Base Case.

12 *Two other arguments*
In this section I wish to formulate, in terms which conform to the present account, two other traditional revisionary arguments, and to discuss them briefly.[21]

The first argument is that from the existence of double vision. My interest in this argument lies in setting out its treatment of its Base Case, that is the case of double vision. I shall not discuss whether it would be plausible to generalise, from the Base Case, any revisionary conclusion as to what is generally d-perceived. (It is worth remarking, though, that the ubiquity of double vision induced by focussing would make it hard to limit damage once the Base Case claim had been conceded.)

The problem raised by double vision is that there is (we are all prepared to grant) only one appropriately placed external object, but there are (or seem to be) two, and therefore distinct, visually presented items, two items we can demonstratively think about. The two premises are then:

(21) *That-L* (i.e. the leftmost of the visually presented items, whatever it is) is not identical with *that-R* (i.e. the rightmost of the visually presented items, whatever it is).

---

[21]Both these arguments are variants of the argument from illusion. I treat them separately because what I have called the critical claims in them are particularly interesting.

(22) There is only one appropriately placed external object (call it E).

It follows that:

(23) Either *that-L* is not identical with E or that *that-R* is not identical with E.

Given what is built into the notion that E is the appropriately placed external object, (23) can be re-stated as:

(24) Either *that-L* or *that-R* is not an external object.

However:

(25) It is implausible to treat *that-R* and *that-L* (whatever they are) differently.

The only plausible conclusion is:

(26) Neither *that-R* nor *that-L* is an external object.

It seems to me that this captures in the framework which I am recommending the core of the traditional argument based on double vision. It also makes it clear that the only way to challenge the conclusion is to deny premise (21). Surely both (22) and the logic and plausibility claims yielding (26) are hard to reject. However, once scrutinised, (21) is hardly self-evident. It is quite possible to say, contrary to (21), that:

(27) *That-L = That-R.*

To sustain (27), double vision has to be thought of as involving a double sighting of a single object. On that conception the identity judgement (27) is correct. Our perception puts us in touch with a single object in such a way that we can demonstratively think about it twice. So, by affirming (27) we can avoid any revisionary conclusions based on this phenomenon.

The second argument which I wish to set out is the so-called time-lag argument. This is based on what has to be conceded once the consequences of the fact that light travels at a finite speed are considered. In order to set out the problems in my terms I shall assume that we are dealing with a case where we are, as we would commonsensically say, looking at a star (call it S) which in fact exploded, and so ceased to exist, one thousand years ago.

The explosion is, of course, a long way from being registered by the naked eye. The difficulty that is raised by such a case can be formulated in the following argument:

(28) *That* (the demonstratively graspable and visually presented thing, whatever it is) exists now.

(29) Star *S*, which would be the appropriately placed external object, does not exist now.

It follows that:

(30) *That* is not identical with *S*.

It also follows that:

(31) *That* is not an external object.

This conclusion is evidently revisionary. What can we say about it? It is clear that the second premise, (29), might be questioned; thus, it might be suggested that (31) does not follow, because the star is not the appropriate external object, that is, the object which the visually presented thing would be if it were an external object. However, it is also possible to query (28). We might say that in the circumstances in which it is envisaged that the argument is being used, we should actually count (28) as false. What is true rather is:

(28*) *That* (the demonstratively identifiable thing) does not exist now.

It is often assumed in discussion of 'exists' that sentences like (28*) cannot be true. If that assumption is correct then the present response is not admissible. But, once the significance of such an assumption for other philosophical arguments, like the present one, is seen, it is also possible to treat the truth of (28*) both as enabling us to avoid the time-lag problem, and also as revealing that the dogma about the impossibility of truth for such sentences should not be accepted. Thus I am suggesting we should regard the finite speed of light as enabling us at *t* to demonstratively think about items which no longer exist at *t*. That is why a sentence like (28*) can express a truth.

13 *Conclusion*

The way the argument has developed will almost certainly have given the impression to people who have offered, or who accept, different elucidations of 'direct perception' that they are committed to disagreeing with the leading proposal here. This need not be so, and I wish to be as conciliatory as possible at this stage. Since 'direct perception' has been used in so many discussions, and there are a number of fundamental notions we need the terminology to express, the expression can, of course, quite properly and without engendering disagreement, be elucidated in different ways. The crucial question, as I see it, is whether or not the present proposal succeeds in articulating, making explicit, and organising arguments around, a notion which should be recognised as *one* of those which is central to the debate and which the terms in question need to be recognised as sometimes expressing.[22]

---

[22]This paper was finished while I was on leave at Williams College, Williamstown, Mass. I wish to express my gratitude to my own college, Exeter College, Oxford, for permission to be on leave, and to Williams College, and especially Professor Dan O'Connor, for the marvellous conditions I enjoyed there. I also wish to thank Tim Crane for his patience and guidance.

4   Experience and its objects

E. J. LOWE

This paper has three parts. In the first I give an account of the nature of sense perception which lays special emphasis on the role of experience in perceptual processes. In the second I say why a capacity for sense perception as I define it is indispensable for any being that can genuinely engage in belief and judgement about the world. And in the third I criticise modern computational accounts of human perception for treating sensory experiences as effectively epiphenomenal in processes of perceptual cognition.

I

What is it to perceive something by sense? An answer which I have proposed elsewhere (Lowe 1986b), and which I wish to defend here, goes as follows. (I state it for the special case of vision, but believe that it may be extended in appropriately modified form to the other sense modalities.) One *sees* an object, I suggest, if and only if one's visual experience is directly causally dependent on certain properties of that object in such a fashion that one is thereby enabled (with the aid of certain background knowledge, maybe) to form a fairly reliable judgement as to what those properties are. These properties will then qualify as *visible* (to the observer) properties of the object that is seen. As it stands, this proposal is somewhat schematic, and details need to be filled in at various places. This I shall do in due course. But first certain possible queries and objections of a more general nature should be addressed.

One objection might be that it is circular to define seeing in terms of visual experience. But that would only be so if I also proposed to define visual experience in terms of seeing, which I do not. I do not, for instance, want to define a visual experience as one caused by stimulation of the natural organ of sight, the eye, by light. An experience qualifies as a visual experience purely by virtue of its intrinsic phenomenal or qualitative character – or so I would claim. It is true that such experiences are normally caused by light impinging on the retina of the eye, but they can also apparently be caused by direct stimulation of certain parts of the cortex, as the well-known findings of Wilder Penfield suggest (see Penfield and Roberts 1959, pp. 51ff.). It is not inconceivable that a congenitally blind person (one whose eyes or optic nerves were damaged beyond repair) should be capable of enjoying such experiences and have sight conferred artificially by being fitted with a prosthetic device. The device would not necessarily have to be sensitive to light in the spectral range to which the natural eye is sensitive: indeed, there is no reason in principle why it should not be sensitive to some form of energy other than electromagnetic radiation. So what qualifies an experience as visual has nothing to do with its causal provenance (at any stage earlier than the cortex, at least). Qualitative character is what counts – and I shall say more about it later.

A second objection might be that in insisting that seeing involves having visual experiences I am ignoring the phenomenon of so-called 'blindsight'.[1] Blindsight subjects, in whom the striate cortex has been (wholly or partially) destroyed by injury, disease or surgical intervention, are capable of discriminating the locations of light stimuli and even of distinguishing elementary differences of shape or form in them, but without the benefit of enjoying visual experiences of any sort (at least in that part of the visual field corresponding to the damaged part of the cortex). It is significant, however, that the subjects themselves resolutely *deny* that they see the stimuli in question, and have to be asked to 'guess' their locations and shapes. Even after learning that their 'guesses' are highly accurate (though they are less so than the visual judgements of normal subjects), they still deny that they *see*, and continue to think of themselves as just 'guessing'. I think that they are right to deny this, and hence that the phenomenon of blindsight actually confirms my definition. Seeing *does* require having visual experiences. Note too that my definition requires that the subject be enabled to form a fairly reliable *judgement* as to the relevant properties of the seen object: so that the blindsight subject is disqualified as a seer not

---

[1]See Weiskrantz 1986, upon which my description and interpretation of the phenomenon are heavily dependent.

only by virtue of lacking the appropriate experiences, but also because his discriminations apparently have to take the form of 'guesses' rather than judgements. Finally, I should in any case stress that my opening question was 'what is it to perceive something *by sense*?', and thus I would urge that even if we allow that in some sense blindsight subjects do perceive – and perhaps even see – things, they do not enjoy a mode of *sense* perception. I shall return to the issue of blindsight later, in an attempt to explain why sense perception is indispensable for creatures genuinely capable of belief or judgement.

Another general issue I should address concerns the extent to which my definition makes seeing an *epistemic* process. First of all, it will be observed that it does not follow from my definition that if a person sees an object he must thereby acquire knowledge (or even belief) about it. And this is as it should be: for it is clear that very often one sees objects of whose very existence one is quite ignorant at the time of seeing them. Thus it can happen that at the time of being presented with an array of visible objects one fails to notice certain of them, but that one is able to recollect their presence at a later time. This requires that one must indeed have *seen* them at the earlier time – for one cannot recollect what one has not experienced. However, on the other hand, my definition of seeing is not wholly *non*epistemic, for it recognises that seeing should at least provide a *possible* means of gaining knowledge about the object that is seen – though it allows, too, that the realisation of that possibility may depend crucially upon the subject's store of background knowledge. Someone who knows nothing about telescopes may *see* a distant galaxy when peering through the eyepiece of a telescope, but the experience will not issue in any reliable judgement concerning that celestial object, as it would in the case of an astronomer's observation.

But now it may be objected that the clause concerning background knowledge in my definition is too lenient, in that it forces me to say that ordinary folk *see* their own retinal images whenever they are looking at their everyday surroundings – for, certainly, anyone with a specialised knowledge of physiological optics can form fairly reliable judgements concerning properties of his retinal images on the basis of the visual experiences he enjoys in such ordinary situations.[2] This is the 'problem of the proximal stimulus'. The 'problem', supposedly, is to characterise seeing

---

[2] I readily embrace this consequence in Lowe 1986b.

in such a way that only 'distal' stimuli – things like tables and trees, and presumably also distant galaxies – qualify as objects that are *seen*, and *not* things like retinal images and patterns of neural activity in the retina or cortex (unless, that is, they themselves happen to occur as distal stimuli, as when an ophthalmologist investigates another person's eye). But *why* not things like these? As far as I can see, no good reason can be given for excluding them as *bona fide* objects of vision, and the mere fact that ordinary folk would not *say* that they see such objects is just a symptom of their fully excusable ignorance. Perhaps the supposed problem arises from a tacit assumption that objects of vision compete with one another for that status: that if one were always seeing one's own retinal images, one would thereby be prevented from ever seeing one's own everyday surroundings (almost as though the retinal images would 'get in the way'). But that is absurd: when one sees a televised football match, one sees the images on the television screen *as well as* seeing the players, though normally one's attention is focused on the latter. What is perhaps true is that objects of vision compete for *our attention*, so that we cannot *attend* to our retinal images while also attending to our everyday surroundings. But that, if true, is a fact about attention, rather than about vision as such.

Incidentally, when I stipulate that in seeing an object one's visual experiences should *enable* one to form fairly reliable judgements about certain properties of the seen object, I do not mean to suggest that one must form those judgements (when one does) as a result of *inferring* them from judgements about one's visual experiences (though nor do I wish to deny that this may happen on occasion). The seer need not form any judgements about his visual experiences, even when he does form judgements about the seen object 'on the basis of' those experiences. At most the seer needs to be recognitionally sensitive to relevant features of his visual experiences, in the sense that he is capable of noticing or discriminating the presence or absence of these features. I shall come back to this issue later.

I now turn to the task of filling in some more details in what I admitted as being a somewhat schematic account of visual perception. One notion which particularly needs expansion is that of *direct causal dependency*. According to my definition, when a person sees an object, his visual experiences must be 'directly causally dependent' upon certain of that object's properties. The key idea here is that vision involves a certain kind of *responsiveness* to its objects: it is not enough that there merely be *some* sort of causal dependency between visual experiences and things seen. A simple example of the kind of responsiveness I have in mind would be this: when a magnet is passed over a pile of iron filings, the filings *respond* to its movement by the changing pattern they form. Similarly, the television images produced in a 'live' broadcast *respond* to changes in the televised objects – for example, to the movements of players on a football field. When a video-recording of the match is played, the images on the screen are still *causally dependent* upon the original movements of the players – but not 'directly' so, as in the 'live' broadcast: what is missing is precisely the element of *responsiveness*. Giving an explicit definition of this special kind of causal dependency is no easy matter, and I shall not attempt it here. But it seems clear enough that it is this special kind of dependency that is involved in sense perception. This, indeed, is why it is admissible, in my view, to say that one literally *sees* the match in the case of the 'live' broadcast, but not in the case of the video-recording. (Compare hearing someone over the telephone and hearing a recording of their voice.) Note, incidentally, that what disqualifies the video-recording is *not* the time-lag between the events on the field and what appears on the screen – for even with a 'live' broadcast there will still be a small time-lag, which could in principle be made as large as we liked (by reflecting the radio waves from a suitably distant object). The next aspect of my account of visual perception which needs elaboration has to do with the *effects* upon visual experience that seeing involves. I say nothing explicitly about these in my definition, and advisedly so – for I think it would be wrong to try to build an explicit account of them into such a definition. What I do say is that visual experiences have to be affected by certain properties of the seen object *in such a fashion* that the observer is thereby enabled to form a fairly reliable judgement as to what those properties are. Even so, I can and should try to say what would qualify an effect upon visual experience as apt for the role it is here called upon to play. Two questions in particular arise: first, *what* features of visual experience need to be affected by an object if one is to see it, and second, *how* do these features need to be affected? My answer to the first question is that it is features of the *phenomenal or qualitative character* of visual experience that need to be affected, and my answer to the second question is that these features need to be affected in a way which *depends systematically* upon properties of the seen object. The reason for my first answer is that if effects upon visual experience are to enable the observer to *form judgements* about properties of the seen object, those effects must be ones of which the observer is, or at least *can* be, *conscious* or *aware*: and it is precisely the phenomenal or qualitative features of visual experiences of which their subjects are aware. (Recall that blindsight subjects feel unable to make perceptual judgements – as opposed to 'guesses' – concerning light stimuli precisely because they lack any visual phenomenal awareness in the relevant portions of their visual fields. Recall too, however, my earlier denial that judgements about the seen object have to be *inferred from judgements* about features of visual experience – which should allay any worries about the proverbial skills of chicken-sexers and the like.) The reason for my second answer is that only *systematic* dependencies between the properties of seen objects and qualitative features of visual experience will enable the observer to form *fairly reliable* judgements concerning those properties. What is a 'systematic' dependency, though? In general, it will I suggest be some sort of *functional* dependency, in the mathematical sense of the term – the sort of dependency we find, for instance, between ambient temperature and the height of a mercury column in a thermometer. (Note that what makes a thermometer a fairly *reliable* source of information about ambient temperature is precisely that its behaviour is governed by such a functional dependency, subject to the satisfaction of certain background constraints.) I should stress, however, that many of the relationships of functional dependency we may expect to find exhibited in visual perception will be a good deal more complex, mathematically, than this simple analogy might suggest: some of them, for instance, will involve rates of change, or even rates of rates of change, in qualitative features, and hence will require expression in the form of differential equations (perhaps even partial differential equations).

Now, if features of the qualitative character of visual experience are to enter into such relationships of functional dependency, they must of course be susceptible to continuous variation in appropriate ways, or along appropriate dimensions. But I think it is clear that they *are*. Thus the *colour* features of our visual experience vary continuously along the three independent dimensions of brightness (or intensity), hue and saturation. However, *chromatic* colour features are not essential to visual experience, as the possibility of colour-blindness demonstrates, and as the normally sighted can confirm for themselves by the use of filters (or, indeed, just by watching black-and-white television). What *are* essential, though, are the features of *extensity* that are always to be found in visual experience.[3]

---

[3] I borrow the term 'extensity' from Ward (1918, pp. 78ff., 116ff.).

These features also exhibit continuous variation along independent dimensions – in fact, along two such dimensions. A complication arises however inasmuch as we cannot in this case plausibly speak of these as *natural* dimensions as we can in the case of colour variation. What we *can* say though is that the extensive features of visual experience exhibit a two-dimensional or surface-like topology – a claim I have argued for elsewhere (Lowe 1986a). It is of course possible to *select* two orthogonal 'directions' as 'axes' for this topological manifold, labelling them perhaps 'altitude' and 'azimuth', but such a selection would be more or less arbitrary in that many other coordinate systems would serve equally well (including, for instance, systems of polar coordinates).

A further crucial property of the qualitative character of visual experience is this. At any given moment at which a subject is undergoing visual experience, the manifold of *extensive* features of visual experience is manifested in its entirety (unless, indeed, part of the visual field is 'missing', as in the case of some blindsight subjects). By contrast, only a small and fairly arbitrary selection of the *colour* features of visual experience need be manifested at any one time. It is, at least in part, this fact about visual experience which leads us to regard it as the pre-eminently *spatial* mode of experience – in fact, for the sighted it provides the very paradigm of the idea of space or extension. But it is important to realise that this is merely an accident of our psychology and physiology. The 'extensive' features of visual experience are, in reality, no more inherently 'spatial' in character than are the colour features, paradoxical though this may sound. Each set of features constitutes a manifold exhibiting a particular structure, a structure which can be mapped onto that of a certain abstract mathematical space with certain distinctive topological properties. Analogously, the state of an ensemble of physical particles can conveniently be described in terms of an n-dimensional 'phase space'. If we think of the features of visual extensity as somehow more genuinely *spatial* than such features as the momenta of particles in such an ensemble or the colour features of visual experience, this is partly just because when we *imagine* space we represent it to ourselves visually (if we are sighted, at least) – and we tend to do so precisely because visual experience is distinctive in making available to the subject's consciousness a *simultaneously* presented manifold of spatially structured features, namely, the extensive ones. (It is this that sustains our talk of the 'visual field'.)

It should be remarked, however, that another reason why we think of the extensive features of visual experience as somehow more genuinely 'spatial' than other features is that it is these features of visual experience which form the basis of our visual judgements concerning the spatial properties of the physical objects that we see. Yet, of course, a manifold of physical objects is itself *spatial* only by virtue of its structural isomorphism with a certain abstract topological structure, even if it is true that mankind's first scientific knowledge of such abstract structures – embodied in the axioms and theorems of Euclidean geometry – arose from our interest in measuring and comparing the sizes and shapes of physical objects. We shouldn't think of the likeness between the two-dimensional manifold of visual extensity and a two-dimensional physical surface as going anywhere beyond a purely formal structural isomorphism.

Of course, ordinary folk will not describe the qualitative or phenomenal characteristics of their visual experiences in the technical terms of 'brightness', 'hue', 'saturation', 'extensity', and so forth. But it would be wrong to suppose that they are therefore not equipped to describe them *at all* (much less that they are incapable of noticing and recognising them, and indeed with considerable precision). In practice what we do to communicate our awareness of them is to employ constructions involving certain senses of words like 'look' and 'appear'. The senses in question are the *non-epistemic* or *phenomenal* ones: not, thus, the sort of sense that is typically at work in a statement like 'That man appears to be waving at us', but rather the sort of sense that is found in such statements as 'That round plate appears elliptical from this angle' and 'That red surface looks yellow in this light'. The point about such statements is that although they are ostensibly statements about properties of the *objects* of visual experience (plates, surfaces, and so on), in fact what they achieve is to communicate in an oblique fashion information concerning the qualitative character of a subject's visual experience. There is much more to be said on this issue, but it would involve a deviation from the main thrust of this paper to go into it in further detail here. All I would urge at present is that the language of visual appearances affords a means of describing the qualitative character of visual experience quite as effective, in its own way, as that provided by the more austere and technical language of dimensions of qualitative variation (for an exemplification of this, see Lowe 1986a).

It may be objected at this point – if not long before – that I am indulging in the 'myth of sense-data'. Well, yes and no. If 'sense-data' are construed as being private objects of introspection whose properties are incorrigibly known by their subject, I want no truck with them. But insofar as sense-datum theorists are or were attempting to talk about qualitative features of visual experience, I concur with them in thinking that there *is* something to talk about. However, the debate which still goes on between sense-datum theorists and 'adverbial' theorists of sensation I feel to be largely an idle one. The adverbialists are surely right in rejecting an 'act/object' account of sensation – right to avoid 'reifying' sense-data as visual objects possessing visible qualities of shape and colour. But the sense-datum theorists are right in supposing, for instance, that spatial *adjectives* can be legitimately employed to describe certain aspects of the qualitative character of visual experience. For instance, it is perfectly legitimate to say that the manifold of extensive features of my current visual experience is such that a certain rectangular region of it exhibits a certain uniformity of hue. This no more requires us to 'reify' this region as a private object of introspection than the description of a certain region of 'phase space' as possessing some geometrical property requires us to reify that region as a peculiar kind of quasi-physical object existing over and above the ensemble of physical particles with their properties of position and momentum.

Now that we have to hand means of describing the qualitative features of visual experience – whether in the austere terms of dimensions of qualitative variation or in the more homely terms of the language of visual 'appearances' – we are in a position to corroborate my suggestion that when one *sees* an object, certain of its properties stand in relationships of functional dependency to certain qualitative features of one's visual experience: relationships which, furthermore, enable one to form fairly reliable judgements as to what those properties of the seen object are, given that one possesses appropriate background knowledge. Take, then, as a typical example, a case in which a normally sighted subject sees a rigid material object possessing a certain shape – for instance, a flat, circular dinner plate. Typically, the subject may hold the plate in front of him, turning it this way and that as he fixes his gaze on it. During the course of such an exercise – assuming that the subject's eyes are open and the plate is suitably illuminated – the subject will enjoy a sequence of visual experiences whose qualitative character varies systematically with changes in the orientation of the plate relative to the subject's line of sight. For instance as he tips the face of the plate more and more away from a vertical plane orthogonal to his line of sight, it will 'appear' more and more eccentrically elliptical (a fact which could be described more austerely in terms of changes and constancies in the dimensions of variation of visual qualitative features, the relevant changes being in certain aspects of visual extensity).

The functional relationships that govern such systematic covariations are given by the laws of projective geometry – or, more familiarly, by the so-called laws of perspective. Provided that the subject has a working knowledge of these laws (and what I mean by this will emerge later), and provided that he is entitled to certain general assumptions concerning his physical environment (such as that most of the physical objects he is likely to encounter are relatively rigid and stable), such a sequence of visual experiences equips him to form the fairly reliable – and in this case correct – judgement that the object which confronts him is flat and circular in shape. (I shall say more about these provisos later, and try to justify the claim that they may be satisfied in a wide range of circumstances.)

It is worth remarking here that, given the assumption of rigidity, the laws of perspective are in fact remarkably unambiguous in their implications for the shape of seen objects. As David Marr has pointed out, it is a mathematically provable fact that just three different views of four mutually fixed points suffice to determine their geometrical relationships up to a reflection (see Marr 1982, p. 209). In fact, I venture to affirm that the laws of perspective constitute our *main* basis for three-dimensional space-perception. Stereopsis is a relatively unimportant additional luxury, as is demonstrated by the fact that subjects possessing only monocular vision from birth have no difficulty in attaining to perfectly adequate three-dimensional space-perception. (Here I should remark, incidentally, that although stereopsis clearly does make a difference to the qualitative character of visual experience, it does not do so by adding a third dimension to visual extensity: see further Lowe 1986a, p.274.) However, it must be stressed that *motion parallax* is a vital ingredient in the point I am making: a single 'snapshot' view grossly underdetermines the geometrical properties and relations of an array of visible objects, but once motion in the observer and/or the objects is introduced, visual experience specifies its environmental objects geometrically to a remarkably high degree of accuracy – always subject, of course, to rigidity assumptions. (To convince oneself of this, one need only survey the passing scene from a moving railway carriage.) It is perhaps also appropriate at this point to reiterate my earlier remark that the functional dependencies in visual perception include relationships between rates of change, or even between rates of rates of change, in qualitative features and properties of seen objects, so that, for instance, the *motions* and *accelerations* of seen objects must be included amongst their visible properties.

I must briefly deal with one final issue before I close this part of the paper. Many of those who are sympathetic to the notion of sensory experience and accept its vital role in any adequate account of sense perception may none the less feel that in emphasising the *phenomenal* or *qualitative* character or 'content' of visual experience, I have been neglecting another and perhaps more important kind of experiential content, namely, *intentional* or *representational* content. When one enjoys a visual experience, one does not just enjoy a state of qualitative awareness, one enjoys a state which represents – or better, which *presents* – the world as being thus-and-so in one's vicinity. In general, one's visual experience will present the world as containing certain objects with certain properties standing in certain spatial relationships both to one another and to one's own location in physical space. For example, a visual experience might present the world as containing a red cow to the left of a green bush directly ahead of and a little below the point at which one is standing (normally, of course, it would present much more than *just* this).

Now I by no means wish to belittle the importance of such facts about visual experience. In particular, I do not wish to assign this sort of intentional content exclusively to the *judgements* or *beliefs* that we may form on the basis of our visual experiences, rather than to the visual experiences themselves. Even so, I would argue that the task of explaining why visual (and other sensory) experiences have this sort of intentional content is closely akin to the task of explaining how we are able to form perceptual judgements concerning objects in our environment, and hence that to this extent the intentional content of visual experience belongs to the *explanandum* rather than to the *explanans* of a theory of visual perception. In order to explain what it is to *see* an object, it will not do just to take as given the intentional content of visual experiences invoked in the explanation, since that the visual experiences involved in seeing an object should be capable of carrying appropriate intentional content is part of what needs to be explained. My own opinion, thus, is that such intentional content as a visual experience has must ultimately be grounded in its phenomenal or qualitative content – though explaining the nature of the 'grounding' relation involved here is a task of no small magnitude, and one which goes far beyond the scope of this paper. (As I have indicated, however, it is akin to the task of explaining the intentional content of perceptual judgements and beliefs, and so not unconnected with some proposals I make in this paper.) But this at least constitutes my justification for placing the emphasis which I do on the role of phenomenal or *qualitative* content in visual perception, and for saying rather little in the present paper about the *intentional* content of visual and other sensory experiences.

II

I think I have said enough, for the time being, in explanation and defence of my account of what it *is* to perceive something by (visual) sense, though more will emerge in due course. The next question I wish to address is whether sense perception is – as indeed I consider it to be – indispensable for creatures capable like ourselves of genuine judgement and belief. For if it is not, then it is I suggest a subject of relatively little philosophical significance, however interesting it may be from a psychological point of view.

Consider once more the phenomenon of 'blindsight'. It appears that the discriminatory capacities of blindsight subjects are in fact fairly rudimentary, albeit quite accurate as far as they go. Such subjects can for instance discriminate, with a fair degree of precision, the direction of a light stimulus, and can distinguish an 'X' shape from an 'O' shape. But they cannot, it seems, register the presence or absence of a specified kind of physical object, such as a table, in the 'blind' regions of their visual fields. However, it is not difficult to conceive of a blindsight subject who *could* do this – who could 'guess', with a high degree of accuracy, what sorts of physical objects were located at various places in his immediate environment, without benefit of visual experience of any sort (by a causal mechanism involving the eye, and without the aid of other sensory cues). But can we intelligibly extend this thought-experiment to conceive of a subject who, *from birth*, was deprived of *all* modes of sense perception and yet possessed instead blindsight (of the sophisticated sort just hypothesised) and perhaps also 'deafhearing', 'numbtouch' and so forth as well? I think it is clear that we cannot. For consider again the less extreme hypothesis of the 'sophisticated' blindsight subject who, we suppose, enjoys other modes of sense perception and formerly enjoyed normal visual perception. We have no difficulty in supposing that he could at least *entertain the thought* that a table, say, was located at such-and-such a distance and direction from him, and hence that he could 'guess' this and turn out to be right. But the reason why we have no difficulty in supposing this is that we have no difficulty in understanding how such a subject could possess the *concept* of a table: for we can assume that he knows what tables *look* like, or at least what they *feel* like. (For the same reason, we can assume that he possesses some concept of what it is for an object to occupy a position in physical space relative to himself.) But we can't assume this in the more extreme case: indeed, in that case we have to assume that the subject has *no idea* what a table, or any other physical object, *looks* like, *feels* like, *sounds* like, or *tastes* like – in short, how it *appears* to any sense. And that means, I suggest, that we cannot intelligibly attribute to such a subject any physical concept, nor, hence, any thought involving physical concepts. This still perhaps leaves open the possibility that such a subject might possess purely abstract concepts, though it is strongly arguable that these in fact require a substratum of physical concepts. And if that is so the lesson would appear to be that genuine thought of any sort – and hence genuine belief and judgement – is only possible for a being endowed with sense perception. The point is hardly a new one, I confess, since it may be summarised in the Kantian slogan 'thoughts without content are empty'.

One of the obvious implications of this conclusion is that it is impossible to endow a computer with genuine cognitive states without equipping it with suitable sense modalities. This is not to deny that an ordinary computer may contain information-bearing states. But genuinely *cognitive* states like belief are not just informational states, because cognitive states have conceptual content and structure, which mere informational states do not. The pattern of rings in a tree trunk is an information-bearing state – it carries information about the tree's age, amongst other things. But there is all the difference in the world between such a state and a *belief* that the tree is such-and-such a number of years old. It is true that books, and other written records, carry information in a richer, conceptually articulated sense, inasmuch as the sentences they contain have compositionally structured semantic content assignable to them; but, of course, such content is only derivative, depending as it does on the capacity of intelligent beings with genuine cognitive states to interpret what is written. Accordingly, such sentences provide no adequate model for the cognitive states of intelligent beings. Sentences in a 'brain code', analogous to the machine code of a computer, cannot then provide an adequate basis for the conceptually articulated cognitive states that we find in human beings – and again I would urge that what such a purely computational account of human cognition crucially neglects is the internal relation between conceptual content and the qualitative character of sensory experience. (A detailed account of that relation is, however, a mammoth task which goes far beyond the ambit of this paper.) To possess any physical concepts at all a being must know how at least some physical objects appear to at least one sense modality. This does not, I hasten to point out, rule out possessing concepts of *unobservable* physical objects, though it does rule out the possibility of a being for whom *no* physical objects were conceived of as observable.

So one reason why a being genuinely capable of belief and judgement must have a capacity for sense perception is that without this it could possess no states with conceptual content. But another reason can be given too, and this is that without a capacity for sense perception a being has no adequate basis upon which to correct its beliefs and judgements – and having an ability to do this is partly constitutive of having an ability to believe and judge at all. In order to appreciate this point, imagine that in addition to our ordinary senses a subject were endowed with an 'extra-sensory' faculty rather like the 'sophisticated' kind of blindsight hypothesised a moment ago, but differing from it in that the deliverances of this faculty would take the form not of 'guesses' but rather of *beliefs* – beliefs to the effect that objects of such-and-such sorts were located in such-and-such places in the subject's vicinity. Thus, on a particular occasion, the subject might suddenly find himself acquiring a belief that a red wooden table was standing in the corner of the room, even though he had detected no such object there by sense (either because he hadn't looked in that direction, or because the light was out, or whatever). We can further suppose, if we like, that the deliverances of this faculty are very often correct. We cannot, however, suppose them to be *infallible*, without invoking supernatural powers.

Now the question we must address is this: what are we presuming when we describe the deliverances of this faculty as *beliefs* that the subject acquires? At the very least, I suggest, we are presuming that the subject is capable of taking a critical stance towards them: that he has at least some idea of what would constitute evidence for or against the deliverances, and hence how he might go about confirming or disconfirming them. In a word, to qualify as genuine beliefs the deliverances must be open to *correction* by the subject. (Of course I don't mean that he must be able to tell, infallibly, whether or not they are correct, only that he should have available some rational strategy for trying to detect errors in them. Incidentally, if this seems to rule out the possibility of animal belief – and I am by no means sure that it does, at least for the higher mammals – then recall that we can still attribute *informational* states to them which fall short of belief.) Now, of course, in the case hypothesised none of this is problematical: for the subject in that case can check the deliverances of the special faculty against the evidence of his senses – he can, for instance, go and *look* for a red table in the corner of the room. It is true that this is not the *only* means he has of weeding out erroneous deliverances of the faculty, since he may be able to weed out some because they conflict with other well-entrenched beliefs that he already has. For instance, if the faculty prompts him to believe that a round square table stands in the corner of the room, he may reject its deliverance because it conflicts with his logical beliefs; if it prompts him to believe that his Aunt Jemima is standing in the corner, when he firmly believes that she is dead, then likewise the deliverances of the faculty may be overridden. However, it is clear that these alternative means of checking the deliverances of the faculty can only play a secondary role to that played by sense perception (and here we should note that when the subject does correct the deliverances of the faculty by appealing to already well-entrenched beliefs of his, many of these will originally have been acquired through sense perception in any case). So we see that it is only in virtue of possessing capacities for sense perception that a subject could genuinely acquire beliefs in the *non*sensory manner which the faculty involves: and hence we see that it is incoherent to suppose that there could be a being *all* of whose capacities for sense perception were replaced by faculties like the one hypothesised.

The lesson is, once again, a not unfamiliar one, since it is the basic thought underlying all traditional empiricist epistemologies – namely, that the acquisition of belief must make contact at some point with sensory experience. It will not do, then, to regard perception *merely* as a mode of belief-acquisition, since this precisely leaves out the crucial contribution of *experience*.

An objection which might be raised here is that it cannot be experience itself, but at most only our beliefs about our experience, that provide a basis for correcting other beliefs of ours: so that the process of checking and adjusting our corpus of belief must after all be one which takes place wholly from *within* that (constantly changing) corpus. Beliefs, on this view, can only be corrected in the light of *other beliefs*, albeit often in the light of beliefs *about our experience*. But I don't accept this, not least because I don't consider that we need to have, or in general do have, the sorts of belief about our experience which this proposal would require us to. When, for instance, I check my belief that there is a red table in the corner of the room by going and having a look, *is* it the case that I must *form a belief that I see a red table there* in order to satisfy myself that my original belief was correct? Surely not: I am satisfied simply provided I enjoy the requisite sort of visual experience. (I don't even have to *believe* that I am having such an experience, much less that in virtue of having it I am seeing a red table.) The assumption behind the objection that I am dismissing would appear to be that beliefs can only be confirmed or corrected by *processes of inference from other beliefs*, but I can see no good grounds for regarding this assumption as true. However, I am now verging on some large and difficult questions of epistemology, which I cannot address within the ambit of the present paper.

One question which I should perhaps address at this point, though, is the question of why it is that in *actual* cases of blindsight, in contrast to our hypothesised case of the subject with the special extra-sensory faculty, the subject's discriminations issue in 'guesses' rather than judgements or beliefs. Couldn't the blindsight subject learn to trust his ability to discriminate stimuli to the extent that his natural response was indeed one of belief? Perhaps so – rather as someone whose 'hunches' about horse race winners were constantly borne out might eventually cease to have 'hunches' and just acquire straightforward *beliefs* about future winners. But the trouble I suppose is that the blindsight subject has no adequate conception of *what it is* that he has to learn to trust. Compare the case of someone who has his vision restored after being blind (in the normal sense) since infancy: he may indeed have to learn to trust his new-found mode of experience. But then at least he is *aware* of what it is that he has to trust as providing a basis for belief. The blindsight subject's problem, however, is that he lacks all awareness of the provenance of his 'guesses', and has no means of determining (internally, at any rate) whether a given 'guess' issues from his blindsight faculty or not. It is not as though a special feeling comes on when the faculty is working, to tell him that it is in operation (as I suspect we imagine happens in the case of the horse race predictor). And this I think should caution us not to take the hypothesised case of the extra-sensory faculty too seriously after all: I suspect that, as described, it is probably of doubtful coherence even if we do grant the subject ordinary modes of sense perception as well. If so, however, this just serves to emphasise all the more how vital genuine sense perception is to the process of belief-acquisition.

III

I want to conclude with some mildly critical remarks about modern computational approaches to perception, again with special emphasis on visual perception. Perhaps the best representative of such an approach is the late David Marr, whose work surely transcends all other in this field in its originality, sophistication and methodological awareness. My complaint is that the goal which theorists like Marr set themselves, though highly relevant to the technology of artificial remote-sensing and kindred matters, is not at bottom the right goal for one concerned to understand the nature of human visual cognition (not that I think that their work has no relevance at all to the latter issue, I hasten to add). In essence, the goal which such theorists set themselves is one of discovering how a (largely geometrical) description of the three-dimensional physical environment can be computed from information encoded in two-dimensional optical images produced by the focusing of light scattered from surfaces in that environment (see Marr 1982, pp. 36ff.). There is some attempt to constrain the choice of computational algorithms for this task by what is known about the neurophysiology of the human eye and brain, but in general the level of 'implementation' (as Marr calls it) is kept fairly firmly in the background (see Marr 1982, pp. 24ff.). I have no particular complaint about that, but what I do object to as importantly misguided is that the computational approach treats visual experiences (if indeed it deigns to mention them at all) as effectively just epiphenomenal. An admirably explicit admission of this is made by Steven Pinker, who writes that subjective experience

> is noncontroversially epiphenomenal if one subscribes to the computational theory of the mind in general. In no computational theory of a mental process does subjective experience *per se* play a causal role ... subjective experience, if it is considered at all, is assumed to be a correlate of ... processing. (Pinker 1985, p. 38)

As I remarked a moment ago, the objective which the computational approach sets itself is one that *is* highly relevant to the problem of designing artificial remote-sensing devices, and this in itself brings out one reason why that approach may be expected to throw less light on human visual cognition than its proponents hope. The point is that in designing such a device one would of course not attempt to endow it with *general intelligence* as a means to enabling it to accomplish its design goals, partly because so little is understood about the nature of general intelligence but also because this would be a strategy of overkill and massively wasteful of computational resources. So for practical purposes the problem of designing such a device has to be seen as that of programming a fundamentally *unintelligent* machine to compute three-dimensional environmental descriptions from two-dimensional optical images. That is a complex problem, of course, as Marr's work makes clear. For instance, one needs to find efficient algorithms to detect 'salient' features like edges, terminations and perhaps texture gradients in the optical array of light intensities, and then further algorithms to compute the angles and distances of physical surfaces from such data, accommodating along the way problems arising from the occlusion of some of these surfaces by others, variations in the ambient illumination, the presence of shadows, and so forth. And even that is only a beginning along the road to a fully three-dimensional object-centred description of the physical environment.

But, I would urge, the complexity of the computational problem involved here arises not least from the fact that there is in this case no possibility of calling on the resources of *general intelligence*, and indeed nothing like visual *experience* for general intelligence to operate upon. An artificial remote-sensing device has to generate environmental descriptions from optical inputs quite *unintelligently*, and of course that is a laborious and complicated task for it (or, more properly, for its designer). But human perceivers, it seems safe to affirm, do *not* operate in this way. We have and use the benefits of *visual experience and general intelligence* to acquire knowledge of our visible surroundings. As I see it, the task which early stages of the human visual processing system have to perform is to deliver to us visual experiences which fairly faithfully reproduce salient aspects of the geometrical structure of the retinal image (I ignore, for simplicity's sake, the complications of stereopsis and chromatic colour vision, neither of which are essential for visual perception). That is certainly no small information-processing task. But thereafter general intelligence can be brought into play, as we shall see.

It surely cannot be dismissed as irrelevant to human visual cognition that we *do* in fact enjoy visual experiences whose qualitative characters display to a striking degree a fundamental isomorphism with the geometrical structures of the retinal images which give rise to those experiences. For instance, if there is a small rectangularly shaped region of relatively uniform light intensity in one quadrant of the retinal image, this will normally translate into a similarly shaped and correspondingly located region of relatively uniform intensity in the extensive space of visual experience enjoyed by the subject – more or less, at any rate. (We should not, incidentally, be misled here by myths about the alleged poverty of the retinal image: the human eye is in fact a remarkably fine optical instrument with a high degree of resolution and little refractive distortion or blur in the normal circumstances of vision: see Gibson 1950, pp. 112, 116.)

Now, *why* do we (unlike blindsight subjects and artificial remote-sensing devices) enjoy visual experiences thus related to our retinal images? Not in order to allow us to acquire knowledge of the properties of those retinal images, to be sure (though we *can* put our experience to this use if we are so minded, provided we possess the appropriate background knowledge which, however, ordinary folk generally lack). Nor do we plausibly enjoy them purely as epiphenomena of neural processing in the optical pathways of the brain (an 'explanation' of the last resort). The answer, I suggest, is that what this state of affairs equips us to do is precisely to acquire a knowledge of the three-dimensional layout of surfaces surrounding us. And the reason why it so equips us is that that layout is fairly accurately specified (at least, once motion parallax is introduced) by the geometrical structure of the retinal image in conjunction with the laws of perspective (subject, once again, to certain rigidity assumptions). That is to say, by making the geometrical structure of the retinal image available to general intelligence in the form of conscious visual experience, the visual system renders a knowledge of the geometry of our physical environment possible for us in virtue of our implicit grasp of certain principles of projective geometry.

It is worth remarking here that recognition of the above-mentioned power of the retinal image to specify its environmental causes was one of J. J. Gibson's major contributions to the understanding of visual perception in his early work, particularly in his book *The Perception of the Visual World*. What was, however, peculiar about his position then and subsequently was that he was reluctant to acknowledge the need for the information encoded in the optical array at the retinal surface to be made available to consciousness in the form of visual experiences. To the limited extent that he allows talk about the qualitative character of visual experience at all, in terms of what he calls the 'visual field', he is usually at pains to play down its cognitive significance. Workers in the computational paradigm, like David Marr, have taken Gibson to task for failing to appreciate how much processing of the retinal image is needed to make its information usefully available to the percipient (see Marr 1982, pp. 29ff.), though they too markedly downplay the significance of visual experience, as we have already seen from Pinker's remarks. I shall return to this curious agreement between opponents a little later.

However, to make the answer I gave a moment ago begin to seem acceptable, I must now explain the sense in which we can be said to possess an implicit knowledge of the laws of perspective and how that knowledge may be presumed to be deployed in the process of visual cognition. In the first place, then, I do not think that a possession of such knowledge *in the form I suppose it to take* should be regarded as particularly taxing intellectually for creatures with our level of general intelligence. I have thus no hesitation in attributing such knowledge to quite young human infants. Of course, I am *not* supposing that we all implicitly grasp certain principles of projective geometry in the form in which those principles would be expressed in textbooks of analytic geometry. Rather, our implicit grasp of those principles manifests itself in our ability to recognise what a wide variety of three-dimensional objects *look like* from a wide variety of points of view: that a pyramidal object looks thus-and-so at such-and-such an angle, and so forth. I am not even supposing that we have an ability to *describe* all these objects and how they look, merely that we are recognitionally sensitive to these facts. And this is a capacity which I believe we all do possess from infancy (indeed, it may quite conceivably be to some degree innate).[4] Some of us, it is true, can *utilise* this geometrical knowledge in more ways than most folk can: for instance, artists and draughtsmen can use it to *depict* how an object looks, as well as to *recognise* it – though even they cannot state explicitly, in mathematical terms, the precise projective relationships concerned, much less compute specific numerical values for the quantities involved. But in the ordinary process of visual perception the knowledge in question is deployed purely at a recognitional level, to motivate judgements about the spatial properties and relations of surrounding objects. No elaborate process of *inference from judgements* about the qualitative character of visual experiences and the

---

[4]For findings which support this view, see Bower 1989, pp. 9ff.

laws of perspective need be invoked here, however, and only a gross intellectualist bias could make one suppose this necessary.

(I should add that I take a very similar stance towards the role of rigidity assumptions in visual cognition. These too need not constitute judgements on the part of the subject and operate on an unreflective level in normal circumstances. Likewise they may well have some innate basis, and don't require to be acquired from experience – indeed *can't* be to the extent that they guide us in the formation of the perceptual judgements that we make on the basis of experience. As to their precise content, this is a complex matter and partly one for empirical psychological research, though what is at least clear is that visual perception would simply be impossible in a world in which physical objects exhibited very much less stability of form than they actually do.)

An objection which might be raised against the approach to visual cognition that I am advocating is that it is just a cheat – that it has 'all the advantages of theft over honest toil'. The complaint would be, then, that I am somehow just assuming as given most of what needs to be explained. I don't agree. I don't, in particular, think that there is any vicious circularity involved in my characterising our implicit knowledge of the laws of perspective in terms of our capacity to recognise how variously shaped objects *look* from various points of view. For I do not regard that capacity as involving perceptual knowledge about a class of *visible properties* of physical objects, their 'looks' (recall my earlier remarks about the communicative purposes of the language of visual appearances). Rather, what this recognitional capacity reflects is an implicit grasp of the laws of functional dependency between the geometrical properties of visible objects and the extensive features of visual experience – and these laws, as we have seen, are precisely the laws of perspective. (Incidentally, it is true enough that if physical space were not locally Euclidean and light did not travel in straight lines, then an object of a given shape would not necessarily look how it actually does from a given angle. But that just reflects the fact that the laws of perspective are not wholly *a priori* principles of pure projective geometry.)

Of course, what my approach *does* assume is general human intelligence – a big mystery, to be sure – but it is no business of a theory of *visual perception* to give an account of general intelligence. Indeed, as I see it, the problem with the computational approach is that it seeks to throw light on human visual cognition *without* invoking general intelligence. As I remarked earlier, that is indeed a sensible strategy if one's goal is to design an artificial remote-sensing device: but that is not what the human visual system *is* (even allowing for the fact that it is natural rather than artificial). For the plain fact is that *we* use our visual experiences and general intelligence in arriving at judgements concerning our visible surroundings, whereas a remote-sensing device possesses neither (and is additionally incapable of making judgements in any case). Of course, these last remarks do not apply to blindsight subjects, who have no visual experiences upon which to turn their general intelligence. Hence it is at least conceivable that visual discrimination in their case *does* operate as it might in an artificial remote-sensing device (moreover, such subjects, as we have seen, do *not* make visual *judgements*). It has in fact often been hypothesised that we have *two* visual systems, only one of which survives in the blindsight subject (see Weiskrantz 1986, p. 162). But then my thesis is that the other, and dominant, visual system is the one which requires to be understood in the way that I propose.

But perhaps it will be objected now that 'general intelligence' *cannot* play anything like the role I take it to in processes of visual cognition, because to suppose that it does is to overlook the extent to which perceptual processes are 'modular', and so 'informationally encapsulated' or 'cognitively impenetrable'.[5] It may be urged that evidence of this is provided, for example, by studies of the various forms of visual agnosia (see Humphreys and Riddoch 1987) – conditions in which subjects suffering from lesions in specific areas of the visual cortex display quite specific disorders of visual recognition, such as prosopagnosia (the inability to recognise familiar faces by sight). For the subjects in question do not, by and large, suffer from any general intellectual impairment.[6]

However, I am not convinced that this sort of objection to my approach is valid. First of all, it appears that many types of visual agnosia involve lesions at locations in the cortex (for instance, in the occipital lobes) at which information from the left and right halves of the retinas is still being processed separately,[7] and hence at a stage prior to the production of

---

[5]See Fodor 1983, pp. 47ff., and Pylyshyn 1984, pp. 214ff., 269.
[6]Fodor makes precisely this point: Fodor 1983, p. 99.
[7]This certainly seems to be true of the case studied by Humphreys and Riddoch: see Humphreys and Riddoch 1987, p. 30, where the patient is described as suffering from 'extensive brain damage in both occipital lobes'.

unified whole-field visual experience.[8] And my proposals only concern what happens *after* the production of such experience. Visual agnosia may, then, be a consequence of the visual system's failure to present the subject with visual experiences whose qualitative content is fully determinate and clearly organised at both local and global levels. On this view, the ability to recognise faces may be specifically affected just because it requires a particularly fine sensitivity to the overall organisation of detailed features, and not because there is a specific 'face-recognition module' in the human visual system which can be selectively affected by damage to dedicated neural circuits. The introspective reports of visually agnosic subjects would seem to confirm this diagnosis. They say, for instance, 'I can see the whole face – the bit I am looking at ... is quite clear ... but everything else is ... as though there was a thin layer all over it or as though it was out of focus' (quoted in Humphreys and Riddoch 1987, p. 87).

In any case, there is considerable evidence, both direct and indirect, that perceptual systems in humans are *not* in fact all that strongly 'encapsulated' or 'cognitively impenetrable'. For example, although we are strongly habituated to interpreting our visual experiences in term of three-dimensional scenes, we can (*pace* Fodor 1983, p. 54) very easily switch to a 'flat', 'pictorial' interpretation, given sufficient motivation and a little practice. Again, there is the evidence provided by experiments with inverting spectacles and other devices for displacing the retinal images systematically. These experiments show that human subjects (unlike, be it noted, less intelligent creatures such as birds and reptiles) are able to adapt remarkably well to such inversions, and indicate that the adaptations do not involve any basic reorganisation of early visual processing but rather a cognitive adjustment on the part of the subject to his visual experience (see Gregory 1972, pp. 204ff.). This conflicts with the suggestion, characteristic of the 'modular' view, that visual recognitional processes are substantially 'hardwired', or possess a relatively fixed neural architecture (see Fodor 1983, p. 98, and Pylyshyn 1984, pp. 215, 269).

As a final example, there is the evidence provided by experiments with 'tactile visual substitution systems' (TVSS), which enable even congenitally

---

[8]Unification would appear to take place in the infero–temporal cortex, which lies 'several synapses beyond the striate cortex' (the latter being in the occipital lobe): see Weiskrantz 1988, pp. 196–197. It was in the temporal lobe that Penfield's previously mentioned electrical stimulations of the cortex elicited visual experiences (Penfield and Roberts 1959). By contrast, stimulation of the striate cortex only gives rise to reports of scattered 'phosphenes': see Weiskrantz 1986, p. 171.

blind adult subjects to achieve three-dimensional quasi-visual perception of objects in their immediate environment, in the course of a training period of the order of three weeks.[9] If different perceptual systems like touch and vision were strongly 'encapsulated', it is hard to see how such rapid adaptation of one, so as to confer on it characteristics of the other, could be achieved through exploratory learning. In view of their complete novelty in a tactile employment, the 3D geometrical recognitional capacities developed and exploited by congenitally blind TVSS users are evidently not capacities that are specific to the domain of tactilely presented information.[10] Nor, in view of their rapid development, can they plausibly be associated with a fixed neural architecture. They would appear, in fact, to be essentially the *same* capacities as those that normally sighted subjects deploy in recognising objective shape from perspectival changes – whence we may reasonably conclude that in the normally sighted too these capacities are not 'hardwired' components of the visual system. (This does not, however, preclude the possibility – which I tentatively endorsed earlier – that the tacit geometrical knowledge involved here may have some innate basis: for I am only concerned to challenge the suggestion that this sort of knowledge is 'encapsulated' in specific perceptual processing modules, as opposed to being an endowment of general intelligence.)

In sum, it emerges that human beings are able to respond remarkably flexibly to their sensory stimulations, and that their perceptual recognitional capacities can be substantially developed and modified, even in adulthood, through intelligent adaptation to changes in the format of these stimulations. If I am right, it is only because we can be *aware* of such changes, by virtue of possessing conscious experience, that we find such adaptation possible. The advantage over less intelligent creatures which such adaptability confers on us is easy to appreciate, and helps to make an evolutionary explanation of the emergence of consciousness quite thinkable. More to the point, though, the clear implication is that, in human beings at least, general intelligence does indeed have an important role to play in processes of perceptual recognition – a role which the often strongly *habitual* character of such

---

[9]See further Bach-y-Rita 1972, and Guarniero 1974. For discussion of some of the implications, see Morgan 1977, pp. 197ff. For discussion of analogous experiments using auditory substitutes for vision with congenitally blind infants, see Bower 1989, pp. 26ff.
[10]'Domain specificity' is, according to the 'modular' view, one of the leading characteristics of perceptual systems: see Fodor 1983, pp. 47ff.

processes should not be allowed to obscure. (Habits don't have to be stupid, nor need they be unamenable to intelligent modification.)

At this point let me return briefly to my earlier observation that one major respect in which advocates of the computational approach to visual perception and advocates of J. J. Gibson's 'ecological' approach are in agreement, despite their many differences, is precisely in their playing down of the role of *conscious visual experiences* in visual perception. The focus of both of these schools is on the question of how the mind-brain can extract environmental information from the light energies encountered by the eye. And that is of course also my concern, at least in part. But the point is that neither of these schools considers as a solution to this problem the possibility that what the human visual system does is to supply the subject with qualitatively structured visual experiences from whose character the subject can extract environmental knowledge by the intelligent (albeit habituated) deployment of a body of implicitly grasped principles, such as those principles of projective geometry whose grasp we manifest (according to my claim) in our perspectival recognitional abilities.[11]

Why, however, is there this concurrence in downplaying visual experience? Partly, no doubt, it reflects a continuing hostility amongst psychologists to subjectivity and introspective awareness, which are exclusively associated (I think mistakenly) with a forbidden Cartesian paradigm of the mind. And in the case of the computational school there is the additional consideration that no-one has the slightest idea how to set about *designing* something to be a recipient of visual experiences, within the computational paradigm. Of course, it is not news that 'qualia' and consciousness pose problems for a functionalist conception of the mind, but it is worth emphasising the point that this is no 'mere' philosophical or metaphysical difficulty, but impinges directly upon the viability of computational explanations of specific human cognitive capacities, like visual perception. Nor does the fact that I myself have little to offer by way of an explanation for the phenomenon of consciousness, and more particularly for the genesis of qualitative states of visual awareness, constitute the basis of a legitimate objection to my own approach to visual

---

[11]Of course, the computational approach *does* invoke something like tacit knowledge of projective geometry (and likewise of rigidity constraints) in its account of visual cognition, so that my opposition to it is by no means unqualified but is focused rather on the questions of where that knowledge resides within our cognitive economy (e.g. whether it is 'encapsulated') and how it is deployed (e.g. whether we exercise it in forming judgements on the basis of the qualitative character of visual experiences).

perception: for at least I do justice to the inescapable fact that such states *occur* and play a vital role in the process of seeing. Better this than to try to explain visual perception *without* reference to visual experiences. For that is to adopt the wrong *explanandum*, and at best offers the prospect of an explanation of blindsight.

One final objection to my emphasis on the role of visual experiences in visual perception might, however, be this: if, as I say, visual experiences possess qualitative or phenomenal characteristics exhibiting a structural isomorphism with certain geometrical properties of the retinal images which give rise to them, how does it *help* for us to have visual experiences *in addition to* retinal images? In order to extract environmental information from *experiences*, won't we need to process *them* in very much the same way in which retinal images are supposed to be processed by early stages of the visual system? Won't we, for instance, have to possess some way of detecting edges, terminations, texture gradients and so on *in the qualitative array of experiential features* constitutive of a visual experience? No we won't, for this is to overlook one of the crucial differences between visual experiences and retinal images, namely that the former are constituents of consciousness whereas the latter are just a species of physical object (in the broadest sense of the term). We do not have to *detect* structure in our visual experiences, for what they are is precisely *structured states of awareness*. Visual experiences are not objects of visual perception – items that we *see*. By contrast, retinal images are indeed precisely this, by my account (see Lowe 1986b, pp. 279-281). They are, as I say, physical objects (in the broad sense), being patterns of electromagnetic energy-distribution with location and dimensions in physical space. Their crucial role in the process of human visual perception arises from the fact that they encode highly specific information about properties of the environmental objects that are of direct concern to us. Visual experience makes this information available to us by more or less replicating relevant features of the retinal image in the structural organisation of phenomenal awareness, which general intelligence then enables us to decode by exploiting our implicit grasp of such principles as the laws of perspective. That, at any rate, is the story that I have tried to tell in this paper. If it has at times the air of (what some would regard as) old-fashioned empiricism, that is not something which I find in the least embarrassing.[12]

---

[12]I am especially grateful to Peter Smith and Tim Crane for comments on earlier versions of this paper.

5   *Scenarios, concepts and perception*

CHRISTOPHER PEACOCKE

1   *Scenarios*

A perceptual experience represents the world as being a certain way. What is the nature of the content it represents as holding? How is our mastery of observational concepts related to these perceptual contents? In the course of addressing these questions, I will be identifying two kinds of representational content on which we can draw in giving accounts of concepts which have peculiarly close links with perception.

The representational content of experience is a many-splendoured thing. This is true not only of the remarkable range of detail in the perceptual content, but also of the range of different, and philosophically interesting, types of content that can be possessed by a particular experience. I begin with what is arguably the most fundamental type of representational content. The sense in which this type of content is arguably the most fundamental is that representational properties of other sorts all in various ways presuppose the existence of this first type of content.

I suggest that one basic form of representational content should be individuated by specifying which ways of filling out the space around the perceiver are consistent with the representational content's being correct. The idea is that the content involves a spatial *type*, the type being that under which fall precisely those ways of filling the space around the subject which are consistent with the correctness of the content. On this model, correctness of a content is then a matter of instantiation: the instantiation by the real world around the perceiver of the spatial type which gives the representational content in question.

We can sharpen up this intuitive formulation. There are two steps which we have to take if we are to specify fully one of these spatial types. The first

105

step is to fix an origin and axes. The origin and axes will not be a specific place and set of directions in the real world. This is precisely because at the moment we are fixing a type which may potentially be instantiated at many different places in the real world. Nevertheless, it is important that the origin and axes be labelled by certain interrelated properties. It is this labelling by interrelated properties which helps to constrain what are instantiations of the spatial type we are determining. Thus, for instance, one kind of origin is given by the property of being the centre of the chest of the human body, with the three axes given by the directions back/front, left/right and up/down with respect to that centre.

The use of a particular set of labelled axes in giving part of the content of an experience is not a purely notational or conventional matter. The appropriate set of labelled axes captures distinctions in the phenomenology of experience itself. Looking straight ahead at Buckingham Palace is one experience. It is another to look at it with one's face still towards the Palace, but with one's body turned towards a point on the right. In this second case, the Palace is experienced as being off to one side from the direction of straight ahead – even if the view remains exactly the same as in the first case.

To say that bodily parts are mentioned in the labelling of the axes is not to imply that the bodily parts are given to the subject in some visual or other sensory manner. It is not necessary, in experiencing something as standing in certain spatial relations to one's own body, to perceive one's own bodily parts. They may even be anaesthetised. The nature of the way in which bodily parts are given when they are appropriate labels for the axes is actually an issue of considerable interest. For present purposes, though, let us just note that we are committed in using this framework to the existence of some such way in which bodily parts are so given.

In giving the content of tactile experience, we would sometimes have to use as origin something labelled with the property of being the centre of the palm of the human hand, with axes defined by relation to parts of the hand. Actually in the specification of the representational content of some human experiences one would need to consider several such systems of origins and axes, and we would need to specify the spatial relations of these systems to one another. There are many other complexities too; but let us keep things simple at this stage.

Having fixed origin and axes, we need to take the second step in determining one of our spatial types, viz. that of specifying a way of filling out the space around the origin.[1] In picking out one of these ways, we need to do at least the following. We need, for each point (strictly one should say point-type) identified by its distance and direction from the origin, to specify whether there is a surface there, and if so what texture, hue, saturation, brightness and temperature it has at that point, together with its degree of solidity. The orientation of the surface must be included. So must much more in the visual case: the direction, intensity and character of light sources; the rate of change of perceptible properties, including location; indeed it should include second differentials with respect to time where these prove to be perceptible.

There is no requirement at this point that the conceptual apparatus used in specifying a way of filling out the space be an apparatus of concepts used by the perceiver himself. Any apparatus we want to use, however sophisticated, may be employed in fixing the spatial type, however primitive the conceptual resources of the perceiver with whom we are concerned. This applies both to the apparatus used in characterising distances and directions, and to that employed in characterising the surfaces, features and the rest. I will return to the significance of this point later.

We are now in a position to say with slightly more precision what one of our spatial types is. It is a way of locating surfaces, features and the rest in relation to such a labelled origin and family of axes. I call such a spatial type a *scenario*.

With this apparatus, we can then say what is required for the correctness of a representational content of the sort with which I am concerned. Consider the volume of the real world around the perceiver at the time of the experience, with an origin and axes in the real world fixed in accordance with the labelling in the scenario. We can call this a *scene*. The content of the experience is correct if this scene falls under the way of locating surfaces and the rest which constitutes the scenario.

It is important to give for experiences a notion of their representational content which is evaluable as correct or as incorrect outright, rather than merely as correct or as incorrect relative to some assignment or other. The point parallels (and indeed is connected with) a familiar point in the philosophy of language. Consider a particular utterance of the indexical

---

[1]Strictly, in giving the content we should consider a set of such ways of filling out the space. By doing so, we can capture the degree of perceptual acuity; greater acuity corresponds to restriction of the set of ways of filling out the space whose instantiation is consistent with the correctness of the representational content. I shall take this qualification as read for the remainder of this paper.

sentence 'He is witty'. A theory should provide a statement of the conditions under which this particular utterance is true outright, rather than merely the conditions under which it is true relative to any given assignment of objects to its indexical elements (Burge 1974). It is the content of the utterance which is assessable outright which concerns particular objects. Similarly, it is the content of a perceptual experience which is assessable outright that concerns particular places. For perceptual experience, I identify such an outright-assessable content with a *positioned scenario*. A positioned scenario consists of a scenario, together with (i) an assignment to the labelled axes and origins of the scenario of real directions and places in the world which fall under the labels, and (ii) an assigned time. For a particular perceptual experience, the real directions and places assigned at (i) are given by the application of the labels to the subject who enjoys the experience – if the origin is labelled as the centre of gravity of the body, the real place assigned to it is the centre of gravity of the perceiver's body; and so forth.[2] The time assigned at (ii) is the time at which the perceptual experience occurs: perceptual experience has a present-tense content.[3] We can then say that the content given by the positioned scenario is correct if the scene at its assigned place falls under its scenario at the assigned time, when the scenario is positioned there in accordance with the assigned directions.

The requirement that any perceptual experience has a correctness condition imposes restrictions on what other forms of perceptual experience, besides those of human beings, are possible. Suppose it were said that there could exist a being whose perceptions have scenario-involving contents which concern an origin, but do not contain labelled axes. Now a correctness condition for a particular experience occurring at a given time is not fixed until its scenario is positioned in the real world. An origin alone does not suffice for this positioning: there will be many different ways of orienting it around the perceiver's location at the time of the experience. Until one of these orientations has been selected as being the appropriate one, no correctness condition has been determined. Even in the case of spherical organisms, existing in a fluid, whose perceptions are caused by the impact of light all over the surface of their bodies, the

---

[2]There are several oversimplifications here; I am aiming to capture the spirit of a position.

[3]The time at which the mental representation underlying the experience is computed, however, may bear a complex relation to the time represented in the content of the experience. See Dennett forthcoming.

scenarios presented by such organisms' experiences must have axes labelled by parts of their bodies. (The parts mentioned in the labelling need not be limbs.) I will return to this labelling later.

I should also emphasise that the positioned scenario is literally meant to be the content itself. It is not a mental representation of the content; nor a specification of a representation; nor a way of thinking of anything. Subpersonal mental representations of different sorts may equally have for their content the same particular component of a scenario. For example, the orientation of a surface at a particular point may be given by specifying its slant and tilt, or equally by specifying components for its representation in gradient space.[4] Mental representations which differ in the way such orientations are represented may nevertheless represent the same scenario as instantiated in their respective subjects' surroundings.

Since we have now touched on the issue of mental representation, it may be helpful for me to comment on the relation between the account being developed here and Marr's $2^1/_2$D sketch. There can be much in a positioned scenario which is not in the content of a $2^1/_2$D sketch. The $2^1/_2$D sketch has only retinocentric coordinates, and does not include illumination conditions. The present material does, though, give a natural framework in which to give the content of a $2^1/_2$D sketch, if such mental representations exist.

Is the present account committed at least to the existence of mental representations with roughly the properties of Marr's $2^1/_2$D sketches? In Marr's work, such representations are computed after the primal sketch and before any 3D models are assigned to shapes in the environment. Is the present philosophical treatment committed to the existence of such a temporally intermediate representation? It is not. What matters for the purposes to which this apparatus will be put is that there exist some mental representation at least part of whose content is given by the positioned scenario. It does not matter if the representation also has other, perhaps simultaneously computed, contents. It will matter that certain systematic connections hold between these scenario-involving contents and other contents that the representations may possess. I will be arguing that the identity of certain other contents depends upon the nature of their links with scenario-involving contents. But again, this does not require the existence of distinct mental representations with roughly the properties of Marr's $2^1/_2$D sketches.

---

[4]For these two ways of representing surface orientation at a point, see Marr 1982, pp. 241–243.

A good theory must elucidate the appropriate correctness conditions for perceptual experiences if it is adequately to distinguish these experiences from states which do not represent to the subject the world as being a certain way. But the importance of elucidating representational content goes far beyond the need to draw that distinction in the right place. By perceiving the world, we frequently learn whether a judgement with a given conceptual content is true or not. This is possible only because a perceptual experience has a correctness condition whose holding may itself exclude, or require, the truth of a conceptual content.

Some conceptual contents are actually individuated in part by their relations to those perceptual experiences which give good reasons for judging those contents. I will give some detailed examples later. But in advance of the details, it should be clear that scenarios are a promising resource for anchoring notions of conceptual content in some level of nonconceptual content. For a scenario is a spatial type, and a positioned scenario is just a spatial type as tied down to a particular location, orientation and time. A spatial type is quite different from a concept. The identity of a concept, as the term is used here, is answerable to Fregean considerations of cognitive significance. A concept is also ultimately individuated by the condition required for a thinker to possess it. A spatial type is not. So a theory of nonconceptual content which employs the notion of a spatial type promises one way in which a hierarchy of families of concepts can be grounded in a noncircular way.

The notion of a positioned scenario I have been employing is one that can give the content of a fully perceptual experience, and can equally give the content of an experience which is hallucinatory. But it would be quite consistent with the apparatus I've introduced to hold that the fully perceptual case has a philosophical primacy, and that nonperceptual cases have to be elucidated by the relations in which they stand to the fully perceptual case. Consider two different scenes, the objects in each of which are distinct, but which are perceived fully veridically, and in the same way. We can regard a scenario as being the type which captures the similarity of two such different perceptual cases. It is then open to us to say that a hallucinatory experience represents the environment as being a scene of such a type, though there is no such scene there. In brief, the scenario account neither exacerbates nor by itself solves epistemological problems.

2   *Scenarios: consequences and comparisons*

There are several desirable consequences of the thesis that the objective content of an experience is given by its positioned scenario.

(a) Writers on the objective content of experience have often remarked that an experience can have a finer-grained content than can be formulated by using concepts possessed by the experiencer. If you are looking at a range of mountains, it may be correct to say that you see some as rounded, some as jagged. But the content of your visual experience in respect of the shape of the mountains is far more specific than that description indicates. The description involving the concepts *round* and *jagged* would cover many different fine-grained contents which your experience could have, contents which are discriminably different from one another.

This fine-grained content is captured in the scenario. Only those ways of filling out the space around you which are consistent with the veridicality of your experience will be included in the scenario. The ways included in the scenario will omit many which equally involve the appropriate mountains being rounded or jagged.

In describing the scenario, of course, we do have to employ concepts. If we are to fix on the scenario uniquely, we will indeed have to use very fine-grained concepts too, to capture the fine-grained content. But it is crucial to observe that the fact that a concept is used in fixing the scenario does not entail that that concept itself is somehow a component of the experience's representational content, nor that the concept must be possessed by the experiencer. The fine-grained concepts have done their work when they have fixed a unique spatial type. We should not confuse the scenario, the spatial type itself, with the infinitely various ways of picking it out. It is the type which is involved in the content of the experience, not descriptions of the type.

Correlatively, we have on this account to recognize the rather indirect way in which descriptions in ordinary language, which are always at least partially conceptualised, help to characterise the way someone is experiencing the world. The ordinary-language characterisation of the scenario can be at most partial.

(b) In some of my own earlier writings, I discussed the senses in which the type of content possessed by perceptual experience is analogue and unit-free (see Peacocke 1986a, Peacocke 1989a). Let us take 'analogue' first. To say that the type of content in question is analogue is to make the following point. There are many dimensions – hue, shape, size, direction – such that any value on that dimension may enter the fine-grained content of an experience. In particular, an experience is not restricted in its range of possible contents to those points or ranges picked out by concepts – *red*, *square*, *straight ahead* – possessed by the perceiver. This fact is accommodated by attributing a scenario content. It is accommodated for characteristics of points in the environment because any values of a perceptible dimension may be mentioned in the ways which comprise the scenario. The restrictions on the environment determined by the veridicality of the experience need not be formulable using concepts possessed by the subject independently of the occurrence of the experience. With some important qualifications to be given below, nonpunctual properties such as shape in the scenario will be determined by the assignments to points. Again there will be no restrictions resulting from the thinker's repertoire of shape concepts on the shapes he may perceive things as having.

The unit-free nature of spatial perception is illustrated by the fact that when we see a table to have a certain width, we do not see it as having a certain width in inches, say, as opposed to centimetres. This is also explained by the distinction between the ways of characterizing a scenario and the scenario itself. Suppose we prescind here from qualifications about perceptual acuity. Then we can say that one and the same restriction on the distance between the sides of the table, one and the same restriction on the ways in which the space around the perceiver can be filled consistently with the experience being fully veridical, is given by doing these two things: saying that the sides are 39.4 inches apart, and saying that they are 100 centimetres apart.

The same point also holds for directions and the units in which they may be measured.

(c) The scenario account provides for the possibility of amodal contents of experience, in the sense that it allows for overlapping contents of experiences in different sense modalities. The restrictions on the environment required by the correctness of a visual experience may overlap with the restrictions required by the correctness of a tactile experience. This can be so if the positions, relative to each other, of the origins and axes for the scenarios of the contents of each experience are fixed by the subject's total conscious state. Both a visual experience, and a tactile experience resulting from stretching out your arm at a certain angle, may represent the existence of a surface in front of you at a certain distance. It is because this is so that, at a higher, concept-involving level, the judgement 'That surface is red and warm' does not, when one is taking one's experience at face value, rest on any identity belief concerning the surface in question. I will consider amodal conceptual contents further below.

There is a very great deal more to be said on all aspects of this account. But even on this very primitive foundation, two considerations support the claim that an account mentioning scenarios cannot be dispensed with in favour of purely propositional accounts of the representational contents in question. By a 'purely propositional' account I mean one which identifies the representational content with a set of propositions (whether built to Frege's, Russell's, or some other specification), where the constituents of these propositions do not involve, directly or indirectly, scenarios.

First, it is hard to see how a purely propositional account can be made plausible without being parasitic on something properly treated by use of scenarios. Suppose you are in a field in the early autumn in England, and see mist in a certain region. Can a theorist specify part of the representational content of your visual experience by means of the proposition, concerning that region, that it has the property of being misty? Consider in particular the Russellian proposition, which has the region itself as a constituent. This proposal seems inadequate for very familiar reasons. Suppose the region in question is to your north. Someone for whom the region is in a north-easterly direction may also see it to be misty, and the same Russellian proposition would be used by this theorist in specifying the content of his experience. But the region is clearly presented in perception in different ways to you and to the other person. Each of you sees it as being in a different direction relative to yourself, and your actions may differ as a result. Any description of the contents of your two experiences which omits this difference is incomplete. If we fill out the propositional theory to include 'ways in which regions are perceived', the advocate of the scenario account will understandably say that these 'ways' are a prime example of something of which only his account gives an adequate explanation.

To this the purely propositional theorist may reply that the relevant aspect of representational content should be formulated not just as '*R* is misty', where *R* is the region in question, but with a conjunction of Russellian propositions: '*R* is misty and *R* is located in direction *D*'. Here *D* is an egocentric direction.

The theorist of scenarios should say that this move is inadequate on either of the two ways of taking it. The two ways of taking it result from two different ways of construing 'egocentric'. Take first the construal on which seeing something to be in egocentric direction D involves merely seeing it as having a certain direction in relation to object x, where in fact x is the perceiver himself. This reading is too weak to capture what is wanted. This is because one can see something as having a particular direction in relation to an object x which is in fact oneself whilst not realizing that the object to which one sees it as bearing that relation is in fact oneself. Examples of persons seen in mirrors suffice to make the point.

This suggests that the propositional theorist needs rather the stronger construal. On the stronger construal, to see something as having an egocentric spatial property is to see it as standing in a certain relation to oneself, where this involves use of the first-person way of thinking in giving the content of the visual experience. But the second consideration I wish to develop is precisely that purely propositional accounts, unlike the theory of scenarios, make impossible an adequate account of the first-person way of thinking.

We have just seen that the pure propositionalist will have to mention the first-person way of thinking in giving his propositional contents of experience. For the pure propositionalist, propositional contents exhaust the nonconceptual representational content of experience. But this position is incompatible with the conjunction of two other principles which we have reason to accept.

One of these principles is what we can call 'Evans' Thesis' (Evans 1982, pp. 223–224). This states that it is partially constitutive of a subject's employing the first-person way of thinking that he is prepared to make, noninferentially, suitable first-person spatial judgements on the basis of his perceptions when these are taken at face value. These will include 'I am on a bridge' when he has an experience as of being on a bridge, 'I am in front of a building', 'There is a dog on my right', and so forth.

The other principle is what I call 'the Principle of Dependence', which states that there can be no more to a concept than is determined by a correct account of what it is to possess that concept. If the Principle of Dependence is true, then we can (with many qualifications and refinements) individuate concepts by filling out this schematic form: concept F is that concept C to possess which a thinker must meet condition $A(C)$. Here the concept F must not be mentioned as such within the scope of psychological states ascribed to the thinker. If it is, we will not have individuated the concept without residue in terms of what it is to possess it (see Peacocke 1989d).

In my judgement, the Principle of Dependence is a powerful tool in the theory of thought and in philosophy more generally. But the application of the Principle which is of interest here is to first-person thought. If we accept Evans' Thesis, then the first-person way of thinking will be individuated in part by the rational sensitivity of present-tense spatial judgements containing it to the content of a thinker's perceptual experiences. But according to the propositionalist, these experiences themselves already have a first-person content which is not itself explained directly or indirectly, in terms of scenarios. So the propositionalist will not have given an account of the first person which respects the Principle of Dependence. An account of mastery of a concept is still circular if it adverts to the enjoyment of perceptual states with a content requiring possession of the concept whose possession was to be elucidated.

This problem is not solved for the pure propositionalist merely by saying that he holds that neither experience nor thought is prior in the individuation of the first-person way of thinking (a 'no-priority' view). As long as it is agreed that part of the account of mastery of the first-person concept involves a certain distinctive sensitivity of first-person spatial judgements to the deliverances of perceptual experience, there is an obligation to say what that sensitivity is without simply taking possession of the first-person concept for granted. If we accept the Principle of Dependence, an account of grasp of the first-person concept must distinguish it from all other concepts. Certainly the pure propositionalist does not have something individuating if he says that the first person (for a given subject) is that concept m such that his judgements about whether Fm display a certain sensitivity to experiences which represent Fm as being the case. This condition will be met by much else, including demonstrative ways of thinking of places in his immediate surroundings. A natural further condition is one which relates first-person present-tense spatial judgements in a particular way to the scenario content of experience. But if this further condition is correct, the resulting treatment of the content of experience is not a purely propositional theory – it employs scenario content after all.

It should not, of course, be any part of the scenario account to deny that the first person has to be mentioned in fully specifying the representational content of perceptual experience. It should insist on first-person contents, as it should equally insist on the partially conceptual character of the perceptual content when one sees something to be a dog, or a tree. The issue is rather, in the case of the first person, whether or not the theorist can say more about the nature of the first-person content. The scenario account can respect the Principle of Dependence applied to the first person in the following way. The scenario account already says that a fundamental type of representational content is given by a scenario, a spatial type which involves a labelled origin and labelled axes. The rational sensitivity picked out in Evans' Thesis should be understood as a rational sensitivity of first-person present-tense spatial judgements to the spatial relations things are represented in the scenario of the experience as having *to the labelled central bodily origin and axes*. This avoids the circularity, and in an intuitive way. Of course we still owe a philosophical account of what it is for one scenario, with one set of labelled axes and origin rather than another, to be the content of an experience. But once we recognise the level of the scenario, there is nothing to make this problem insoluble.

Devotees of the theory of indexical thought will note that points exactly corresponding to those just made about first-person thought can be made about the perceptual-indexical concept *here*. There would equally be a circularity in the philosophical account of mastery of *here* in its relation to perceptual experience if we were not able to make reference to the labelled origin in an experience's scenario.

Though I have been arguing that scenario content cannot be replaced by pure propositional contents, propositional contents (even of a neo-Russellian kind) can still be important in characterizing further features of perceptual content, once we have the level of scenario content in place. I shall be arguing for just such a view in the next section.

3 *A further level of content: and an application*

We have touched on one way in which scenarios can contribute to the individuation of a concept, the first-person concept. I turn now to discuss how some other conceptual contents are individuated in part by their relations to a level of nonconceptual representational content. I will be suggesting that we need to recognise a kind of nonconceptual representational content in addition to the positioned scenario.

How is mastery of such apparently partially perceptual shape concepts as *square*, *cubic*, *diamond-shaped* or *cylindrical* related to the nonconceptual content of experience? In the general framework I favour, the task is to say how the various possession conditions for these concepts mention the

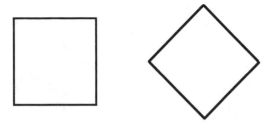

Figure 1

nonconceptual contents of experiences (see Peacocke 1989d). We can take the concept *square* as the example for discussion. The concept intended is the relatively observational shape concept which can be possessed without the subject's awareness of any geometrical definition. It is also a concept which has, inherently, fuzzy boundaries.

We can enter the issues by considering a natural, simple suggestion about what is necessary for possession of the concept *square*. This simple suggestion is built up using the materials we have developed so far. Suppose a thinker is taking his experiences at face value. Suppose too that in the positioned scenario of his experience, the area of space apparently occupied by a perceived object is square. Then, this simple account suggests, the thinker must find the present-tense demonstrative thought that that object is square to be primitively compelling.

This simple account is not circular. It uses the concept *square* in fixing a certain sort of scenario; we emphasised earlier that that does not require the thinker to possess the concept *square*. This simple account can be written out in a way which makes it clearly capable of featuring as part of a longer story which, in the terminology of 'What Are Concepts?', is of the *A(C)* form. Indeed it is plausible that any theory of possession of these relatively observational shape concepts will have at some point to exploit this way of avoiding circularity.

The necessary condition proposed by the simple account is, however, not in fact necessary. That it is not necessary is already shown by Mach's example of the square and the diamond (Figure 1; see Mach 1914, p. 106).

A thinker, taking his experiences at face value and possessing this concept *square*, need not find it primitively compelling (without further reflection) that a floor-tile in the diamond orientation is square. But it can still be that in the positioned scenario of his experience, the region of space

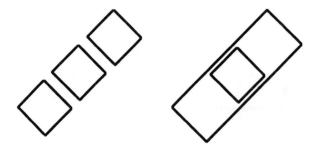

Figure 2

apparently occupied by the floor-tile is square – as indeed it will be if his experience is veridical.

The case illustrates a first respect in which we need to qualify Evans' pioneering discussion of these issues. He wrote that

> To have the visual experience of four points of light arranged in a square amounts to no more than being in a complex informational state which embodies information about the egocentric location of those lights. (Evans 1985a, p. 392)

Four points of light arranged in a regular diamond shape will produce an informational state which embodies information about the egocentric location of those lights. The informational state produced need not be an experience of them as arranged in a square.

Mach's example does not show that scenarios are irrelevant to the difference between the concepts *square* and regular *diamond*. What it does show is that they cannot be used in so simple a fashion; they need to be supplemented with the use of further materials. I doubt that this can be done solely with the materials provided by scenario content. Certainly one should not impose the condition that mastery of the concept *square* is tied in some distinctive way to perception of squares in the orientation of the left-hand square in Figure 1. It is certainly possible to see a square at other orientations as a square. Indeed, as Stephen Palmer has emphasized, one can even, naïvely, see a square at a 45 degree angle as a square, rather than a regular diamond, if the context is right (see Figure 2, from Palmer 1983, p. 301).

Intuitively, the difference between perceiving something as a square and perceiving it as a (regular) diamond is in part a difference in which symmetries are perceived. When something is perceived as a diamond, the perceived symmetry is a symmetry about the bisectors of its angles. When something is perceived as a square, the perceived symmetry is a symmetry about the bisectors of its sides.[5] So intuitively, the simple account should be supplemented by requiring that, for the case it treats, the object apparently occupying the region in question be perceived as symmetrical about the bisectors of its sides. But does perceiving something as *symmetrical* require the perceiver to possess and make use of the concept *symmetrical*? If so, then what we will have done is simply to explain (this part of) mastery of the concept *square* in terms which require mastery of other concepts. We will not have anchored the difference between the concepts *square* and *diamond* at a level of nonconceptual content. If on the other hand there is a sense in which perceiving something as symmetrical does not require possession of the concept *symmetrical*, what is that sense? And how do we capture the nature of the additional content which distinguishes a case in which we have not merely veridical perception of a symmetrical region, but also have that symmetry perceived? I will sketch one way of answering these two questions.

I suggest that perceptual experience has a second layer of nonconceptual representational content. The contents at this second layer cannot be identified with positioned scenarios, but they are nevertheless distinct too from conceptual contents. These additional contents I call *protopropositions*. These protopropositions are assessable as true or false. A protoproposition contains an individual or individuals, together with a property or relation. When a protoproposition is part of the representational content of an experience, the experience represents the property or relation in the protoproposition as holding of the individual or individuals it also contains. I write of proto*propositions* rather than protothoughts because protopropositions contain objects, properties and relations, rather than concepts thereof. I write of *proto*propositions because they are not, on the present account, determined as part of the content of an experience by being fixed by some conceptual content the experience possesses. The protopropositions which enter the representational content of ordinary

---

[5]'People perceive different geometrical properties of the figure when it is seen as a square rather than as a diamond' (Palmer 1983, p. 293). Palmer's paper contains further material of great relevance to a philosophical theory of these matters.

human visual experience contain such properties and relations as SQUARE, CURVED, PARALLEL TO, EQUIDISTANT FROM, SAME SHAPE AS, and SYMMETRICAL ABOUT.[6] These properties and relations can be represented as holding of places, lines or regions in the positioned scenario; or of objects perceived as located in such places. There will of course be many equally acceptable set-theoretic ways of building up such propositions.

Because it is properties and relations, rather than concepts thereof, which protopropositions contain, there is no immediate circularity in mentioning this level of representational content in individuating certain conceptual contents. As always, of course, we will want to have a substantive theory of what it is to be in perceptual states with protopropositional contents.

Protopropositional content is not determined by positioned scenario content. Two experiences can have the same positioned scenario content but different protopropositional contents. Many familiar cases can illustrate this. One illustration is given by the case in which one comes to see two shapes in the environment to be the same – one a tilted version of the other, say, even though the single shape in question is quite unfamiliar. The experiences before and after seeing the identity of shape have the same representational content at the level of the positioned scenario. They differ in that the later experience has amongst its protopropositional contents that the two objects are of the same shape. An even more familiar case is given by certain differences in spatial grouping. When you see a two-dimensional array of elements as grouped in columns rather than rows, your experience has the protopropositional content that certain elements, which are in fact vertically arranged, are co-linear. But there need not be any difference in the positioned scenario content between the case in which the array is seen as grouped in columns and that in which it is seen as grouped in rows.[7]

Protopropositional content plays an important role in memory, in recognition and in the subject's construction of a cognitive map of his world. When a subject perceives some of an object's properties and the relations of some of its parts, his memory of the object and for its

---

[6]I use upper-case letters for a word to indicate that I am referring to the property or relation to which it refers, rather than to the concept it expresses.

[7]The preceding discussion revises the treatment of this case given in Peacocke 1983, without altering the general view required of the relation between sensational and representational properties of experience. For another discussion which treats this case by using propositional contents, see DeBellis forthcoming. DeBellis develops the use of propositional contents in giving the contents of perceptions of Western music.

perceptual type is greatly facilitated. When his perceptual experience has such protopropositional contents, the subject does not have to remember highly detailed scenario contents, with their specifications for each point. There is no need for so much detail, provided he can remember the salient properties and relations in which the object and its parts were perceived to stand. Protopropositional content is equally important to recognition. We may see an object, and thereby acquire an ability to recognize it when we re-encounter it. But the re-encounter will frequently present the object from a different angle, a different distance, and the object's own orientation to its environment may vary too. If there were only a meagre protopropositional content in the original perception of the object, immensely complex operations on a highly detailed content would be necessary for perceptual recognition of the object. But with a detailed protopropositional content, the task is eased. That two lines are straight, that they form a right angle, that an object is symmetrical about one of its axes, can enter the content of two experiences in which the same object is presented at very different angles, distances, or in a different orientation to its surroundings. A corresponding point applies to the construction of a cognitive map. The presence of protopropositional content reduces the demands on the thinker. As he moves, he can register that a certain line is straight, and enter this appropriately in his cognitive map after he has moved away, rather than having to transform one complex scenario content into a corresponding complex content for his map.

The reader will not be surprised to learn that it is this level of protopropositional content which I propose to employ to avert the threatened failure to give an account of the difference between the concepts *square* and *diamond*. When we say that in an experience of something as a square, the symmetry about the bisectors of its sides must be perceived, we are noting a restriction at the level of protopropositional content. An experience in which something is perceived as a square is one whose nonconceptual representational content contains the protoproposition that a certain figure is symmetrical about a line, a line which in fact in the positioned scenario of the experience bisects the figure's sides.

The reader may also have been wishing to protest for some time that there is an argument that the components of content I have tried to capture by the properties and relations of protopropositions are after all really conceptual. Consider the predicative component of the demonstrative content, judged on the basis of perception, 'That line is straight'. Isn't what is judged here of the line the same as the way experience represents the line to be? So if the component of the content judged is conceptual, must not that of the perception be likewise?

My reply is twofold. First, there are many examples which should make us acknowledge that a subject can perceive a property or relation without conceptualizing it. The symmetry of an inkblot shape can be perceived by one who does not have the concept of symmetry. Such a shape does not appear the same to one who does not perceive the symmetry as to one who does. But to perceive the symmetry, the subject does not have to be capable of exercising the concept *symmetrical* in his thoughts, or to be capable of combining it with any singular mode of presentation he possesses. The property SYMMETRICAL features in the protopropositional content of this subject's experience, without being conceptualized by him. Again, there is a difference between hearing the note middle C and the F# just above it, when sounded simultaneously, as an augmented fourth and hearing it as a diminished fifth. I now follow DeBellis (forthcoming) in describing the difference between the two cases in terms of the relations in which the notes are perceived to stand. When they are perceived as an augmented fourth, the F# is perceived as the seventh of the scale with G as tonic, and the C as the fourth thereof. When they are perceived as a diminished fifth, the upper note is perceived as the fourth of the scale with D flat as tonic, and the C as the seventh thereof. There is no question but that the interval can be perceived in either of these ways by someone without even the most rudimentary personal-level knowledge of the classifications of music theory; that is, by someone without the apparatus for conceptualizing the relations he perceives. Finally, as a third case, consider the two most salient ways of perceiving an utterance of the familiar sentence, 'Visiting royalty can be boring'. It seems to me correct to say of an English hearer of an utterance of this sentence that he hears it under one rather than another of its structural descriptions. What this involves in one of the two cases is the hearer perceiving it as, roughly, the royalty of which the boringness is being predicated, rather than that of a certain kind of visit. When heard this way, the components of the uttered sentence are heard as standing in certain relations to one another. But I doubt that the ordinary speaker-hearer has to have, at the personal level, the apparatus for conceptualizing these syntactico-semantic relations. I doubt that the ordinary speaker–hearer has to be capable of thoughts about these syntactico-semantic relations. The ordinary speaker-hearer either hears the utterance as meaning that it can be boring to visit royalty, or hears the utterance as meaning that when royalty visit, they can be boring. It would not be right to say that talk of one structural description rather than another being perceived is merely projected backwards from the sentence being heard as having one complete meaning rather than another. Consider someone who understands much of English, including the '-ing' suffix applied to verbs, but who does not understand the verb 'to bore' as intended in the example. This subject can still hear the sentence under one rather than another of its structural descriptions. The plausible hypothesis, it seems to me, is that far from perception of structural descriptions being projected backwards from perceived meaning, it is rather true that perception of the sentence as structured one way rather than another, or what underlies such perception, positively contributes to the hearer's perception of the sentence as having one meaning rather than another. As in the musical and the spatial cases, the syntactico-semantic relations are perceived but not conceptualized.

The second part of the reply to the imagined objection is concessive, at least to part of the spirit of the objection. There is indeed a conceptual component of the judgement that is intimately related to experiences with protopropositional contents that certain perceived things are straight. But this conceptual content is one which is individuated in part by certain of its relations to such protopropositional contents. As in the first-person case, and certain others to follow, it is not part of the present position that perceptual experiences do not have conceptual contents involving this concept *straight*. They do in general have such a conceptual content. What matters to the present position is that if we are to have a noncircular and individuating account of mastery of this perceptual concept *straight*, that mastery must be related to some feature of experience which does not have to be explained in terms which presuppose possession of the concept. We cannot supply this by relating the mastery to experiences whose positioned scenarios require for their correctness that a certain line be straight: for that can be so without the straightness being perceived. Having the property STRAIGHT in the protopropositional content respects that point, without threatening a circular account of mastery. These points, just made for properties and certain concepts of them, also have structural analogues for objects and perceptual–demonstrative modes of presentation of them.

A congenitally blind man can possess the perceptual concept *square*, and apply it on the basis of his tactile experience of the world. There is a good case to be made that *square* and other perceptual shape concepts are not modality-specific – are amodal, as I will say. There is a natural criterion for the amodality of a concept within the framework of the $A(C)$ form and possession conditions. A concept is amodal if there is no particular sense modality such that the concept's possession condition mentions the thinker's sensitivity of beliefs containing the concept to experiences in that particular modality. Let us adopt that criterion. It treats amodality as a property of the concept itself, as opposed to a property dependent upon one amongst other means of grasping it. By this criterion, the modified simple account of the concept *square* can itself be a fragment of a possession condition for an amodal shape concept. Suppose a possession condition for a concept mentions a sensitivity of certain judgements whose contents contain it to states with scenario-involving contents, or to anything else which can equally be present in more than one sense modality; and suppose too that it does not mention anything else which requires experiences in a particular modality. When these suppositions hold, the concept is amodal. Despite the departure already made from it, this is very much in the spirit of Evans' idea. On the present account, there remains a 'single conceptual capacity' which is exercised both in response to visual experience, and in response to tactile experience, when, in response to experiences of each kind, a thinker judges something to be square (see Evans 1985a, p. 374).

Given the present criterion for the amodality of a concept, it is a *non sequitur* to deny the amodality of a particular concept F solely on the ground that some particular subject can experience things as F in one modality but not in another. For it may be that experiences in one modality have protopropositional contents which are lacking in that particular subject's experiences in the other modality. So, for example, symmetry and parallelism are not, as we actually are, made salient in the protopropositional content of our tactile experience in nearly so wide a range of cases as they are in visual experience. Since this is so, some shape concepts may be applied on the basis of visual experience of an object which are not immediately applied when the object is touched. It does not follow that the concepts are modality-specific in the way the concept *red* is. We may rather be able to explain the difference by citing the different properties entering the protopropositional contents of visual and tactile experiences.

This treatment of perceptual shape concepts is consistent with acknowledging that experiences have conceptual content. In Evans' work, experiences are conceived as not having a conceptual content at all.[8] This part of Evans' conception is not obviously obligatory. It is not clear that there is good reason for denying the overwhelmingly plausible view that we see things as trees or hear a sound as that of a car approaching. However, accepting the overwhelmingly plausible view does not seem to give us a new resource to use in building possession conditions for perceptual shape concepts. If we try to make the possession condition for the perceptual concept *square* a matter of a certain sensitivity to experiences with a content containing the concept *square* we will be open to the charge of circularity. This circularity is parallel to that suffered by the propositional theorist we noted earlier, who tries to make possession of the first-person concept a matter of the sensitivity of thoughts containing it to features of experiences which already have first-person contents. Like that theorist, we would be attempting to individuate a concept by reference to something which already takes for granted the thinker's possession of the concept in question, viz. the capacity to have experiences whose contents contain the concept in question.[9]

The moral we should draw is that though experiences do indeed have conceptual contents, a possession condition for a concept should appeal at most only to the nonconceptual contents of the thinker's experiences, amongst which are the positioned scenarios and the protopropositional contents. If this is correct, then Evans' view that experiences have no conceptual contents was not by itself depriving him of any resource that is legitimately usable in the individuation of particular concepts.[10]

---

[8]See Evans 1982; the view is endorsed by Colin McGinn (1989, p. 62).

[9]This was a problem which was noted, but far from satisfactorily resolved, in Peacocke 1983.

[10]John Campbell has emphasized the philosophical significance of real cases of subjects suffering from visual disorientation – see Campbell 1989. These subjects are able to identify and apparently perceive the shape of objects in their environment, without experiencing them as having any particular (egocentric) location. There is a readable case study in Godwin-Austen 1965. As Campbell says, these cases show another respect in which we need to revise Evans' description, displayed above, of perceiving something as square. For Evans' description apparently leaves no room for the possibility of experiencing something as square without experiencing it as having a particular location. The present account can accommodate the possibility at the level of protopropositional content. Even if an edge *e* and an edge *e'* are not localized in the subject's perception, that perception can still have the protopropositional content that *e* is PARALLEL TO *e'*. The same applies to protopropositional contents about the relations of SYMMETRY and of BEING AT A RIGHT ANGLE TO such-and-such. But for something to be perceptibly square is to be defined in terms of these notions: and so the possibility is allowed that something is perceived as square, without being localized. This does not mean that scenario content drops out altogether from an account of what it is for an experience to have a protopropositional

While the direction of constitutive explanation has so far been running from experience to concept possession, it is essential to allow too that there is some causal explanation in the opposite direction. Once a thinker has acquired a perceptually-individuated concept, his possession of that concept can causally influence what contents his experiences possess. If this were not so, we would be unable to account for differences which manifestly exist. One such difference, for example, is that between the experience of a perceiver completely unfamiliar with Cyrillic script seeing a sentence in that script, and the experience of one who understands a language written in that script. These two perceivers see the same shapes at the same positions; it may be that the positioned scenario and the protopropositional contents of their respective experiences are identical. The experiences differ in that the second perceiver recognizes the symbols as of particular kinds, and sequences of the symbols as of particular semantic kinds. The question of the nature of this difference, and more generally of what it is, constitutively, for an experience to have a conceptual content, remain as urgent and as open as ever.

Obviously the remarks of this section cannot purport to give a full possession condition for the concept *square*. A full possession condition must elucidate a thinker's ability to judge that an unperceived thing is square. Many intriguing issues arise in the attempt to elucidate that ability. One of them is the nature of a thinker's understanding that imperceptibly small things can be square, and that objects too large to perceive can be so too. Another such question is the relation of this understanding to the ability to judge of an unperceived but perceivable thing that it is square. Pursuing these issues would take us too far away from the other topics I wish to discuss. We can note, though, that the partial possession condition developed so far has a bearing on the answers to these questions. Consider, for instance, a thinker's ability to judge of something unperceived but perceptible that it is square. A theorist might try to explain this as follows. Just as the nonconceptual content of perception is given by a spatial type, so that of a cognitive map is given by a way of assigning objects, properties,

---

content containing a given property. It is plausible that a subject must have some ability to use those of his perceptual experiences in which instances of properties are localized to confirm or refute the represented instantiation which occurs without localization. (If this ability has disappeared altogether, and we still want to attribute perceptual identifications without localization, the attribution will be correct because there was once a connection with such abilities.)

relations and so forth in the space itself in which the subject is embedded. So far, this is tempting and plausible. But suppose the theorist goes on to say that to judge that an object at a specified, unperceived location is square is simply for the location in the content-specification of one's map to be assigned something square. That is identical with assigning it something diamond-shaped. But judging that the object there is square is different from judging it to be diamond-shaped. The distinctions between nonconceptual contents discussed above thus infuse our thought about the nonperceptual cases too.

4   *Spatial reasoning and action*

Is nonconceptual representational content autonomous? Is there, or could there be, a creature which is in states with nonconceptual representational contents, even though the creature does not possess any concepts? Some passages in Evans suggest he was tempted by such a claim of autonomy for his nonconceptual contents (1982, pp. 124, 158).[11] But such a thesis of autonomy is not obligatory.

Even for the most primitive level of scenario content, there are strong arguments against such autonomy. Scenario content is spatial representational content. Specifically spatial content involves more than just a sensitivity to higher-order properties of stimulation patterns. I doubt that we could ever justify the attribution of genuinely spatial content to an organism's states, of a kind going beyond such sensitivity, unless the subject were on occasion to employ states with these contents in identifying places over time. Such an identification might on occasion consist in identifying one's current location with one previously encountered. The possibility of such identification is also involved in the subject's appreciating that the scene currently presented in his perception is something to which his own spatial relations can vary over time.

Identification of places over time requires that states with scenario content contribute to the construction of a cognitive map of the world around the subject. It is, in turn, highly questionable whether we can make

---

[11]Evans' position was that a perceptual informational state with a nonconceptual content is an experience only if it serves as input to a '*thinking, concept-applying and reasoning system*' (1982, p. 158 – Evans' italics). He regarded this as a 'further link' of perceptual informational states with nonconceptual content. He also said of the operation of the informational systems which include the perceptual systems that their operations are more primitive than those involving the 'far more sophisticated cognitive state' of belief (p. 124), and speculated that these more primitive operations may be carried out 'in some phylogenetically more ancient part of the brain' (p. 158).

sense of the subject engaging in such construction unless he employs at least a rudimentary form of first-person thought, that is, unless he possesses at least some primitive form of first-person concept. If this is correct, scenario content is not autonomous. On the approach I am advocating, then, nonconceptual content is not a level whose nature is completely explicable without reference to conceptual content at all. It is rather a type of content which, though nonconceptual, cannot be explained except in part by reference to its relations to certain primitive conceptual contents. At the most basic level, conceptual and nonconceptual content must be elucidated simultaneously. The most basic elements of the scheme themselves form a local holism.

To identify places over time requires the subject to be able to integrate the representational contents of his successive perceptions into an integrated representation of the world around him, both near and far, past and present. We can label this the ability to engage in spatial reasoning. Some parts of spatial reasoning may be conceptual. Some, though not conceptual, will still be propositional – we earlier emphasized the role of protopropositional contents in building a cognitive map of the environment. But where spatial reasoning involves only scenario content, the reasoning will be neither conceptual nor propositional.

Spatial reasoning involves the subject building up a consistent representation of the world around him and of his location in it. It is worth remarking on what 'consistent' means here, given that scenario content is neither conceptual nor propositional. One of the distinctive relations to which spatial reasoning is answerable is the following notion of consistency: that of a given perceptual experience's positioned scenario being consistent with a given cognitive map. What this means is that there are ways of filling out the mapped space around the subject such that both of the following are instantiated: (i) the way of locating features in it required by the cognitive map and (ii) one of the ways of locating things in the world sufficient for the correctness of the positioned scenario.

Whenever we claim that a certain role in reasoning is essential to a particular kind of content, we incur an obligation. The obligation is to elucidate the relation between the content's role in reasoning and its correctness (truth) conditions, or the contribution the content makes to such correctness conditions. This is a natural generalization of the obligation to provide, for any given concept, an account of the way in which what individuates the concept also succeeds in determining (together with the world) a semantic value.[12] Ideally, we would like to have a theory of how a role in spatial reasoning determines the correctness of assigning one positioned scenario content rather than another to an experience. The task of providing this theory is one of the many which lie in intriguing regions visible from the main route of this paper. The task is of course not precisely analogous in detail to that which arises for conceptual contents. For in those cases, the concepts are being individuated by their possession conditions; whereas, I have been emphasizing, a scenario (a spatial type) is not. Nonetheless, the obligation to say what it is for one spatial type rather than another to be involved in the content of an experience still exists, and must be met in part by its detailed role in spatial reasoning.

Genuine spatial reasoning must in turn be capable of explaining the spatial properties of a thinker's actions. The spatial property may just be the minimal property of being carried out at a particular location. The fact that such properties are included leaves room for the possibility of an equally minimal case, touched upon earlier. This is the case of a being which is not capable of initiating changes in its own configuration or location, but whose nonspatial actions (such as changes of colour or of the acidity of its surfaces) are controlled by its representation of its own and other things' locations in its cognitive map. Human beings are, though, obviously capable of controlling a much wider range of the spatial properties of their actions, and in the remainder of this section I will consider the role of scenario content in this control. This further role cannot be taken as unconditionally constitutive of having experiences with scenario content, since the minimal case is possible. But the further role is crucial to the content-involving explanation of human action.

To characterize the further role, we must first remind ourselves of the distinctive kind of knowledge a subject has about the position of his limbs and the configuration of his body. As Wittgenstein (1980, volume I, §§770–772, 798) and Anscombe (1962) long ago emphasized, this knowledge is not inferred from, or even caused by, sensations. You can know the position of your own arm even when it is anaesthetized, and even when you are not seeing it or feeling it with another limb. What is important for us is that in the content of this distinctive kind of knowledge, the location of a limb is given egocentrically, in relation to the subject's body. It is given in the same

---

[12]This is the obligation I described in Peacocke (1989d, pp. 6ff.) as that of providing a 'Determination Theory' for any given concept's possession condition. There is a detailed attempt to meet the obligation for the logical constants in Peacocke 1987.

kind of way in which a location is given in the positioned scenario of an experience, where the scenario is labelled with bodily axes.[13]

In characterizing the distinctive type of knowledge in this way, I differ in some respects from Brian O'Shaughnessy's penetrating treatment (1980, volume 2, chapter 10). O'Shaughnessy's insight was that knowledge of the position of our 'bodily extremities' is 'non-conceptual' and 'non-propositional'. But he also says that this knowledge is 'entirely practical'; and that its content 'is exhaustively manifest in a set of physical acts' (volume 2, p. 64). It is certainly not true that a person's knowledge of the position of his limbs and body at a given time is exhaustively manifest in actions he actually performs. Much of this knowledge possessed at a given time is not put to use in action at all. Perhaps O'Shaughnessy would say rather that the distinctive knowledge consists in certain dispositions to act. There must be something right about mentioning dispositions to act, and I will return to them soon. But we will not get a proper understanding of the knowledge in question until we acknowledge its content. For it seems clear that the content of the distinctive knowledge has correctness conditions, which may or may not obtain. As a result of drugs or neural damage, a subject's belief about the location of his hand may be false. We cannot accommodate this just by saying that a false belief is one which, when manifested in action, does not lead to success. A distinction between the success and the failure of an action depends upon a notion of the content of its generating intentional or subintentional state, a content whose correctness condition may obtain (success) or not (failure). And the content of these (sub)intentional states is of the same kind as the content of one's knowledge when one knows that one of them has succeeded.[14]

It is not surprising, given his views, that O'Shaughnessy says that there is a structural parallel between subintentional states and sensations. If what I have been saying is right, the content of the subintentional state has a

---

[13]It is a question worth investigation how the limb is given in this distinctive knowledge. It is certainly not conceptualized descriptively – as a particular finger might be conceptualized as 'the fourth finger on my left hand'. On the way a particular finger is given in the content of the distinctive knowledge, it is potentially informative that it is the fourth on one's left hand. One supposition worth considering is that it is partially constitutive of the way the finger is given in the distinctive knowledge that the intention (or subintention) to move the finger, thus given, from one place to another is one which, when things are working properly, results in that movement of that finger.

[14]It should be emphasized that subintentional states and acts in O'Shaughnessy's sense are not subpersonal in Dennett's sense. The subintentional states are so characterized because their content is not fully conceptualized; but they occur at the personal level.

correctness condition on the external, objective world. The sensation does not. So there is no structural parallel of that sort on my position. Absence of conceptual content does not mean absence of all genuine content.

Now let us return to the further role of scenario content in human action. In supplying a subject with information about the location of things relative to bodily axes, perception supplies that nonconceptual information in a form immediately usable if the subject wants to move his body, or some limb, towards, or from, or to be in some other spatial relation to what he perceives. It is only because the bodily-based scenario-involving contents are common to perception, to our distinctive knowledge of bodily position, and to what is under our immediate (sub)intentional control, that the information in perception is immediately usable in performing actions. When a propositional attitude has a conceptual constituent individuated in part by scenario content it can play an intermediary role between perception and action.

This intermediary role made possible by scenario contents with labelled (bodily) axes explains more fully a connection, which I mentioned in earlier work (1986a, 1989a), between the nonconceptual contents of perception and bodily action. A normal individual, asked to direct the beam of a spotlight in a forest onto a tree 47 degrees to the right of straight ahead, will not, in the sense relevant to action, know where to point the beam. The normal individual does not know which perceptually individuated direction is 47 degrees to the right of straight ahead. He will, though, have no difficulty if the tree in question is marked, so that he can see in which precise direction it lies.

It is helpful here to consider an explicit statement of the subject's practical reasoning in this second case, in which the normal individual has no difficulty in carrying out the task. He forms the intention with this content:

(1) I will move my arm in the direction of that tree.

He also knows from his perceptual experience that

(2) That tree is in the direction d (identified egocentrically, using scenario content).

So he forms the intention with the content

(3) I will move my arm in the direction d.

He can then carry out this intention without further practical reasoning. This description makes it clear that the connections between perception and action rest on two links. The first is the link between the perceptual demonstrative 'that tree' and the availability of the perceptually-based knowledge of (2) which contains that demonstrative way of thinking. The second is the link between the egocentric mode of identification of the directions and the subject's 'basic' actions. If either of these links does not hold for some other mode of presentation in place of 'that tree', such connections between perception and action will not hold, *ceteris paribus*.

Actually even if both these links hold, that is not strictly sufficient for the link between perception and action to hold, because of the phenomenon known as 'optic ataxia'. A subject with optic ataxia cannot reach accurately for visually presented objects; nor can he orient his hand correctly to fit into a slot which he sees. We should not conclude from such cases that the representations which control bodily movements do not involve scenario content. A better hypothesis is that the representations which control the limbs do use scenario content, but that in the cases of optic ataxia the contents of visual experience are *inaccessible* to the motor control systems. That is, we have two different representations, not two different kinds of content (which would need some kind of 'translation' procedure). This is a better hypothesis because subjects with optic ataxia display a 'well coordinated, rapid and accurate pattern of movements directed at the body'.[15]

There are also unusual cases in which two or more systems of labelled axes are properly used in giving the positioned scenario content of a single experience, but in which the spatial relation between those two systems is not specified in the content of that experience. There are, for instance, certain positions in which, when lying on your back, you can twist your arms up behind your head. A piece of furniture touched with a hand of the twisted arm may be experienced as standing in certain spatial relations to one's hand, fingers and wrist, but not as standing in any particular relation to the rest of one's body. In such a case of fragmentation, there is also fragmentation of the person's systems of knowledge which help to explain bodily actions. The subject will know what to do to move his fingers away

---

[15]Perenin and Vighetto 1988, p. 661. See also p. 662: 'None of the patients showed any significant motor, proprioceptive, visual field or visual space perception disturbances'. My thanks to R. McCarthy for this reference.

from the touched furniture, but not, without further reasoning, how to move them closer to his torso.

Of the many substantive questions which arise in this area, one which seems somewhat more tractable than the rest is this: what gives a subintentional state or trying one nonconceptual content rather than another? One subpart of this question concerns the labelling of axes in a scenario. We need to say something illuminating about this labelling which does not take for granted a partially scenario-like nonconceptual content which already has labelled axes.

I should emphasize that the problem here does not concern merely notational variants of particular axes and coordinate systems. One notational variant of the basic human axes would rotate them by 45 degrees, and adjust coordinates in specifying a scenario in a compensating fashion. That this is a purely notational, insubstantial, matter should be especially clear in the case of scenario content – for it is clear here that the variation is solely in means of specifying one and the same spatial type. The important question is rather this: why are axes labelled in *some* way involving particular bodily parts and limbs appropriate in giving the spatial type which is in turn used in giving the content of a trying, and of other subintentional states? We could encapsulate the point by saying that the question is about frames of reference for spatial types, rather than about coordinate systems.

Here is one possible answer. Let me say that two instructions ('tryings') of a given subject are of the same type if they differ only in the reference of their 'now' component. So trying to move one's left hand to a particular position in front of oneself at 9 a.m. and trying to do so at 10 a.m. are instructions of the same type. Now take a given type of instruction with a nonconceptual, partially scenario-like content. I suggest that the frame of reference to be used in labelling the axes of its scenario is that frame with respect to which instructions of the given type always have the *same* effect, when characterized in relation to that frame, in all normal spatio-temporal contexts (and when the efferent nervous system is functioning properly). When an instruction is an instruction to move one's hand in a certain relation to one's body, it will have the same effect, described in relation to a bodily frame of reference, whether the thinker is in London or in Edinburgh. It will not have the same effect if the bizarre choice were made of a frame of reference involving longitude and latitude. Nor would it always have the same effect (when the thinker is functioning properly) in any other frame of reference defined by objects with respect to which the subject can move. Nor will descriptions of the effect in terms of muscle-changes be the same in all spatio-temporal contexts. For they will depend on the starting point of the hand. This criterion can be called the *constancy* criterion for fixing the frame of reference, and so the labelling, of any axes used in individuating the scenarios for a given subject's subintentional states. The constancy criterion is a small first step towards the formulation of a substantive theory of the nonconceptual content of subintentional states.

5 *Conclusion*

I have been arguing that we should recognize scenario and protopropositional contents as forms of nonconceptual representational contents. These nonconceptual contents must be mentioned in the possession conditions for perceptual and demonstrative concepts. A proper appreciation of their role allows us to explain the possibility of noncircular possession conditions for these very basic concepts, and to give an account of the relations between perception, action and a subject's representation of his environment.

At several points, I have indicated philosophical issues arising out of the approach of this paper. Before closing, I wish to mention very briefly some of the links between, and open questions about, the types of nonconceptual representational content I have been discussing and issues in the cognitive sciences.

Suppose, with Roger Shepard (1981), we regard the task of the mechanisms of visual perception as that of computing an inverse of the projective mapping from the environment to the retinal image. From this lofty perspective, we would certainly expect representations with positioned scenario and protopropositional contents to be computed (along the way): for it is the real scene, in our sense, which produces the retinal image. In a content-involving psychology, we would expect the early stages of vision to compute and combine various partial specifications of the scene around the perceiver. The several feature maps, and the integration thereof, studied by Anne Treisman and her colleagues (Treisman and Gelade 1980, Treisman and Schmidt 1982) are just such partial specifications. They also begin to suggest mechanisms by which protopropositional content is made explicit in mental representations. If we want the explanatory power that only a content-involving description of a computation can supply, we should use positioned scenarios and protopropositions in describing the mechanisms outlined in that research.

If the treatment in this paper is roughly along the right lines, an important item on an interdisciplinary agenda should be the construction of a theory of the ways in which the various types of representational content proposed here are mentally represented. We should certainly want to know the relation between these types of content and the theory that mental images are interpreted symbol-filled arrays (Tye 1991, pp. 90–102). It is also important to understand the possibilities for the realization of states with scenario content in connectionist systems. We need to consider the following proposal. We might partition the three-dimensional space around the subject into suitably small cells. Each cell could be represented by a 'binding' unit which is connected to three other elements. These three other elements each represent the values of the cell on the labelled axes of the scenario. The binding unit can then have connections to other assemblies for the features represented as instantiated at that cell; and so forth. Do problems about binding make this too costly and implausible? A third, closely related, area in which we have interdisciplinary questions is that of the mental models discussed in philosophical terms by Colin McGinn (1989).[16] We have the prospect of further understanding, both of mental representation and potentially of content itself, emerging from future work on this interdisciplinary agenda.[17]

---

[16]McGinn indexes mental models with truth-evaluable propositions. If these are built up from constituents solely at the level of reference, I would remarshal the arguments of §2 to argue that mental models need a more discriminating assignment of content. If the indexing propositions are at the level of sense, then we need to mention scenario and protopropositional content. The assignment of these nonconceptual contents to mental models is entirely within the spirit of McGinn's views.

[17]The views expressed here relate also to other writings. Quine (1969, p. 147, pp. 153–154) emphasises the need to give some psychological states contents that are neither conceptually nor linguistically individuated. And Lewis takes the contents of someone's visual experiences to be sets of 'those possible individuals who, according to the content of his visual experience, he himself might be; they share just those properties he sees himself to have. These will mostly be relational properties: properties of facing such-and-such an arrangement of nearby things' (1983a, p. 30): Lewis certainly does not conceive these sets to be linguistically or conceptually individuated. The relation of my account to Lewis' merits more discussion. Here, I just note two major issues. First, is Lewis right to attribute the same kind of content to perceptions as to other propositional attitudes? Second, while Lewis' apparatus captures every positioned scenario content, it assigns no special status to the labelled axes and origins. I think an experience can only have a correctness condition about (say) a particular direction if it has a labelled origin and axes. (Lewis may of course restrict the contents of perception to take account of these theses.)

Earlier versions of this material were presented in 1988–1989 to an interdisciplinary conference on the mental representation of space at King's College Cambridge, to a seminar at Oxford University and to the International Colloquium on Cognitive Science at San Sebastián/Donostia. I thank John Campbell, Adrian Cussins, Martin Davies and Michael Martin for valuable comments.

6   *The nonconceptual content of experience*

TIM CRANE

1   *Concepts and perceptual experience*

To what extent do our beliefs about the world affect what we see? Our beliefs certainly affect where we choose to look, but do they affect what we see when we look there?

Some have claimed that people with very different beliefs literally see the world differently. Thus Thomas Kuhn: 'what a man sees depends both upon what he looks at and also upon what his previous visual–conceptual experience has taught him to see' (Kuhn 1970, p. 113). This view – call it 'Perceptual Relativism' – entails that a scientist and a child may look at a cathode ray tube and, in a sense, the first will see it while the second won't. The claim is not, of course, that the child's experience is 'empty'; but that, unlike the scientist, it does not see the tube *as* a cathode ray tube. One way of supporting this claim is to say that one cannot see something *as* an F unless one has the *concept F*. Since the child plainly lacks the concept of a cathode ray tube, it cannot see it as a cathode ray tube.

Although Perceptual Relativism is hard to believe, this supporting suggestion is not so implausible. After all, when we see (and more generally, perceive) the world, the world is presented to us in a particular way; so how can we see it as being that way unless we have some *idea* or *conception* of the way it is presented?

We need not be committed to a representative theory of perception to think that perceptions in some sense represent the world. We can express this by saying that perceptions have *content*. Now it is a commonplace that the contents of beliefs and the other propositional attitudes involve concepts. The belief that this thing is a cathode ray tube involves, in some sense, the concept *cathode ray tube*. So the line of thought behind Perceptual

Relativism may be expressed thus: seeing an F *as an F* is a state with content. So the content of this perception must involve the concept *F* – for if it did not, why should we say that the experience represents the F in question *as* an *F*? Thus Christopher Peacocke:

> the representational content [of an experience] is the way the experience presents the world as being, and it can hardly present the world as being that way if the subject is incapable of appreciating what that way is.[1]

On the other hand, it is plausible to say that the child and the scientist have something perceptually in common, when (let us suppose) they look at the object from the same position, in the same lighting, with normal eyesight. And this common state need not just be qualitative – not just a matter of their visual sensations, or properties of their visual fields, if there are such things.[2] Rather, there is surely a sense in which their experiences *present* or *represent* the world in the same sort of way. When the child comes to acquire the concept of a cathode ray tube, there is surely something in common between the ways the world was represented before and after this acquisition. Otherwise, how could it come to recognise, for instance, that *that thing* is a cathode ray tube?

So there are reasons for thinking that the concepts perceivers have do affect what they see, and reasons for thinking they do not. I think we should therefore reject Perceptual Relativism in its most extreme form. We should accept that the experiences of two perceivers in a situation such as the one described will be perceptually similar. If this is granted, then the question is: how should a theory of perception classify the similarities between such experiences?

Let us agree that these similarities should be expressed, in some sense, in terms of the contents of the experiences – in terms of how the experiences represent the world to be. To capture the relevant similarities, we would then have to deal with the above suggestion that one cannot have an experience of something *as* an F without that experience involving the concept *F*.

---

[1]Peacocke 1983, p.7; as we shall see, Peacocke has changed his views since this was written.

[2]For sensational properties of experiences, see Peacocke 1983, chapter 1. Michael Tye argues that there are no such things in 'Visual qualia and visual content' (this volume). I should say at this stage that I use the terms 'experience' and 'perception' more loosely than some writers. The way I use 'perceives', 'X perceives that p' does not entail p.

There are two reasonable strategies we could employ. One is to say that the experience does involve concepts, but these are concepts that any two such perceivers will share. So, for instance, the infant and the scientist would experience the cathode ray tube as (perhaps) tubular, grey, shiny etc. The common content of their experiences would be given in terms of *observational* concepts that they both possess (see McGinn 1989, pp. 59ff.). The second strategy is to say that what they have in common is (at least) an experience with content, but content that is *nonconceptual*: it does not, in some sense, 'involve' concepts. It is this strategy I shall examine in this paper.

The claim that experiences have nonconceptual contents is a familiar one in recent philosophy of perception.[3] But what does the claim really mean? Saying that an experience has a content that does not 'involve' concepts is, as yet, too vague. We need to know more about *concepts*, *contents* and the notion of a mental state 'involving' concepts before we can really understand the claim.

In this paper, I shall try to give enough of an account of these notions to yield a notion of nonconceptual content – one which is at least consistent with the leading theories of nonconceptual content. In Section 2, I shall consider how the term 'nonconceptual content' should be defined. In Section 3, I shall give a sketch of what it is for a state to be 'composed of concepts' or have conceptual content, and derive from that a sketch of what it is for a state to have nonconceptual content. I shall then argue, in Section 4, that this notion of nonconceptual content does apply to perception.

2   What is nonconceptual content?

What is this nonconceptual content supposed to be? I shall begin with three examples of states that philosophers have claimed to have nonconceptual contents.

First, there are perceptual experiences – perceiving that it's raining, that the cat is on the mat and so on.[4] Second, there are the states of the so-called 'subpersonal' computational systems like the visual system – states which have content, but whose content is not (unlike the first sort of state)

---

[3]See, in particular, Dretske 1981, chapter 6; Evans 1982, pp. 122–129, and pp. 154–160; Peacocke 1986a; Peacocke 1989c; and Peacocke's 'Scenarios, concepts and perception' (this volume); Cussins 1990. The proposal has some affinities with the account of the individuation of experiences in Millar 1991.

[4]See Peacocke 1986a; Peacocke 1989c; and Peacocke, 'Scenarios, concepts and perception' (this volume); cf. Dretske 1981, p. 155 fn. 7, and p. 162.

phenomenologically salient.[5] Third, there are the states that, following Dretske, we may describe as carrying 'information' in the sense of communication theory. To take a well-known example of Dennis Stampe's (1977), if a tree has 70 rings, then it is 70 years old. Thus this state of the tree's has a content – it carries the information that the tree is 70 years old (see Dretske 1981).

What makes these all examples of states with nonconceptual contents? Let's start by assuming that all these states do actually have contents.[6] To say that any state has content is just to say that it represents the world as being a certain way. It thus has what Peacocke (this volume) calls a 'correctness condition' – the condition under which it represents the world *correctly*. It is in this minimal sense of 'content' that perceptions, the states of the visual system, and the tree's rings all have content.

It is well known that we will need to add more to this minimal definition to capture the kind of content beliefs and other propositional attitudes have. So we may say that the content of a belief is a Russellian Proposition, or a set of possible worlds, or something more fine-grained yet, like a Fregean Thought. But whatever the contents of beliefs are, we should not assume at the outset that just because experiences (and the other states mentioned) have content, they have the same sort of content that beliefs have.

This minimal definition of content does not mention concepts. It does not seem to be part of a state's having a correctness condition that the state (or its content) 'involves' concepts. Yet we tend to assume that beliefs (or their contents) involve concepts. What does this mean?

It might mean that the concepts are literally the constituents of the belief. So when someone believes that the sun is shining, this belief state is literally composed of the concepts *sun* and *shining*. Or it might mean that the concepts are the constituents of the *content* of the belief: it is the content *The sun is shining*, rather than the belief state as such, that is literally

---

[5]See Evans 1982, p. 104 fn. 22; Campbell 1986, p. 172; Davies 1986; and Cussins 1990. Colin McGinn labels nonconceptual mental content 'subpersonal content': 'the kind of content routinely attributed by cognitive scientists to information-processing systems of which the subject has no awareness' (McGinn 1989, p. 163).

[6]Some philosophers dispute whether information in Dretske's sense is really content (see e.g. Cussins 1990, p. 392). For my purposes, it doesn't really matter if they are right, since I ultimately want to argue that perceptions have nonconceptual contents, and these are not just states with Dretskean informational content. So the fate of Dretskean information as content does not matter to me – I use it only as an example. Others (e.g. Stich 1983) deny that computational states too have content. I do dispute this; see Crane 1990.

composed of the concepts *sun* and *shining* – just as the sentence 'The sun is shining' is composed of its constituent words.

If this is what it is for a state to have *conceptual* content, then a state with *nonconceptual* content is one which is not composed of concepts. So if experiences have nonconceptual contents, then they do not have concepts as constituents. The experience of the sun shining is not composed of the concepts *sun* and *shining*. Or perhaps it is the *content* of the experience that is not composed of these concepts. So perhaps the idea is this: just as conceptual content is content that is composed of concepts, so nonconceptual content is content that is not composed of concepts. Conceptual content is 'structured' content, and nonconceptual content is 'unstructured' content.

But on the face of it, this definition will not explain why the examples I mentioned above are all examples of nonconceptual content. For the mere fact that a state has a structured content (in this sense) seems neither necessary nor sufficient for its being conceptual.

It is not necessary because it seems that some conceptual and nonconceptual states can share contents. When I believe that the sun is shining because I see that it is, then in an obvious sense I believe what I see. What I am believing is surely in some sense the same as what I am experiencing – namely, *that the sun is shining* – the way the world is represented to be, or the content, in the minimal sense of that term mentioned above. But if experiences have nonconceptual contents, and beliefs do not, then how can this apparently obvious fact be explained? How can the belief have a structured content if the experience hasn't?[7]

It is not sufficient because it seems that the contents of computational states can be structured without being conceptual. According to certain computational theories of vision, light is reflected onto the retina, and the information it contains is processed – by algorithms that compute functions – to form a representation of the scene perceived. The states involved in this process represent visually perceptible properties of the scene: properties such as reflectance, illumination, and the orientation of edges of objects.

Now many think it obvious that the contents processed by the visual system do have constituents. For the theory assigns structure to these states, analysing them – as it may be – in terms of concepts such as that of a *zero-crossing* (Marr 1982). But if a concept just is a constituent of a content, then

---

[7]At the end of §4 of this essay I shall suggest an answer to this question. The present point is that it is hard to see how it can be correctly answered if we simply define nonconceptual contents as 'contents that are not composed of concepts'.

the constituents of these computational contents will be concepts by definition: some of the states of a perceiver's visual system will have contents with zero-crossing-representations as constituents, and will thus be composed of concepts, including the concept *zero-crossing*. But these were supposed to be states with nonconceptual contents.

So the mere idea of a content that is not composed of concepts does not help to explain the idea of nonconceptual content. To this it may be said: so much for the idea of nonconceptual content. If the only sense we can make of the idea of a concept is as the constituent of a representational state (or of the content of that state), then why not just define 'concept' thus and have done with it? It is not, after all, as if the everyday notion of a concept is clear enough to be saved for systematic philosophy; and what can be saved applies just as well to these allegedly 'subpersonal' states as to beliefs.

But this reaction is premature. My point so far is only that the idea of nonconceptual content should not be defined simply in terms of having constituents. This does not mean that there is nothing in the idea of nonconceptual content. It's just that it shouldn't be defined that way. What I need to show is how it should be defined.

To get a better grip on the notion of nonconceptual content, take the simplest of our three examples: the tree's rings. Why should anyone think that this state does not 'involve' concepts? The answer is obvious: the state of the tree cannot involve concepts in any sense, since the tree has no mental states, and so *a fortiori* possesses no concepts. When we describe the tree as representing its age, or as carrying the information that it is 70 years old, we do not suppose that the tree possesses the concept of a year – or indeed any other concept. However, we think that when someone believes that they are 70 years old, they presumably cannot believe this unless they possess the concept of a year – *whatever* concepts may be. The believer needs to possess the concepts; the tree doesn't.

To generalise from this: for something, X, to believe that a is F, X must possess the concepts a and F. But for X to merely represent that a is F, X does not have to possess these concepts. It is in the latter case that X is in a state with nonconceptual content. Rather than being defined merely in terms of the content's having constituents, the notion of conceptual content is now defined in terms of whether its constituent concepts need to be *possessed* in order for something to be in that state.

Adrian Cussins has recently outlined and defended this idea (see Cussins 1990, pp. 380-401). It will be instructive to look at the way he sets the issues out. Cussins begins by defining conceptual and nonconceptual *properties*:

> A property is a conceptual property if, and only if, it is canonically characterised, relative to a theory, only by means of concepts which are such that an organism *must have* those concepts in order to [instantiate] the property. A property is a nonconceptual property if, and only if, it is canonically characterised, relative to a theory, by means of concepts which are such that an organism *need not have* those concepts in order to [instantiate] the property.[8]

Conceptual and nonconceptual content are then defined as 'content which consists of conceptual properties' and 'content which consists of nonconceptual properties' respectively.

This definition is not entirely straightforward, and a few comments are in order. First, it is obvious that according to the definition, almost all properties are nonconceptual, since there are very few properties that require an organism to have a concept of the property in order to instantiate it. And that is how things should be.

But it looks initially as if some obviously conceptual properties come out as nonconceptual on this definition. Suppose, for the sake of argument, that the type-identity theory is true: mental properties are identical with brain properties. Then my instantiating the property *thinking about Vienna* is my instantiating a certain brain property – call it 'B'. But I need have no concept of the property B in order to instantiate it – I don't need to be a neuroscientist in order to think! So B is a nonconceptual property. But then so is the property *thinking about Vienna*, since it is identical with B. But surely you have to have a concept of Vienna in order to think about it?

Cussins' answer is not that *thinking about Vienna* and B are different properties, but that specifying that property as 'B' does not, from the point of view of the theory of content, specify it in the right way. It is not what he calls a 'canonical characterisation' of the property. A theory canonically characterises something when it describes it in terms of the properties that it treats as essential to that thing. Content, Cussins says, is 'canonically characterised by a specification which reveals the way in which it presents the world' (see Cussins 1990, p. 383 fn. 25). So describing my instantiation of the property as B does not reveal the way the world is presented to me –

---

[8]Cussins 1990, pp. 382–383. I replace Cussins' 'satisfy' with 'instantiate', since the term 'satisfy' is more usually applied to predicates rather than properties.

the world is not presented, in that instantiation, as containing instances of *B*. This is why 'B' is not a canonical characterisation of the property.

Second, it is plain from this that although 'B' is not a canonical characterisation of the property for the purposes of the theory of *content*, it will be canonical for, say, neuroscience. This is why Cussins says that canonical characterisations are 'relative to a theory'. He thus leaves open the possibility that the same property could be canonically characterised as conceptual by one theory, and as nonconceptual by another.

The route from conceptual and nonconceptual properties to conceptual and nonconceptual content is straightforward. A state with conceptual content – e.g. a belief – is one such that the subject of that state has to possess the concepts that canonically characterise its content in order to be in that state. Any state with content that does not meet this condition has a nonconceptual content. More strictly, we can use Cussins' definition to construct a definition of nonconceptual content as follows:

> For any state with content, *S*, *S* has a nonconceptual content, *P*, iff a subject *X*'s being in *S* does not entail that *X* possesses the concepts that canonically characterise *P*.

This definition can now be applied to the examples I introduced at the beginning of this section.

(1) Experience: *X*'s seeing that the sun is shining does not entail that *X* has the concepts of *the sun*, or *shining*. That is, in order to see that the sun is shining, a subject does not *have* to possess these concepts (though of course he or she *may* possess them).

(2) The visual system: in order for a subject's visual system to compute its solution to the complex equations that take retinal information as input and a 3D description of the scene as output, the subject does not have to possess the concepts that canonically characterise these equations (though again, he or she may possess them). You don't need to know the theory of vision in order to see.

(3) The tree's rings: in order for the tree to represent or indicate that it is 70 years old, it does not have to possess the concepts *70*, *year* and *being old*. This is just as well, since it wouldn't be able to possess these concepts anyway.

Saying that it makes sense to *apply* the definition of nonconceptual content to these cases is not, of course, saying very much. We still have to establish that there are any mental states which have nonconceptual content. To do this, we must probe the definition further.

A state with conceptual content, C, may be defined in terms of the conditional: if X is in C, then X possesses the concepts that canonically characterise C. The point, therefore, is not that conceptual contents have constituents and nonconceptual contents don't – as we saw above, this won't work. It is rather that X needs to 'possess' these constituents in order to be in the state.

But what is it to 'possess' these constituents, these concepts? It cannot simply be a matter of having the literal parts of the state 'written' inside one's head. (After all, the tree has 70 rings; in no sense does this amount to possessing the concept 70.) There must be more to possessing a concept than being in contentful states that have constituents. But what more?

It seems, then, that to understand what concepts are, we need to understand what it is to possess a concept. Indeed, Christopher Peacocke has recently advanced an even stronger thesis, his 'Principle of Dependence': that 'there can be *no more* to the nature of a concept than is determined by a correct account of what it is to possess the concept'.[9] In the next section, I will try to give an argument for this Principle.

3 Concepts and contents

So what is it to possess a concept? It is often said that thought requires the possession of concepts (see Evans 1981, p. 132). This can seem almost tautological, as can its converse: there is no possession of concepts without thought. This latter truism is almost self-evident: it is hard to make sense of a thinker whose mental life just consists of a series of concepts, with no intentional states of which they are 'constituents'. So we may conjecture that a concept, C, is possessed by a thinker, T, only if T is in intentional states in whose contents C figures. But is the former truism just as obvious? Why should thought require the possession of concepts?

Consider my possession of the concept *cheese*. According to the above conjecture, I only possess this concept if I am in intentional states in which the concept *cheese* figures. Suppose, for example, I believe that cheese is nutritious. It will not be possible for me to have only *this* belief about cheese, since I cannot believe that cheese is nutritious (call it 'P') without

---

[9]Peacocke 1989c, p. 2 (my emphasis); cf. also Peacocke 1989b, p. 51, where Peacocke says that 'the idea that a concept is individuated by a correct account of its possession' is 'a master key' to the theory of concepts.

having certain beliefs that are the obvious logical consequences of this belief – the belief that not(P & not-P) for example.[10] These beliefs are uninteresting consequences of P, but there are more interesting beliefs I must have too, that are not related to P by logic alone. For example, if I believe that cheese is nutritious, I must believe that cheese is edible, and arguably, if my belief is genuinely to be about cheese, I must believe that cheese is made of milk.

This list of beliefs could be extended; but there is no need to do so to underline the familiar point that having one belief entails having a lot. While there is, arguably, nothing incoherent in supposing that a mental life could consist of just one sensation, it seems plainly incoherent to suppose that it could contain just one intentional state. If a thinker has a belief, then he or she must also have many others. These beliefs will be either those related logically to the original belief (P or not-P) or those related by what we can call the 'semantic' properties of their contents (the belief that cheese is nutritious and the belief that cheese is edible).

So if I can't have the *concept* of cheese unless I have beliefs in which the concept figures – whatever concepts are – then I can't have the concept if I only have one belief about cheese. For I can't have only one belief about cheese. Since intentional states come not in single spies but in whole battalions, then since possession of concepts needs intentional states, it needs a multiplicity of them.

Moreover, the reason why there has to be this multiplicity is that beliefs have to stand in these relations to other relevant intentional states in order for them to have the contents they do. The upshot of the 'cheese' example is that the belief just wouldn't be *about cheese* unless the thinker had the other relevant beliefs. The much-discussed 'holism of the intentional' resides not simply in the fact that there must be a multiplicity of intentional states if there are to be any, but in the fact that the content of any one intentional state depends, to some extent, on the contents of the others. Indeed, it is this latter fact that *explains* the former.

But a thinker's beliefs about the world are also sensitive to perceptual evidence, and in some cases, their contents are partly defined by the perceptual evidence that a thinker would take as counting in their favour. Someone could not believe that it's raining unless they were disposed to regard a perception of drops of water falling from the sky as evidence for

---

[10]People do not *always* believe the logical consequences of what they believe, of course. I am here skating over a number of complications, in order to give the general picture.

this belief. Intentional states stand not only in logical and semantic relations to one another, but also in evidential relations to perceptions. All these three kinds of relations help to fix the content of a given intentional state.

But what does this tell us about concepts and their possession? These uncontroversial points about holism do not answer our initial question about why thought requires the possession of concepts. To answer this question, we next need to ask why a theory of the mind needs the notion of a concept at all.

When looking for the notion of the *content* of an attitude, there are straightforward dissections we can make in the anatomy of the mind – we can dissect people into their mental properties and their other properties; then we can dissect their mental properties into their intentional states and their nonintentional mental states; and we can dissect their intentional states into their attitudes and the contents of these attitudes. That gets us down to whole contents, the bearers of truth values. But where do concepts fit in? What do we add to the claim that people have beliefs, desires, intentions (and so on) about cheese by saying that they have the *concept* of cheese? Why talk about concepts at all? (See Hart 1983.)

To answer this, we need to know what the idea of a concept is meant to explain. Frege writes:

> The task of our vernacular language is essentially fulfilled if people engaged in communication with one another connect the same thought, or approximately the same thought, with the same proposition. For this it is not at all necessary that the individual words should have a sense and meaning of their own, provided only that the whole proposition has a sense. Where inferences are to be drawn the case is different: for this it is essential that the same expression should occur in two propositions and should have exactly the same meaning in both cases. It must therefore have a meaning of its own, independent of the other parts of the proposition.[11]

Frege was concerned here with language, but a parallel point can be made for thought. If we simply wanted to represent facts, then our beliefs would only need to have 'whole' contents. All that would matter would be whether

---

[11]The quotation is from a letter from Frege to Peano (29 Sept 1896) in Frege 1980, p. 115. I am grateful to Bill Hart for drawing my attention to this passage. Notice, of course, that the term 'proposition' in this context means what I mean by 'sentence', and the term 'thought' means what I call 'content'.

a content was true or false. The *fact* might have constituents (particulars and properties) but they would have no reflection in the content, since (to echo Frege) they would as it were have no role, no 'meaning of their own'.

But once we consider the role our beliefs play in reasoning, then it starts to become clear why their contents need constituents. A thinker who believes that *a is F*, and that *b is F*, and that *a is not b* will be disposed to believe that *at least two things are F*. Surely the states in this inference cannot just have unstructured contents, or or we would not be able to explain its validity. And if we cannot explain this, we cannot explain why the constituent beliefs have the contents they do – according to the holistic proposal just outlined.

To recall Frege's remark: it is essential that the same (type of) 'part' of the content should occur in the two states, and that 'it should have exactly the same meaning in both cases' – i.e. the parts should be tokens of the same *semantic* type. So in the simple example above, the states must both contain *F* as a part. I say that it is only a terminological variant of this to say that they must contain the *concept F*.

To account for the inferential powers of these beliefs, then, the thinker's beliefs should contain an element common to their contents: the concept *F*. What I want to suggest, then, is that concepts are the *inferentially relevant constituents of intentional states*. To discern conceptual structure in a thinker's thoughts, we need to look (as it were) not 'down' into the propositional content, but 'up' into the nature of the intentional states themselves. The idea is to derive the psychological notion of a concept from facts about the inferential relations among beliefs.[12]

The notion of *possessing* a concept is then naturally explained as follows. To possess a concept is to be in intentional states whose inferential relations are an appropriate function of their contents. The elements in a thinker's network of intentional states are essentially inferentially related to one another. Concepts are the constituents required to explain these inferential relations. So a thinker could not be in the relevant intentional states unless they contain concepts. Since possessing concepts entails that one is disposed to make certain inferences, then possessing concepts entails that one's

---

[12]The idea is not new, of course. Compare Gareth Evans' remark that 'behind the idea of a system of beliefs lies that of a system of concepts' whose structure 'determines the inferential properties' of the beliefs (Evans 1981, p. 132). John Campbell (1986) has argued from inference to structure, but not in the very general way suggested here. Campbell's strategy is to examine certain primitive patterns of spatial reasoning, and show how they thereby exploit the conceptual structure of the thoughts involved.

intentional states are 'composed' of concepts. This establishes the link we sought at the end of Section 2, between a state's being *composed* of concepts and its subject *possessing* concepts.

To say that beliefs have conceptual structure because of their inferential relations is not yet to say anything about the mechanism that underpins this structure. The structure of this mechanism need not mirror the inferential structure of beliefs. The mechanism could be a giant 'look-up table' that 'infers' the 'belief' that *at least two things are F* from the inputs *a is F*, *b is F* and *a is not b* simply by having the first 'belief' written, as it were, at the intersection of the others.[13]

But I do not need to be committed to any *a priori* claims about mechanisms. My definition of a concept is a claim about the relations between beliefs, not a claim about their underlying mechanisms. This is why the definition does not commit me to the Language of Thought (LOT) hypothesis (Fodor 1987, appendix), for that is precisely the claim that the structure of the mechanism of thought mirrors its inferential structure. To say that beliefs are inferentially related to one another, and that they therefore have a structure that makes this possible, does not entail that this structure is underpinned by anything *syntactic* – in any interesting sense of 'syntactic'. Maybe the underpinning mechanism is that of a connectionist network. The LOT hypothesis is independent from the present claim about concepts.[14]

This proposal about concepts is not *ad hoc*, for at least two reasons. First, it explains why the claim that there is no thought without possession of concepts is not just a vacuous slogan. We should distinguish between the content and having an attitude with that content – in Frege's terminology, for example, between the Thought and its 'grasping'. I claim that if contents are to be grasped at all, their inferential relations must be grasped. That is, according to my definition of possessing a concept, contents must be grasped by means of the thinker possessing certain concepts. So there is no thought without possession of concepts because states can have the contents they do only if they have inferentially relevant structure.

---

[13]For a giant look–up table, see e.g. Clark 1989, p. 56. I have learned much from Barry Smith on this issue.

[14]This paragraph merely glances at a number of complex issues. For the idea of syntax as used in the LOT hypothesis, see Crane 1990. Martin Davies (forthcoming) has argued, ingeniously, that the conceptual structure of thought needs the truth of the LOT hypothesis. But I agree with Fodor and others that the LOT hypothesis should rather be thought of as the best empirical explanation of conceptual structure.

Second, the proposal offers us an independent motivation for (something like) Peacocke's Principle of Dependence, that 'there can be no more to the nature of a concept than is determined by a correct account of what it is to possess the concept'.[15] A correct account of possessing a given concept, *C*, would on my proposal involve a specification of the beliefs one has to have in order to have any belief about *C*s. The account would have to specify what those beliefs are, and how they are related.[16] The constituent, *C*, of these relevant beliefs is invoked only to explain the inferential relations between them. Since that is what the concept *is*, then of course there is no more to its nature than is given in an account of its possession.

We can now return to nonconceptual content. In Section 2, I said that a state, *S*, has conceptual content iff *X*'s being in *S* entails that *X* possesses the concepts that characterise *S*. In this section I have argued that a concept is an inferentially relevant constituent of an intentional state; and that possessing a concept is therefore being in states with inferentially relevant constituents. So *S* has a conceptual content iff *X*'s being in *S* entails that *S* has inferentially relevant constituents, and this requires that *X* is in other states which are inferentially related to *S*.

Similarly for nonconceptual content. *X* is in a state with nonconceptual content iff *X* does not have to possess the concepts that characterise its content in order to be in that state. Since possessing a concept is being in intentional states whose contents are appropriately inferentially related, then a state with nonconceptual content is one whose contents are not so related. So in order to be in such a state, one does not have to be in other inferentially related states of the kind that give the contents of beliefs their conceptual structure.

4   *Belief, experience and nonconceptual content*
What has all this got to do with experience? I think that this proposal about concepts provides us with a two-stage argument for the nonconceptual content of perceptual experience. The first stage is to show why, contrary to what some philosophers think,[17] perceptions are not beliefs. The second

---

[15]Peacocke argues that inferential role is necessary for the possession of certain concepts – see his remarks about the concept of conjunction in Peacocke 1989b, pp. 51–52.

[16]Which beliefs these are for any given concept would thus determine whether 'prototype' or 'definition' theories of that concept are correct. See Putnam 1975 and Fodor 1981.

[17]See especially Armstrong 1968, chapter 10, and Pitcher 1971. I would also count as belief theories those theories which employ notions like 'judgement' (Craig 1976) or

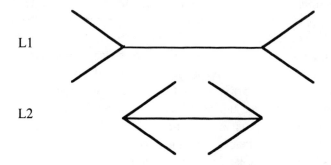

Figure 1 – The Müller-Lyer Illusion

will be to show how this entails that perceptions have nonconceptual contents.

Any theory of perception must explain how perceptions can give rise to beliefs – what makes it the case that we can believe what we see. The belief theory of perception gives a simple answer to this: perceptions just *are* beliefs, acquired in a certain way.

One standard objection to this is that we often do not, and cannot, believe what we see. Consider the famous Müller-Lyer Illusion, where a perceiver, *P*, is presented with two lines of equal length, one with arrows going out (*L1*), the other with arrows going in (*L2*), and suppose *P* does believe that the lines are the same length. No matter how strong this belief of *P*'s is, *P* cannot help but see *L1* as longer than *L2*. A theory that holds a straightforward equation of perception with belief has to say, on the face of it, that the perceivers have contradictory beliefs. But this is implausible. Surely it's better to say that they are in two states with different contents, perceiving that *L1* is longer than *L2*, and believing that *L1* and *L2* are the same length.[18]

It will not do to explain the illusions in terms of a 'prima facie but suppressed' inclination to believe that *L1 is longer than L2* – in Armstrong's words, in terms of 'a state which would be a belief state but for the inhibiting effect of other, contrary beliefs' (Armstrong 1968, p. 140). For there would still be an unexplained component – the difference

---

'hypothesis' (Gregory 1970) – notions which must be defined in terms of belief. Many of the arguments for the belief theory are disposed of by Jackson 1977.

[18]Compare the curious 'Waterfall Illusion': see Frisby 1980, p. 100, and Crane 1988a.

between this state and other, *non*perceptual, inclinations to believe. When conclusive evidence is presented against my nonperceptual inclination to believe that *p*, this inclination should vanish. But when conclusive evidence is presented against my (alleged) inclination to believe that *L1* is longer than *L2*, this alleged inclination remains. (Happy, therefore, are those who believe and have not seen.) Perceptions are resilient to conclusive counter-evidence in such a way that precludes their definition simply in terms of inclinations to believe (see Crane 1988b).

None of this, of course, prevents us being *normally* disposed to believe what we perceive. Perceptions (unlike desires, for instance) are representations of how the world *is*, and thus 'made true' by the facts. In Searle's terminology, they have 'mind-world direction of fit' (Searle 1983, p. 53). Perceptions seem to 'aim' at truth in something like the way beliefs do. But the way perceptions aim at truth is not the same as the way beliefs do. For part of what it is for belief to aim at truth is shown by Moore's so-called 'paradox': the absurdity, for all *p*, of asserting 'I believe that *p* but not *p*'. Yet as the Müller-Lyer Illusion shows, there are values of *p* for which asserting 'I perceive that *p* but not *p*' is perfectly coherent. There is thus no Moorean 'paradox' of perception.

So one clear reason perceptions are not beliefs – and there are others – is that they are not revisable in the light of either other perceptions or beliefs that the perceiver has. Although perceptions do normally involve inclinations to believe, they cannot be identified with these inclinations, since unlike inclinations to believe, they are resilient to conclusive counter-evidence.

In Section 3 I claimed that beliefs were holistically related to one another by at least three kinds of inferential relations. The first were the logical or deductive relations. The second were what I called the 'semantic' relations. And the third were the evidential relations. I claimed that since beliefs would not have the contents they do if they did not stand in these relations, then standing in these relations was essential to beliefs. Moreover, it is because beliefs stand in these relations that they have conceptual structure.

Now take the case of evidential relations. Certain beliefs are partly characterised by the evidence – perceptions and other beliefs – that believers count for or against them. They are therefore revisable on the basis of such evidence. But as we have seen, perceptions are not like this. While they may *be* pieces of evidence, they are not *revisable* on the basis of other evidence – whether that evidence is another belief or another perception. Moreover, if conceptual structure is *only* imposed by these evidential relations and the other inferential relations, then perceptions will not have conceptual structure. This is why their contents will not have inferentially relevant constituents: they will not be composed of concepts.

Although perceptions are unrevisable, the conclusion that they have nonconceptual contents will not follow from this fact alone. For they may yet stand in some of the other inferential relations that are essential to beliefs. Do these other relations hold between experiences?

Take the deductive relations first. On the face of it, it seems plain that there is no such thing as deductive inference *between* perceptions. If I perceive that *a is F*, and I perceive that *a is G*, there is no such thing as inferring the perception that *a is F and G*. If *a*'s *F*-ness and its *G*-ness are both perceptible at the time of the two perceptions, then the content of my perception is surely *a is F and G* in the first place. But if *a*'s *F*-ness and its *G*-ness are not both perceptible on the same occasion, then I can only infer the *belief* that *a is F and G*. That is, if I perceive the fact that *a is F and G*, then there is one perception; but if I don't, there are two perceptions and one belief. Either way, there seems to be no deductive inference between perceptions.

Or consider the case of contents of the form *P & not-P*. One of the deductive constraints on beliefs is that we cannot have explicitly contradictory conscious beliefs. But, in the case of certain striking visual illusions – notably the 'Waterfall Illusion' – we can have contradictory perceptions: a conscious perception with an explicitly contradictory content (Crane 1988a). So once again, perceptions lack certain individuating features of beliefs.

However, matters are not quite as straightforward as this.[19] Can I see that the table is brown and rectangular without also simultaneously seeing that it is brown? Surely not. So why doesn't this mean, on my account, that the content of the perception must have constituents of some sort – a constituent that 'means' *rectangular* and one that 'means' *brown*?

To say that perceptions lack inferential structure of the kind typical of beliefs does not mean that they are entirely unstructured. But reflection on this example shows that there is an important difference between the *kinds* of structure involved in the cases of perception and belief. The difference is that in the case of perception, there is strictly speaking no such thing as the

---

[19]I am indebted to Mark Sainsbury for pressing this objection.

perception of the brownness of the table, in isolation from the perception of its rectangularity. It is simply not possible to perceive that the table is brown without also perceiving its actual shape.

Of course, it also isn't possible to *believe* that the table is brown without believing that it has a shape. But the difference is that whereas the perception is of the table's *actual* shape, the belief is merely that the table *has* a shape. It would be possible for someone to believe that there is a brown table in a certain room without having any beliefs about its definite size or shape. It would be enough to believe simply that it *has* a definite size – somewhere between the size of the room it's in, and the size of a shoebox, perhaps; and a definite shape – round, rectangular, or hexagonal etc. But it would not be possible for a normal perceiver to see a brown table in the room without also seeing its actual size and shape.

Dretske expresses this distinction by saying that the perception of the table contains 'more specific, more determinate' information than the belief about the table.[20] The mere belief that there is a brown table in the room is less specific and determinate than the perception, in the sense that its correctness is compatible with more possibilities. The correctness of this belief is compatible with the table being 6 feet long, or 4 feet 6 inches – and so on. Within certain obvious limits, the belief about its colour and location doesn't rule any of these out. The perception that the table is brown, on the other hand, rules out many more possibilities. There are far fewer ways the length of the table can be that are consistent with the correctness of the perception; so the content of the perception is more specific in that it rules out more possibilities.[21] (This distinction captures the important and nonmisleading sense in which perceptions are more like pictures than statements.)

We may put the point thus: the content of the perception that the table is brown *already contains* the perception of its shape. But the mere belief that the table has a shape can only be *inferred* from the belief that the table is brown, plus the *general* belief that whatever has a colour has a shape. The

---

[20]Dretske 1981, chapter 6, p. 137. This is what he means by saying that the content is coded in *analogue* form. Note that Dretske means 'information' in his own sense, but in this context it can be easily read as 'content'. In this context, see also Peacocke, 'Scenarios, concepts and perception' (this volume) §2.

[21]I do not think, however, that the content of an experience should be represented in standard possible worlds terms – whatever their merits for the contents of beliefs – since it is possible to have contradictory experiences: experiences whose contents would be sets of impossible worlds. Again, see Crane 1988a.

belief about the shape arises, plainly, from a process of reasoning. But the perception of the shape doesn't, for the obvious reason that you *can't* have a perception of the general fact that whatever has a colour has a shape, since such general facts are not perceptible. But as we have seen, you don't *need* such a general 'perception' in order to perceive the shape of the table and its colour – which is just as well, since it can't be had. So although it is possible to infer ascriptions of perceptions from one another, this doesn't entail that the perceptions *themselves* enter into deductive relations.

This brings me to the question of whether those relations that I called 'semantic' – those relations between contents that are not just a matter of logic – apply to perception. The idea was that if you have the belief that *p*, then there are certain other beliefs that you *ought to have* if that belief is to have the content *p*. Once again, perception doesn't share this feature of belief: to perceive that *p*, there are no other *perceptions* that you *ought to* have. There is no 'ought' about it. You simply perceive what the world and your perceptual systems let you perceive. If these systems go wrong, then they can produce states with contents – e.g. contradictions – that the belief system would not tolerate. But unlike the case of beliefs, failing in this way does not stop the perceptions from *having* those contents. (A Davidsonian might put this point by saying that perception is not subject to the 'constitutive ideal of rationality': see Davidson 1970, p. 213.)

So I conclude that the structure in the contents of perception is not conceptual structure: that is, the inferential structure of the contents of beliefs. But how then should we understand its structure? My general account of nonconceptual content does not entail one particular answer to this question. But it is consistent with the most fully developed current theory of nonconceptual content – Peacocke's theory of 'scenario content'.[22]

Peacocke's idea is that the content of a perception can be given by specifying a *scenario*: a set of ways of filling out the space around the perceiver with properties (colours, shapes, temperatures and so on) relative to an origin and a family of axes. The origin will depend on the position and posture of the perceiver. When specifying a given scenario, we will of course use concepts that pick out the various aspects of the scenario – the properties that constitute it. But, Peacocke claims, 'the fact that a concept is

---

[22]See Peacocke 1989c, Peacocke 1989b and 'Scenarios, concepts and perception' (this volume). The last paper introduces a distinction between scenarios and another 'level' of nonconceptual content, the 'protoproposition'. I do not need to discuss this refinement here.

used in fixing the scenario does *not* entail that that concept is somehow a component of the experience's representational content' (Peacocke 1989c).

This claim fits neatly into my account of nonconceptual content. According to the argument of Section 3, to say that concepts are not components of contents is to say that the subject does not have to possess the concepts used to characterise the content in order for his or her state to have such a content. Applied to scenarios, this means that the subject's being in a state with a scenario content does not entail that he or she possesses the concepts that characterise the scenario. And this in turn means that the subject does not have to be able to make inferences involving beliefs about the properties of the scenario, in order for his or her *perceptual* states to have such contents. And this seems right: surely if experiences have such scenario contents, we should not expect perceivers to have beliefs about all the myriad properties that characterise them, and make inferences involving those beliefs. So although a scenario content does have a *structure*, it does not have inferential structure – and so does not have conceptual constituents.

There is still an outstanding issue. How will this picture of perception explain the relation between perception and belief? Perceptions cause beliefs, and these perception-caused beliefs interact with other beliefs inferentially. It may then be asked: how can my account of the content of perception answer our question about the relation between perception and belief? Why doesn't this inferential relation impose structure?

My answer is this: when a perception that *p* causes a belief that *p*, the *whole* contents of these two states are of the same type – *p*. The (causal) relation between perception and belief takes place at the level of whole contents. But on the perception side of this transaction, the contents are not composed of concepts: concepts come later when thinkers employ the beliefs they thus formed, and the desires they have, in reasoning – belief *conceptualises* the content of perception. So treating the transition from perception to belief in terms of whole contents allows us to explain how perceptions have contents that can be the contents of beliefs. It is crucial here to remember the argument of Section 3: the idea of a content was not explained as a combination of concepts. We extracted the idea of a concept from the idea of a system of beliefs; we did not extract the idea of the content of a belief from an antecedently given idea of a concept.

That completes my argument for the nonconceptual content of perception. But what about the other two examples of nonconceptual content that I mentioned at the beginning of Section 2? Will my account apply to them too?

I have nothing to say on the subject of the rings of the tree representing its age. Since for me, possessing concepts entails at least having beliefs, then since the tree has no beliefs, *a fortiori* it possesses no concepts. And I need not take a stand here on the controversial issue of whether the tree is in a state with *content*.

The case of the visual system is more complex. As I said in Section 2, many people think that the contents of states attributed by computational theories of vision are nonconceptual. But these theories often describe the stages in visual information-processing in terms of making inferences.[23] So if these theories are right, how can my argument possibly apply?

I shall end this paper by sketching an answer to this question. There is an important difference between the ways in which intentional states are inferentially related in thought, and the way computational states are related. The inferences a thinker is disposed to make, on which the conceptual structure of his or her thought depends, are constrained only by rationality, which allows the mind to range over its whole territory for its material. The resources of the visual system are, by contrast, severely restricted. Although we can treat it as deducing consequences from premises, the contents of these premises are not holistically related in the way the contents of beliefs are.

Consider, for example, how Irvin Rock explains one striking effect of the Julesz random dot stereograms:

> it would seem that the perceptual system 'knows' certain laws of optics that normally obtain, and then 'interprets' seeming departures from these laws in such a way as to be compatible with them. (Rock 1983, p. 10)

Although it may well be correct to attribute to the visual system representations of certain laws of optics, this is not the same as what goes on when we know or believe laws of optics. To echo a remark of Gareth Evans: to make sense of this case, we do not need to suppose that the visual

---

[23]See Segal 1989, at p. 192. Cf. Marr: 'the true heart of visual perception is the inference from the structure of an image about the structure of the real world outside' (Marr 1982, p. 68).

system is capable of entertaining contents about any other sort of law.[24] But this is precisely what we *do* suppose when attributing to someone a belief about a law – we suppose that the subject can make inferences about laws, and thus entertain other contents about laws. If subjects couldn't do this, then they wouldn't have the concept of a law.

But this isn't so with the visual system – for its states to have content, they do not need to be so holistic. And I have argued here that the holistic constraints of rationality are the only motivation for postulating concepts. So the fact that the visual system does not meet these constraints helps explain why it possesses no concepts. And this would be why its states are not *composed* of concepts, in the sense I have defended in this paper.[25]

---

[24]I have in mind a well-known passage from Evans 1982, p. 104: 'When we attribute to the brain computations whereby it localises the sounds we hear, we ipso facto attribute to it representations of the speed of sound and the distance between the ears, without any commitment to the idea that it should be able to represent the speed of light or the distance between anything else.' See also Davies 1989.

[25]Earlier versions of this paper were presented at University College London, the Department of History and Philosophy of Science, King's College London, and at the Universities of Sheffield, Stirling and York. I am grateful to the audiences on these occasions, and especially to John Campbell, Bill Hart, Stephen Makin, Mike Martin, Hugh Mellor, Alan Millar, Philip Percival, Tom Pink, Mark Sainsbury, Barry Smith and Michael Tye for discussions and written comments that have helped me greatly with the paper.

7   *Visual qualia and visual content*

MICHAEL TYE

Many philosophers take it to be evident that visual experiences have, over and above their representational contents, intrinsic, introspectively accessible properties in virtue of which they have those contents. Such properties, which are held to ground the subjective character or phenomenal 'feel' of the experiences, I shall call 'visual qualia'. Many an argument there has been about whether qualia, visual and otherwise, can be accommodated within a physicalist view of the mental or whether they are special, irreducible properties. I have come to think that at least as far as visual experience is concerned these arguments are badly misguided. I now believe that there are no visual qualia.[1] So the question as to whether they are physical or irreducible simply does not arise.

This position will undoubtedly strike those (including my erstwhile self: Tye 1986; Tye 1989, chapter 6) who have engaged in debate about the nature of qualia as puzzling indeed. Isn't it just *obvious* from introspection that there are visual qualia? Surely the only real question, many will say, concerns the *status* of such qualia. Challenges to their existence are no more worthy of serious consideration than challenges to the existence of tables and chairs. In what follows, I shall try to show not only that no good reasons have been adduced for believing in visual qualia but also that, upon proper reflection, the most natural view is that there are none.

The paper is divided into three sections. In Section I, I say some more about what sorts of properties of visual experience visual qualia are

---

[1]Actually I hold the broader view that there are no perceptual qualia, since I believe that the arguments I give below may be extended *mutatis mutandis* to the other senses. The outright rejection of qualia, both perceptual and nonperceptual, is defended by Dennett 1988; also by Harman 1989. I am sympathetic with the general views expressed in these articles (and in several places I am indebted to Harman's discussion in particular) but there are many aspects of each with which I disagree (e.g., I do not wish to deny that there are pain qualia).

supposed to be and what it is I am committed to in denying their existence. In Section II, I discuss a variety of arguments and examples that purport to show that there are visual qualia. Finally, in Section III, I make some brief comments on the overall significance of my attempt to account for visual experience without qualia.

I

Consider a painting of a tiger. Viewers of the painting can apprehend not only its content (i.e., its representing a tiger) but also the colours, shapes, and spatial relations obtaining among blobs of paint by virtue of which it has that content. It is sometimes supposed that being aware or conscious of a visual experience is like viewing an inner picture. So, e.g., on this conception of vision, if I train my eyes on a tiger in good light, I am subject to a mental picture-like representation of a tiger, introspection of which reveals to me both its content and its intrinsic, nonintentional features by virtue of which it has that content. These intrinsic, nonintentional features are not literally colours and shapes of parts of my mental quasi-picture, as in the case of a real picture. After all, it would obviously be absurd to suppose that parts of my brain are orange and black striped when I see a tiger and it is surely no less absurd to suppose that parts of my soul are. So whether visual experiences are physical or not, even on a pictorial conception, their introspectible, intrinsic properties are not colours and shapes.

Anyone who believes that there are visual qualia must at least believe that visual experiences are like pictures to the extent that they have intrinsic, nonintentional features which are accessible to introspection and by virtue of which the experiences represent what they do.[2] In denying that visual experiences have qualia what I am denying is that there are any intrinsic, nonintentional features of which the subjects of the experiences can be aware and by virtue of which the experiences have their contents. This is not to say, of course, that the contents of the experiences are not themselves introspectible. Nor is it to say that visual experiences do not have intrinsic, nonintentional features. If, as is widely believed, visual experiences are

---

[2]'By virtue of which' here does not mean *solely* by virtue of which. No-one holds that the content of a visual experience is completely fixed by its qualia just as no-one holds that the content of a picture is completely fixed by the colours and shapes of its parts.

neural items, they will certainly have intrinsic physico-chemical properties.[3]

The rejection of visual qualia is *not* tantamount to a rejection of the view that there is nothing it is like for the subjects of visual experiences. On the contrary, the view, at least as I accept it, is that what it is like to have a visual experience (what I earlier called the 'subjective character' of the experience) is determined by aspects of its representational content.[4] So, I maintain that any two visual experiences that are alike in all their intentional properties are alike in their subjective characters. To refute my position it suffices to specify a clear counter-example to this generalization. I know of no such counter-examples. In the next section I shall consider a variety of putative counter-examples together with a number of other objections.

II

The argument from introspection
Standing on the beach in Santa Barbara a couple of summers ago on a bright sunny day, I found myself transfixed by the intense blue of the Pacific Ocean. Was I not here delighting in the phenomenal aspects of my visual experience? And if I was, doesn't this show that there are visual qualia?

I am not convinced. It seems to me that what I found so pleasing in the above instance, what I was focussing on, as it were, were a certain shade and intensity of the colour blue. I experienced blue as a property of the ocean not as a property of my experience. My experience itself certainly wasn't blue. Rather it was an experience that represented the ocean as blue. What I was really delighting in, then, were specific aspects of the content of my experience. It was the content, not anything else, that was immediately accessible to my consciousness and that had aspects I found so pleasing (see Shoemaker forthcoming). This point, I might note, seems to be the sort of thing G. E. Moore had in mind when he remarked that the sensation of blue is diaphanous (see Moore 1922, p. 22). When one tries to focus on it in introspection one cannot help but see right through it so that what one actually ends up attending to is the real colour blue.

There is another rather different way in which a straightforward appeal to introspection might be made on behalf of qualia. The visual experience I

---

[3]In my view, subpersonal processing of (some of) these introspectively inaccessible properties plays a role in the awareness of content.
[4]This is to oversimplify a little. See my discussion of blind 'sight' in Section II below.

had that day in Santa Barbara, as I stood entranced by the colour of the sea, was, to my consciousness, very similar to a colour photograph I might have taken of the same scene. My experience, then, was a picture-like representation of the sea, and my awareness of it was something like my viewing a picture. Since, as I noted in the last section, pictures evidently have accessible intrinsic qualities by virtue of which they represent the world, so too, by analogy, do visual experiences.

The most obvious problem with this appeal is that it is not at all clear that my visual experience, while viewing the ocean, was *really* similar to a colour photograph of the ocean. The only undeniable similarity here is between my experience and the experience I would have undergone had I viewed an appropriate photograph. The fact that these experiences are similar shows nothing about the way in which their contents are encoded. What I deny, then, is that the *format* of visual representations – the way in which they encode their contents – is given in introspection. What introspection reveals are simply aspects of the contents themselves.

The second objection I have is simply that even if visual experiences are, in an important sense, picture-like, it evidently does not follow that they have qualia. One could hold, e.g., that visual experiences have intrinsic qualities by virtue of which they represent while denying that these qualities are introspectively accessible (see Harman 1989). Such a position still permits the possibility that visual experiences are picture-like, e.g., with respect to the representation of spatial relations.[5] But it leaves no room for qualia.

The argument from hallucination

Suppose that Paul hallucinates a pink square object. Then there is something that Paul hallucinates. But what Paul hallucinates is not a real pink, square, physical object – Paul, after all, is hallucinating not seeing. So what Paul hallucinates must be a mental object, an idea or an appearance. Now mental objects are not literally coloured nor do they literally have shape. So the terms 'pink' and 'square' in application to what Paul hallucinates must pick out special properties of which Paul is directly aware. These properties are qualia. Since seeing can be indistinguishable from hallucinating, visual experiences generally relate their subjects to mental objects, the intrinsic,

---

[5] In something like the manner suggested by Stephen Kosslyn for mental images. For a summary of Kosslyn's views here, see Tye 1988 and Tye 1991.

introspectible properties of which are responsible for the subjective character of the experiences.

I lack the space to comment on all that is wrong with this argument. When Paul hallucinates in the above case he has an experience *of* a pink square object. This experience has content – it represents a pink square object. *There is*, then, a definite content to Paul's hallucinatory experience. But there is no object, mental or otherwise, that Paul hallucinates. Furthermore the fact that Paul's experience has a certain content no more requires that there really be a pink square object than a picture's representing a three-headed monster, say, requires that there really be any monsters.

Consider the following parallel. Paul wants a blue emerald to give to his wife. There are no blue emeralds. It does not follow that Paul wants the idea of a blue emerald to give to his wife. That he already has. What he wants is that his wife be given a blue emerald (by him). His desire, then, is the desire it is in virtue of its having a specific content. When Paul reflects upon or introspects his desire what he is aware of is this content rather than any peculiar qualities of a special mental particular upon which his desire is directed. Likewise when Paul hallucinates a pink square what he introspects, I maintain, is the content of his hallucinatory experience. This, it seems to me, is the common-sense view. The idea that the terms 'pink' and 'square' in the context 'Paul hallucinates a pink square' stand for special, phenomenal qualities of which Paul is aware and hence have entirely different meanings from those they have in, say, 'The piece of glass is pink and square' is, on the face of it, very strange indeed. The argument from hallucination does nothing to make this idea palatable.

Visual qualia without visual content
Here is a related argument. Suppose you look at a bright light and turn away. You have an after-image that is red and round, say. In this case you are subject to a visual experience but your experience has no representational content. What it is like for you, then, cannot be determined by aspects of the content of your experience. Rather it must be due to visual qualia (see Jackson 1976).

It seems to me no more plausible to take the terms 'red' and 'round', as they apply to an after-image, as denoting intrinsic qualities of the image than it is to take the terms 'loud' and 'high-pitched', as they are employed in connection with the graphical representations of sounds, as denoting intrinsic qualities of oscilloscope readings. People who work with such readings frequently use terms like 'loud' and 'high-pitched' in application to the readings themselves. (This example is due to Ned Block 1983, pp. 516–517.) It is obvious that in this usage what the terms really mean are 'represents loud' and 'represents high-pitched' respectively. Analogously it seems to me that what the terms 'red' and 'round' signify, in application to an after-image, are representational properties of the after-image experience. One who has a red, round after-image is subject to a visual experience produced by looking at a bright light, the content of which is that something – typically a region of space – is red and round. There is, then, I claim, a definite content to the visual experience after all.

What it is that Shoemaker likes

Sydney Shoemaker presents an interesting argument for the existence of gustatory qualia (see Shoemaker forthcoming). Although my concern is with visual experience, I shall consider Shoemaker's argument since it applies *mutatis mutandis* to the visual case.

Shoemaker tells us that he likes the taste of Cabernet Sauvignon wine. This, however, is not all that he likes when he sips the wine. For the taste is some chemical property of the wine – some combination of esters, acids, and oils – and this chemical property could be detected visually with suitable laboratory equipment. In *these* circumstances using his visual sense, Shoemaker opines, he wouldn't like the taste. What, then, is it about the taste that he really likes? Well, perhaps it is the fact that he has a gustatory experience *of* that taste, i.e., an experience in a certain sense-modality that represents the relevant chemical property. Shoemaker concedes that he does like having such experiences and that his liking them is crucial to his liking the taste. But what he likes about them, he insists, is not that they have a certain content (this, he thinks, is established by the visual case above in which he has visual experiences with the same content) nor that they are produced by certain sense-organs. Rather, according to Shoemaker, what it is he likes about those experiences is what it is like to have them, in other words, he claims, their qualia.

One way of attacking the above argument is to try to show that it requires an illegitimate substitution of terms within an intensional context. Suppose that I am drinking Cabernet Sauvignon and that I react in the same way as Shoemaker. I might state my satisfaction as follows:

(1) What I like about these experiences is that they represent this
taste.

If (1) is taken to assert that what I like about certain experiences and a
certain taste is that the former represent the latter then Shoemaker is
justified in rejecting (1) for his own case on the grounds that he finds the
relevant taste unappealing when presented visually. (Assuming that the taste
is indeed a chemical property of the wine. I am prepared to grant this
assumption *arguendo* but it is contentious.)

(1), however, may also be taken to be referentially opaque with respect
to the occurrence of 'this taste'. And if it is so taken then Shoemaker's
appeal to the visual unattractiveness of the taste is irrelevant. That such an
interpretation of (1) is possible is evidenced by examples such as the
following: Oedipus, after having decided to marry his mother without
knowing who she was, might have said truly

(2) What I like about my forthcoming marriage is that it will unite
me with this woman.

Clearly (2) would be transformed into a falsehood by the substitution of
'my mother' for 'this woman'.

Shoemaker concedes that this reply to his argument is a reasonable one.
Nonetheless, a question arises as to how (1) is to be understood under a
referentially opaque reading of 'this taste'. For, as Shoemaker certainly
realizes, if qualia are to be avoided, (1) had better not be taken to assert that
what is liked about the relevant gustatory experiences is that they represent
the taste of Cabernet Sauvignon via their having certain qualia (see
Shoemaker forthcoming).

How, then, is (1) to be understood? This question is best answered in the
context of my second criticism of Shoemaker's argument, which is that he
fails to rule out a further possible alternative account of what it is that he
likes about his gustatory experiences while drinking Cabernet Sauvignon.
Granting now that what he likes about those experiences is not just their
content – this, by the way, is not obvious even putting aside the point above
since there will inevitably be a number of straightforward differences in
content between the visual and gustatory cases (e.g., in the former the
relevant chemical property will be represented as being instantiated outside
the mouth some distance away from Shoemaker's body) – and granting also
that what he likes is not just that the experiences are produced by certain

sense-organs, still it does not follow that what he really likes here are gustatory qualia. For it seems to me reasonable to claim that what Shoemaker likes about the experiences is that they are gustatory experiences having a certain content. It is this package of content plus species which he finds so appealing – the presentation of a certain content in a certain mode of experience. In proposing this alternative I am assuming that a sufficient condition for an experience's being gustatory is that it have an appropriate functional role.[6] Of course, this functional role is not given to one in introspection. Introspection, I maintain, reveals nothing about the inner nature of the property of being gustatory. (Just as hearing reveals to one nothing about the nature of sound, for example.) It merely informs one that the property is being tokened just as, for example, it sometimes informs one that the properties of being a thought or being a desire are tokened.

We are now in a position to specify what it is that (1) asserts, when 'this taste' is read opaquely, without appeal to qualia. In my view, (1) may be taken to say that what I like about certain experiences is that they represent a certain taste gustatorily, that is, that they are gustatory experiences representing that particular taste.

Shoemaker (in personal correspondence) rejects this proposal of mine on the grounds that 'the way Cabernet Sauvignon tastes to me might change in such a way that, once I have accommodated to the change, my Cabernet Sauvignon-produced gustatory experiences have the same representational content as my earlier Cabernet Sauvignon-produced gustatory experiences did but are ones I find very unpleasant – and this might happen without my ceasing to like the way Cabernet Sauvignon *now* tastes to me'. I am not persuaded by this reply, however. If the way Cabernet Sauvignon tastes to me changes, the gustatory experiences it produces in me will, I claim, represent it as having a *different* taste from the one it had earlier. So, contra Shoemaker, there *will* be a change in the intentional content of my gustatory experiences. (For more on alleged cases of qualia inversion, see the example of the Inverted Spectrum discussed below.)

The conclusion I reach, then, is that the Cabernet Sauvignon example can be handled without admitting that gustatory states have qualia.[7]

---

[6]In my view, this functional role can only be fully specified by *a posteriori* scientific investigation. I should add here that Shoemaker does quickly reject the view that what he likes is a combination of the content of the relevant experiences and their being produced by certain sense-organs. This view is similar to my proposal, but it is one that I too reject.

[7]In fairness to Shoemaker, I should note that he does not himself view the example as decisive. See his comments in Shoemaker forthcoming.

Blind 'sight'

Albert is a very remarkable man. He is blind and he has been so since birth. Nevertheless when he faces objects and concentrates fiercely, thoughts pop into his head – he knows not where they come from – about the visual properties and relations of the objects. These thoughts are so detailed that *content-wise* they are just as rich as the visual experiences sighted people have in the same circumstances. Indeed were one to pay attention merely to the contents of Albert's thoughts, as expressed in his verbal descriptions of what is before him, one would be convinced that he is seeing. But Albert has no visual experiences. For Albert there is experientially no difference between his thoughts on such occasions and his thoughts when he ruminates on mathematics or art or life in general. In each case thoughts just occur and he is introspectively aware of no more than the contents of his thoughts. There is, then, an enormous felt difference between Albert and his sighted fellows at the times at which Albert seems to be seeing. This difference is one that Albert himself would come to appreciate in detail were he to gain sight. It is a difference that can only be explained on the assumption that Albert's inner states lack visual qualia.[8]

Not so. There is another explanation. In my view, what introspection tells me when I see something is not only the content of my visual experience but also the kind of experience it is. The crucial difference between Albert and myself when we face the same scene is that I am introspectively aware that I am undergoing a *visual experience* with a certain content whereas Albert is introspectively aware that he is undergoing *thoughts* with that content. This difference is a felt difference – it is given in introspection – and it is why I, on the basis of my experience, believe that I am seeing something whereas Albert does not. What makes my experience a visual experience is not, I maintain, its having certain visual qualia. After all, there is surely no short straightforward list of the relevant qualia even if there are such entities as qualia. The property of being a visual experience is not itself classifiable as a visual quale either. For one thing, it is certainly not a property in virtue of which its tokens have their contents; for another, in my view, ontologically it is on a par with the properties of being a thought and being a desire. What is sufficient for my experience to be a visual experience is, I believe, that it have the

---

[8]A case like that of Albert was suggested to me in conversation by Stephen Stich.

right functional role.[9] Albert has no inner states that token *this* functional role but if he gains sight he will, and thereby he will come to appreciate what it was he lacked before.[10]

What, I think, the case of Albert does show is that the remarks of G. E. Moore I mentioned earlier about the visual experience of blue being diaphanous are in one respect inaccurate. When one introspects this experience one is aware not only of the real colour blue upon which it is directed but also of the fact that it is a visual experience. This is why in reporting what one is introspecting one will say that one has a *visual experience* of blue. Were qualia presented to one on such occasions there would surely be words to describe them. But our reports cite only the contents of our inner states and their species. Qualia are never mentioned.

The inverted spectrum

Tom has a very peculiar visual system. His visual experiences are systematically inverted with respect to those of his fellows. When Tom looks at red objects, for example, what it is like for him is the same as what it is like for other people when they look at green objects and vice versa. This peculiarity is one of which neither he nor others are aware. Tom has learnt the meanings of colour words in the usual way and he applies these words correctly. Moreover his nonlinguistic behaviour is standard.

Now when Tom views a tomato, say, in good light his experience is phenomenally, subjectively different from the experiences you and I undergo. But his experience has the same representational content as ours. For his experience is the sort that is usually produced in him by viewing red objects and that usually leads him to believe that a red object is present. So he, like you and me, in viewing the tomato has an experience that represents the tomato as *red* (see Shoemaker 1975; Churchland 1984, pp. 39–40). The only way that Tom's experience can be subjectively different from yours and mine, then, is if it has a different visual quale. The intrinsic phenomenal quality in virtue of which his experience represents the tomato as red cannot be the one in virtue of which our experiences represent it as red. Rather his

---

[9]As in the earlier case of the property of being gustatory, a full specification of the relevant functional role is a matter for scientific psychology. Aspects of this role depend, I believe, on visual experiences having a special format (which is itself, of course, a matter for scientific investigation).

[10]Knowing what it is like to see things requires that one undergo visual experiences. This is why Albert doesn't know what it is like to see.

is the one in virtue of which other experiences of ours represent grass and leaves, for example, as green.

One might respond to this argument by denying that a behaviourally undetectable inverted spectrum is possible.[11] There is another response available, however, that seems to me intuitively very satisfying. Contrary to what is claimed above, I believe that the difference between Tom and the rest of us when he views a tomato is that his experience, unlike ours, represents it as *green*. How is this possible? After all, the content of Tom's experience must be given to him, for the difference is a subjective one. But if the content is given to him then he must be introspectively aware that his experience represents the tomato as green. Unfortunately he is aware of no such thing. He sincerely asserts that the tomato is red and even that it looks red to him. Moreover, as was noted above, his experience is the sort that in him is typically produced by viewing red objects.

The answer, I maintain, is as follows: Introspection leads Tom astray. He forms a false belief about the content of his experience.[12] This content is certainly something *of* which he is introspectively aware but it is a content which he misclassifies. He takes it to be the content *red* and so he believes, on the basis of introspection, that he is undergoing an experience that represents red. In reality his experience represents green. *This* representational difference is what is responsible for the subjective difference between his experience and ours. Tom's mistake is due, of course, to the fact that he is unaware of his peculiarity. He does not know that his visual system is producing experiences with atypical contents. He thinks he is normal and he knows that the experience he undergoes viewing the tomato is subjectively like those he undergoes viewing other red objects. So he thinks that his experience represents red.

Perhaps it will be said that I haven't explained how Tom's experience can represent green when it is an experience of the subjective sort that is

---

[11]This is the line taken by Gilbert Harman 1989. One problem that confronts such a line is that even if Tom's peculiarity is ultimately behaviourally detectable, it appears that some possible inversions are not, e.g., inversions pertaining to the experiences of creatures who see the world in black, white, and varying shades of grey. See here Shoemaker 1975.

[12]This position, together with an internalist conception of knowledge which requires Tom to cite the belief that his experience represents a red object in any adequate justification of the claim that the tomato before him is red, entails that he does not know that the tomato is red. Indeed, more generally, it entails that he does not know the colour of anything on the basis of vision despite his excellent performance. (I owe this point to Sydney Shoemaker.) Since the conclusion reached here is obviously false, I maintain that the above internalist conception of knowledge must be rejected.

normally produced in him by viewing red objects and which normally produces in him the belief that something red is present. My reply is that his experience is also of the subjective sort that is normally produced in people generally by viewing green objects and that normally produces in them the belief that something green is present. Why should the former fact outweigh the latter in assessing what the content of his experience is? If we wish to pay equal attention to both facts, perhaps the most natural thing to say is that, relative to humans generally, Tom's experience represents green but, relative to him, it represents red. Since our experiences, on viewing the tomato, represent red for humans generally, there is, as before, a representational difference between Tom and us upon which to ground the subjective difference.

It is important to realize that I am not implicitly offering a reductive analysis of properties of the type, representing F (for group X), in my comments above in terms of properties of the type, being of the subjective sort that is normally brought about (in group X) by viewing F objects etc. Since the relevant subjective sorts are, on my view, themselves properties of the type, being a visual sensation that represents F (for group X), this would create a vicious circularity. I assume that properties such as representing green (for humans) have a complex causal/relational basis in nature, but I deny that this basis requires for its specification the concept of a subjective sort. This is easily illustrated by reference to the case of Tom.

In my view, visual experiences are constituted by brain states. So, Tom's visual experience, when he views a tomato, has various intrinsic physical properties. Now since I deny that there are visual qualia, I deny that any of these properties are introspectively accessible. But I hold that among them is some property P which is standardly tokened in humans generally as a result of their viewing green objects and which is standardly caused in Tom as a result of his viewing red objects. So I hold that Tom's experience has the property of having an intrinsic physical property that is appropriately caused in the relevant populations by both red and green objects. This is sufficient, I claim (in crude, first approximation and ignoring relevant behavioural effects of P), for Tom's experience to represent green relative to humans generally and red relative to Tom.[13]

---

[13]Let me stress that the condition sketched here is *only* intended to be sufficient for Tom's experience to represent these things; it is *not* intended to be necessary. In general, I doubt that illuminating, naturalistic, necessary and sufficient conditions can be given for representational content.

It is important to realize that even given the population relativity of content, on the above approach, the property of representing F (for population X) cannot be identified with any of the intrinsic properties of the experiences that are its tokens. For the former property is both introspectively accessible and F-involving while the latter are neither.

I want now to turn to another version of the inverted spectrum argument for visual qualia. Suppose that there is a species of creatures half of whom have visual experiences that are the inverses of the other half. These differences arise as a result of naturally evolved differences in the retinas of the two groups. Surely, in this case, it is implausible to maintain that when two of the creatures (one from each group) view a tomato in good light one has an experience that represents the tomato as green. But if both creatures' experiences represent the tomato as red then the phenomenal difference in their experiences cannot be accounted for representationally. So visual qualia must be postulated.

Once properties of the form representing so-and-so are taken to be population-relative,[14] this argument loses its force. Both of the creatures' visual experiences represent the tomato as red *but only relative to their own groups*.[15] There is, then, a difference in content. So the inverted spectrum still does not compel us to accept visual qualia.

The same conclusion holds, I maintain, for cases of intra-subjective inversion. If my visual apparatus is systematically tampered with so that objects that earlier looked red to me now come to look the way green objects used to look (and vice versa), my experiences will change from representing those objects as red to representing them as green (and vice versa). In this case, the relevant background population for these attributions of content is myself prior to the operation on my visual system.

Let us now move still further afield from the commonplace realm.

Twin Earth

Jones is watching a cat. On Putnam's planet, Twin Earth, Jones' doppelgänger is watching a creature that looks just like a cat but is genetically and biologically very different (see Putnam 1975). Jones and

---

[14]There are, I might add, any number of properties of this sort. Consider, e.g., the property of being the loser.

[15]In making these remarks as well as the earlier ones on population relativity I am influenced by David Lewis 1980. I do not endorse Lewis' combination of functionalism and type physicalism, however. For criticism of Lewis here, see Tye 1983.

Twin Jones are subject to retinal images that exactly match and their brains are in exactly the same physico-chemical states. Intuitively, then, their visual sensations are phenomenally identical. But the contents of their sensations are different. Since Twin Jones has never seen or heard of cats (there aren't any cats on Twin Earth only twin cats) and the beliefs he forms on the basis of his visual experiences are never of the type 'This is a cat', Twin Jones' experience represents not that there is a cat but rather that there is a twin cat present. So the phenomenal sameness obtaining between Jones' and Twin Jones' visual experiences cannot be grounded in a sameness of content. Rather it must be grounded in the experiences sharing identical qualia.

This argument forgets that Twin Jones' visual experience represents much more than just that a twin cat is present. It also represents the location of the twin cat relative to the viewer, its shape, colour, orientation, and a myriad of other surface details. These aspects of the content of Twin Jones' visual experience will also be found in the content of Jones' experience. I maintain that the phenomenal sameness obtaining between their visual experiences is traceable to these shared aspects.

It may seem that if our conception of the phenomenal is one which ties it to aspects of representational content then we must reject the widely held view that subjective, phenomenal states of consciousness supervene on brain activity (as is implicitly supposed in the above Twin Earth argument). The matter is complex, however. The relevant aspects of content, as far as the phenomenal is concerned, are those that pertain to *directly* visible features, e.g., colour and shape. If it is supposed that a visual experience that (relative to normal perceivers) represents red, say, is an experience that bears some complex relation R to normal perceivers and red objects then, on my view, a person who lives in a world without red objects, and whose brain is artificially stimulated so that it is in exactly the same overall brain state as that of a normal human being on earth who is viewing a red object in daylight, will *not* be subject to a phenomenally identical visual experience. But if it is held instead that a visual experience that represents red (relative to normal perceivers) is an experience that, given normal perceivers, would bear relation R to them and red objects were there such objects, then, on my view, in the case just described, the absence of red objects will not generate the same result. So, on the former approach to content, my position requires a rejection of the thesis that physically identical brains must support phenomenally identical states of consciousness; but this is not required on the latter approach.

Which of the two approaches is to be preferred? It is evident that the latter will not do for *all* aspects of the content of visual experience. For, as applied to the earlier case of Jones, it entails the falsehood that Jones' experience represents not just a cat but also a twin cat.[16] The former, however, seems intuitively too restrictive. Furthermore, both approaches make the dubious preliminary assumption that naturalistic necessary and sufficient conditions can be stated for the case of a visual experience's representing red. So, I am actually inclined to accept a weaker alternative, namely that a visual experience represents red if and only if it stands in the representation relation to redness, whether or not redness is instantiated, relative to the appropriate perceivers. There is, I believe, a naturalistic *sufficient* condition associated with this of the sort I sketched earlier; but I do not believe that there is anything stronger. Nothing in the final approach entails that in a world without red objects *no* visual experiences (including those produced by artificial stimulation of the brain) will ever represent red. So I do not see that the phenomenal–neural supervenience thesis is directly threatened by my position.

Peacocke's puzzle cases

In *Sense and Content* (Peacocke 1983), Christopher Peacocke presents a number of ingenious cases designed to show that sensory experiences have qualia or, as he calls them, 'sensational properties'.[17] Peacocke's first case is as follows: Suppose I view two trees of the same size, one twice as close as the other. My visual experience will represent the two trees as being of the same size – assuming, as will normally be the case, that the more distant tree does not really look smaller to me. But there is surely a sense in which the trees look different. This, according to Peacocke, can only be accounted for by supposing that the two trees have a different size in the visual field. And size in the visual field is, so Peacocke claims, a sensational quality or quale.

---

[16]Assuming, of course, that the internal differences between cats and twin cats do not bear on relation R (as seems plausible).

[17]There is one difference between Peacocke's 'sensational qualities' and perceptual qualia. According to Peacocke, sensational qualities are not qualities in virtue of which perceptual experiences have their contents. (Peacocke does not say what the relationship is between sensational qualities and content.) This difference, however, does not make a difference as far as my criticisms are concerned.

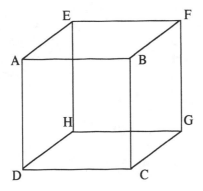

Figure 1

There is another possibility. The reason that the trees look different is, I believe, that it visually appears to me that if the trees were moved into line, the nearer one would completely obscure the other but not vice versa. This, in turn, is because my visual experience represents the nearer tree as being larger from here (the viewing position), that is, it represents it as subtending a larger visual angle. The difference Peacocke alleges to be due to different qualia, then, is, I maintain, due to aspects of the experience's representational content.

Peacocke rejects this proposal on the grounds that experiences like mine can be had by people who lack the concept of a visual angle. If by this Peacocke means to assert that people who lack the linguistic capacity to apply correctly the term 'visual angle' or who have never heard of the term can have experiences like mine then we may quickly agree. But it surely does not follow that *these* people cannot be subject to experiences that represent certain facts about visual angles. If Peacocke has something else in mind by the concept of a visual angle then he must *show* (a) that lacking the concept precludes a person from undergoing a visual experience that represents anything about visual angles and (b) that lacking the concept does not preclude a person from undergoing an experience like mine. Without such a demonstration it seems to me that Peacocke's first case is indecisive.

Peacocke's second case appeals to a contrast between binocular and monocular vision. If I view a situation with both eyes and then close an eye, things will appear different to me. This difference, according to Peacocke, is not representational. The one experience represents things as being just as

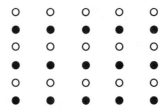

Figure 2

they are represented as being by the other. So the difference must be due to a difference in qualia.

The claim I reject here (not surprisingly) is the claim that there is no representational difference. When I view the situation with both eyes I see a little more of the objects and there is an increase in the determinacy of my representation of object distances. An appeal to qualia is not required.

Peacocke's third example is a case in which a wire cube is seen first as having one face in front of the other and then with the relative positions of the two faces reversed (see Figure 1). Although there is a change in the experience here something in the experience remains the same. This constant feature of the experience is, Peacocke maintains, a sensational quality.

The obvious response to this example is that the experience represents the cube as having a variety of unchanging spatial properties relative to the point of view and that this is really all that remains constant in the experience. For example, both before and after the 'aspect' switch side ABCD is represented as being lower than and somewhat to the left of side EFGH, side AEHD is represented as being level with and wholly to the left of side BFGC, and so on.

Other aspect switches are no more problematic for my position, I might add. Consider, for example, the pattern in Figure 2 (which Peacocke mentions a little later). We may see this pattern either with the dots running from the bottom to the top or from the left to the right. How is this to be accounted for? Answer: There is a difference in content in the two experiences. Each experience represents the pattern as being composed of certain groups of dots. In the one case the groups form rows while in the other they form columns. It is because the experiences represent the pattern as falling into these groups that the perceiver will judge the pattern similar to Figure 3(a) in the former instance and similar to Figure 3(b) in the

(a)   (b)

Figure 3

latter. The overall conclusion I reach, then, is that there is no need to postulate visual qualia in order to account for the subjective aspects of our visual experiences. It suffices to admit that such experiences are visual and that they have contents. Qualia may be eliminated.

III

Why does it matter whether visual qualia can be avoided? The answer, I suggest, is that with the rejection of visual qualia certain aspects of visual experience become less puzzling. Let me explain.

Any adequate account of the subjective or phenomenal aspects of our visual states ought to yield an understanding of why those states have those aspects. Why, for example, does having a visual experience of blue 'feel' the way it does and not some other way? It is hard to see how any satisfying answer can be given to this question if the phenomenal aspects of such experiences derive from visual qualia.

Suppose, e.g., that there are visual qualia and that such qualia are non-physical and irreducible. Then the 'felt' aspect of the visual experience of blue is a matter of its having a special, nonphysical property. It is the presence of this property that gives the visual experience its distinctive 'feel'. Does this really offer us any enlightenment? Apart from the usual concerns about the emergence and causal role of such properties we may still wonder why the visual experience that has the content blue is associated with this irreducible felt quality rather than some other – why, for example, it does not have the felt quality of experiences that represent red. This surely is an impenetrable mystery.

Suppose now that visual qualia are physically reducible. Then the 'felt' aspect of the visual sensation of blue is a matter of its having a certain physico-chemical property. This is, I think, an improvement on the above alternative – it dissolves the worry about the causal role of qualia, for example – but again it does not begin to explain why the visual experience that represents blue should 'feel' as it does.

On the proposal I have made there is a simple explanation. Introspection tells us that the visual experience that represents blue differs from the visual experience that represents red. This 'felt' difference is, I claim, solely a matter of content. Since the colours represented by the two experiences are different, the experiences themselves are introspectively distinguishable. The reason, then, that the visual experience of blue 'feels' as it does is that it could not 'feel' any other way. The 'felt' aspect simply cannot be divorced from the representational aspect.

The onus now lies with the advocate of qualia. I have tried to show that the rejection of visual qualia is defensible against a variety of objections and that it is not only intuitively satisfying but also well motivated.[18] From the present perspective it is not surprising that debates about the nature of visual qualia have not come to any clear resolution. The disputants in these debates have been trapped by a mistaken picture of visual experience, a picture that has led them to disagreements that lack any real substance.[19, 20]

---

[18]For a discussion of the relationship between the elimination of visual qualia and the nature of imagistic representation, see Tye 1991, chapter 7.

[19]I have been asked whether the views I defend in this paper are incompatible with the basic framework of the adverbial approach to visual experience which I have defended elsewhere (see, e.g., Tye 1989 and Tye 1984). The answer, in brief, is 'No'. Although I speak above as if there are visual experiences, I believe that it is possible to analyse this talk without quantification over sensory objects or events along adverbial lines.

[20]I would like to thank Justin Broackes, Tim Crane, Jim Hopkins, Terry Horgan, Christopher Peacocke, and Sydney Shoemaker for helpful comments.

8   *The projective theory of sensory content*

THOMAS BALDWIN

The philosophy of perception is dominated by trichotomies: traditional discussions focused on the relative merits of direct realism, indirect realism, and phenomenalism (see e.g. Moore 1959, pp. 32–59). But these discussions confused issues in metaphysics and epistemology with those that concern perception alone. More recent discussions have moved on to a new trichotomy concerning the nature of perceptual representation: representative theories of perception, adverbial theories, and informational theories.[1] Yet it cannot, I think, be said that this trichotomy forms a Hegelian triad; the search for a synthesis is still on. In this paper I shall present one possible solution – what I shall call the projective theory.

I

Since the merits of the projective theory are best appreciated in the context of a critical survey of the members of the current trichotomy, I shall briefly discuss these, starting out from the approach characteristic of informational theories. These theories are the result of the application of a broadly functionalist treatment of mental representation to perception; so the content of perceptual representations is taken to be exhaustively determined by the causal role of such representations in bringing information about the environment to bear upon the control of behaviour. It does not matter here whether perceptual representation is reduced to belief, which makes the connections with behaviour straightforward, or whether (more plausibly) it is regarded as a distinct state which feeds information

---

[1]For the first, see Jackson 1977; O'Shaughnessy 1980, volume 1, chapter 6. For the second, see Chisholm 1977; Tye 1984 and 1989, chapter 5; and for the third, see Armstrong 1968, chapters 10 and 11; Gibson 1968.

into the holistic web of belief in such a way that the cognitive implications of perception can, on occasion, be disregarded in the light of other beliefs. The important point is that the content of perceptual experiences is defined by reference to their causes and effects.

The familiar objection to this approach is that it omits the role of sensory experience, which contributes an essential subjective aspect to the content of perceptual representations such that only those who have the appropriate sensory experiences know what it is like to enjoy such representations. Thus we contrast normal vision with blindsight: the subject with blindsight somehow employs his eyes to gather information about his environment which he can integrate into his behaviour – but, lacking visual experience, he lacks the type of perceptual representation we enjoy. Again, in our own case we may learn about our proprioceptive receptors which enable us to maintain our normal posture and orientation, and even to ride bicycles. But lacking any determinate postural sensations (except when things go wrong and we feel giddy), we may feel disinclined to talk here of *perceptual* representations at all – despite the causal role of proprioception in bringing information about bodily orientation to bear upon behaviour.

Upholders of the informational approach will, of course, reject this objection. They do not deny the existence of sensory experiences; all they deny is that these experiences make a distinctive contribution to the content of the perceptual representations with which they are associated. Rather, it is said, these experiences just manifest an ability to recognise directly relevant features of the environment (see Lewis 1983b and Lewis 1990). Thus, to take a possible extension of our own abilities, migrating birds are said to be able to navigate around the world because, unlike us, they can sense the earth's magnetic field and locate themselves in relation to it. And the difference between these birds and ourselves is not that they enjoy magnetic qualia of a kind that we are deprived of, but just that they have a natural cognitive ability which we can only reconstruct through the use of compasses.

I do not find this response to the familiar objection persuasive. The appeal to the presence of natural recognitional abilities does not capture the role of sense experiences in making perceptual representations conscious. For all I have said, a migrating bird's magnetic sense could be for it just as proprioception is for us. Thus this response does not undermine the inclination to regard sensory experiences as contributing their own sensory qualia to the content of the conscious perceptual representations. The intuitive ground for this is that it is difficult to envisage how perceptual representations could be conscious unless they possess an intrinsic structure which presents, or makes available to the subject, their represented content: it is, for example, because my lawn currently *looks green* to me that it looks to me *to be* green. I take this to be an instance of the general truth that there is no 'pure' consciousness of content, no message without a medium. This is a disputed hypothesis (O'Shaughnessy 1980, chapter 14) and in the absence of a satisfactory general theory about the nature of consciousness, I am not sure how to argue for it. There are, however, two points that can be made in support of the restricted thesis concerning perceptual consciousness, which is all that need concern us here. First, the fact that we can enjoy different perceptual representations of the same facts – e.g. spatial facts – is obviously to be explained by reference to the different types of sensory experience which give rise to the different representations – e.g. visual and tactile. And this difference, in turn, seems to rest on the different sensory qualities characteristic of different types of sensory experience. Secondly there are disagreements concerning perceptions which are most naturally understood as involving differences in intrinsic sensory qualities. My wife and I agree well enough concerning what is green, what is blue, and what is turquoise; but we disagree, concerning particular turquoise samples, whether they are nearer to blue or to green. Disagreements of this kind are in fact common (see Hardin 1988, pp. 76–80). Doubtless there is a neurophysiological explanation of these disagreements, but such an explanation does not provide a non-sensory description of the content of the disagreement.

This line of argument should be distinguished from that which seeks to find cases in which there is a perceptual-type experience with conscious qualities that are not just apparent qualities within the situation apparently represented (see O'Shaughnessy 1980, chapter 6, and Peacocke 1983, chapter 1). The strongest candidates for cases of this kind are abnormal experiences such as tinnitus and visual after-images, which strike us, subjectively, as of the same type as the sensory experiences that accompany perception. For since these experiences lack any obvious representational content, one seems bound to characterise their content in terms of intrinsic sensory qualities. But this line of argument should be handled with caution. The projective theory I shall present implies that even after-images and their ilk have a minimal representational content. So it would be strategically incoherent for the projective theorist to rely on a nonrepresentational account of them in order to make the case for intrinsic sensory qualities. Yet despite these provisos, I think there is some weight to be attached to the appeal to these abnormal experiences. For since their representational content is at most minimal, it does seem right that we need to be able to appeal to intrinsic sensory qualities to characterise their content. However, as I have indicated, the projective theorist will need to handle these cases carefully; so I shall return to them once the projective theory has been presented.

My general conclusion, therefore, is that the different modes of sensory experience contribute distinctive sensory qualities to conscious perceptual representation. But this is no intellectual resting-place; it is instead the starting-point for debates about the nature and role of these sensory qualities in perception. A preliminary move here must be to identify some sensory qualities. The obvious candidates are the traditional sensible qualities – colour, sound, taste, odour, texture, temperature – and I shall be content with these. Indeed, I shall largely concentrate on the familiar case of colour and discuss its relationship with visual perception. Four points can be quickly made about this case. First, if one thinks of after-images and other abnormal visual experiences, it seems clear that the content of these experiences is largely to be given in terms of colour. So if the intrinsic sensory qualities of visual perception are to be given partly by extrapolation from these abnormal experiences, colour must be included. Secondly, it seems uncontentious that conscious visual perception depends upon the experience of colour (though not necessarily chromatic colour). For, as Berkeley observed, if we think away colour, we think away all visual space and the possibility of conscious visual representation. So there is reason for thinking that the presence of this sensory quality makes conscious visual representation possible; equally, and this is the third point, apparent colour does not determine the content of visual representation, and even if one adds in the spatial distribution of colours within a visual field, the point remains. Perceptual representation involves conceptual content as well as the non-conceptual content contributed by sensory qualities and the other features of sensory fields. Lastly, although one who adopts a traditional secondary quality treatment of physical colour has to take a view of this kind of the experience of colour, the converse does not hold. One can take a realist, non-dispositional, view of physical colour, while relying on our experiences of colour to individuate these physical colours as typical causes of these experiences, and on the public presence of these physical colours to coordinate and calibrate individual quality spaces (see Peacocke 1983, chapter 2).

So far I have spoken in a deliberately vague way about the intended status of these sensory qualities within conscious perception. The natural way to think of them is as phenomenological qualities of any experience which is a conscious perception, and this leads directly to the position of the adverbial theorist, who treats visual experiences of colour as 'sensing bluely, redly, greenly' and so on. For the adverbs can be regarded as specifying types of visual sensation as individuated by their phenomenological qualities. The familiar difficulty for the adverbial theorist concerns the spatial articulation of sensory fields.[2] A satisfactory account of this matter is essential for a solution to Jackson's 'complement property' and 'many property' objections, which focus on the difficulty the adverbial theorist faces in explaining how a single perception can combine apparently incompatible sensory qualities in a distinctive way (see Jackson 1977, pp. 60ff.). For it is not at all easy to understand how this spatial articulation can itself be understood in purely adverbial terms. Merely employing spatial adverbs ('on the left-ly' etc.) to suggest that the spatial articulation is itself a further sensory quality offers no solution – it simply adds further adverbs for which Jackson's problems can be raised.

Tye (1984, 1989) has argued that this problem can be overcome by expressing the spatial articulation of a sensory field through the use of higher-order operators which form complex combinations of the sensory qualities expressed by adverbs from simpler ones. Thus in a case in which something looks both red and circular and something else looks both green and square, Tye proposes that we say that the subject senses coincidentally redly and circularly, and coincidentally greenly and squarely, though not coincidentally redly and squarely, nor coincidentally greenly and circularly. As Tye recognises, one might object that these operators just abbreviate references to areas within a non-physical visual field (perhaps along the lines of the operators employed in Quine 1960), and thus that they subvert his aim of elucidating spatial articulation without introducing reference to purely sensory objects. In order to repudiate this objection, therefore, Tye says that the use of these higher-order operators is to be explained by reference to the identity, or distinctness, of physical objects with the appropriate qualities in the visual space of the normal subject whose sensing

---

[2]This point was recognised by Moore, in his response to Ducasse's early formulation of the adverbial theory: see Moore 1942, p. 687h.

is described through the use of adverbs governed by these operators. Sensing coincidentally redly and circularly is thus to be the experience of a normal subject when viewing a red circular object; similarly, sensing separatedly redly and greenly is to be the experience of a normal subject when viewing a red object spatially separated from a green object.

So far as I can see, this move does indeed provide an adequate response to the objection Tye has in mind; but it succeeds only at a high cost. For, whereas one would normally associate the adverbial theory with an internalist account of the sensory content of perception, once the structure of sensory qualities is explained in the manner proposed by Tye, the account is transformed into a strongly externalist one, since the sensory content of sense experience is now characterised by reference to the properties of physical situations that are the normal causes of sense experiences of the appropriate type.[3] As a result it is vulnerable to familiar objections which seem to me powerful; I will mention two, both from Jackson's critical discussion of accounts of this kind (Jackson 1977, pp. 34–37). First, there is the problem of Hume's missing shade of blue: suppose I have a vivid after-image which is of a shade of blue such that nothing, in fact, is that shade of blue. Since there is no physical object of the appropriate shade to be the 'normal cause' of this kind of experience, the account does not seem to accommodate this case. One might try to go counterfactual, but then the difficulty is to characterise that in virtue of which an appropriate counterfactual is true without reference to the phenomenology of the after-image. Secondly, there is the problem of providing a non-circular account of normal conditions: for example, the Müller-Lyer figure quite normally produces the visual illusion that one of a pair of lines of equal length is longer than the other. There need be nothing abnormal about the conditions under which the figure is viewed when the illusion is seen: on the contrary, to escape the illusion one has to adopt the quite abnormal technique of looking sideways at the piece of paper on which the figure is printed. So the normal cause of the characteristic appearance of the Müller-Lyer figure seems to be just a Müller-Lyer figure itself – in which the lines which appear to differ in length have the same length.

These objections, which can be readily multiplied (see Hardin 1988, pp. 59ff.), arise from Tye's externalist account of content – according to which the spatial articulation of the visual field is defined in terms of the

---

[3]The resulting account is similar to that advanced in Peacocke 1983, pp. 20–21.

structure in visual (and thus physical) space of the normal causes of visual experience. Manifestly, an alternative response to Jackson's objections to adverbial theories is available: the position of the representative theorist. Such a theorist holds that there is an intrinsic spatial articulation of the visual field, and other sensory fields, which is not simply borrowed from the spatial structure of their normal causes. There are then two ways in which this position can be developed. One can either take it that this intrinsic spatial articulation is achieved by relationships within physical space itself (this is Jackson's position – Jackson 1977, pp. 102–103), or one can take it that it requires an 'inner' space distinct from the physical space of the objects represented in perception. The first alternative comes close to the projective theory I discuss below, and I shall say more about it then; so at present I shall discuss only the latter strategy, which is the more common one, and I shall concentrate on O'Shaughnessy's formulation of it.

According to O'Shaughnessy's representative theory of visual perception our visual field is constituted by a two-dimensional array of visual sensations which the mind 'projects' onto physical space in accordance with causal connections between the structure of physical space and the intrinsic spatial structure of the visual field.[4] One issue here is whether it is right to regard the visual field as merely two-dimensional. O'Shaughnessy defends this Berkleian thesis by maintaining that the visual perception of depth always requires the introduction of the conceptual content that accompanies the mind's projection of the visual field onto physical space; and he further maintains that, since the optical information reaching the visual system, which is supposed to determine the spatial structure of visual sensations, can always be specified in two-dimensional terms, there is no way in which the visual sensations themselves can acquire a significant three-dimensional structure. To all this, however, the obvious response is that those of us who enjoy binocular vision do make use of optical information concerning the relationships between the different two-dimensional patterns of light reaching our eyes which enables the visual system to create a nonconceptual three-dimensional visual field. The famous patterns created by Julesz are decisive demonstrations of this fact (see Julesz 1971). But I am not sure how much this issue matters to O'Shaughnessy: certainly many representative theorists have been happy to locate visual sensations, or sense-data, in a

---

[4]O'Shaughnessy 1980, pp. 168–192. Although I here criticise O'Shaughnessy's position, I should acknowledge that my own position owes a good deal to him, especially to his discussion of the sense of touch.

three-dimensional space (see Price 1932, pp. vii–viii). So perhaps O'Shaughnessy could concede the point without any substantive alteration to his position.

The real issue that the representative theorist faces is that of explaining unequivocally what the intrinsic spatial structure of a sensory field amounts to. What is it for our visual sensations to be 'arrayed' in a 2D (or $2^1/_2$D or 3D) 'psychological map'? (See O'Shaughnessy 1980, p. 176.) O'Shaughnessy writes that 'the psychological datum is, not merely a set of simultaneous visual sensations, but in addition their standing to one another in relations like next-to, farther-off-than etc.'[5] I agree about the datum; but not the interpretation of it. It is central to O'Shaughnessy's account that the psychological map be not merely descriptive of appearances; something with existential implications is required, since the mind's projection of visual sensations onto physical space is supposed to depend upon a causal correlation between the location of visual sensations within the visual field and the location of their causes in physical space. Hence the natural way to interpret O'Shaughnessy's account is by reference to a photographic analogy (or some 3D variant of it); for we can distinguish in the case of a photograph between the intrinsic space of the photograph and the space of the things represented by it, and there is a causal correlation between these two spatial systems. But any such analogy falters at a crucial point – namely that it is because photographs are themselves physical that the photographic images constitute a space distinct from the space represented in the picture. Since the only physical space in which visual sensations are located is the brain, and their spatial relations there do not constitute the spatial content of conscious visual experience, there is no material analogue in the case of visual experience upon whose intrinsic spatial structure the mind can project its conception of visual space.

II

It is now time for me to try to advance the discussion by introducing the projective theory. The basic idea of this theory is that sense experience incorporates a reference to regions within the subject's egocentric sensory space – which is just a region of physical space organised from the subject's 'point of view' (or point of hearing, smelling etc.) – and that the sensory

---

[5] O'Shaughnessy 1980, p. 171. The second of these is a curious example for O'Shaughnessy to cite, since it is naturally understood in three–dimensional terms.

quality which identifies the type of an experience is given as 'projected' into the region of space referred to in the experience. This sounds silly at first: it sounds like the suggestion that the subjective quality is itself actually in physical space – or at any rate that this is how things appear to us – and one wants to respond that, although illusions are an unavoidable feature of perception, the senses cannot be that silly – to present to us that which is merely subjective as if it were objective, out there before us. Indeed I think it is because Descartes thought that this illusion is an unavoidable feature of the senses that, even when he has exorcised the threat of the evil genius, he tells us (in the sixth meditation) that we should still be wary of accepting that things are as they appear to be. C. D. Broad was, I think, one of the first philosophers to identify a position of this kind (he calls it 'The Critical Scientific Theory'); but he thought it was an absolute non-starter:

> Now this muddled mixture of theories is not consistent with itself or with the facts. It is inconsistent with itself for the following reason. When I look at a penny, the brown colour that I see is seen spread out over the round contour. Similarly with the cold temperature that I feel. We are asked to believe that there is brownness without shape 'in me', and round shape without colour out there where the penny is, and yet that in some mysterious way, the shapeless brownness 'in me' is projected into the round contour of the penny 'out there'. If this be not nonsense I do not know what nonsense is.[6]

In fact, however, it is not quite this nonsense that the projective theory proposes; for a further feature of the theory is that the sensory qualities lead a double life – both as intrinsic qualities of experience and as apparent qualities of the objects of experience. So the idea is that the intrinsic spatial reference of sense experience converts the subjective sensory quality of sense experience into the apparently objective quality of a physical object located before the subject. Thus by projecting the sensory qualities of sensation out into physical space, sense experience attains that phenomenologically primitive intentionality, whereby a blue sensation becomes a sensation of blue.

This last point can be developed by comparing the projective theory with the adverbial theory. The projective theorist accepts the adverbial theorist's treatment of subjective colour – to have a blue sensation is to sense bluely.

---

[6]Broad 1923, pp. 273–274. This passage is cited in Mundle 1971, p. 147. Mundle here advances, and then in a postscript withdraws, a projective theory.

But she rejects the adverbial theorist's treatment of the sensory spatial properties (however this is worked out in detail), and in its place proposes an essentially relational account of these properties. When, as it is said, my visual field has a blue square patch on the left and a red circular patch on the right, the projective theorist holds that I sense bluely with reference to a square region of visual space on my left and redly with reference to a circular region of visual space on my right. And the primitive intentionality thesis is that sensing bluely with reference to a square region of visual space is having a visual experience as of a blue square on one's left – i.e. it appearing visually that there is a blue square on one's left. In such a situation, of course, there may be no blue square on one's left: the occurrence of the sensation only provides an appearance, a perceptual representation, of a blue square there – not the reality itself. So the primitive intentionality of sense experience permits the non-existence of its object, as it should. But the reference to a region of space is to a region of real, physical, space; and though the reference here remains intentional in the sense that it is to a region of space under a specific description – as a region identified within egocentric space – it is not intentional in the sense that it does not carry existential commitment. In this case, therefore, the two familiar criteria of intentionality (referential opacity and lack of existential import) come apart.

There is also a useful comparison to be made here with Jackson's representative theory (Jackson 1977). The projective theorist agrees with Jackson that the spatial articulation of sensory fields is achieved by intrinsic reference to regions of physical space. In this case the disagreement concerns the way in which the content of perception is then handled. Jackson develops an act-object account which leads him to suppose that the direct objects of sight are non-physical visual sense-data, and it is these sense-data that he then holds to be located in physical space. The projective theorist, who will object that such non-physical items cannot have actual physical locations, rejects the act-object model which leads Jackson to introduce sense-data. Instead, she maintains that even the non-conceptual content of perception is quasi-propositional – consisting of the appearance to the subject that certain qualities are present in certain regions of space, which appearance the projective theorist will seek to ground in the intrinsic sensory qualities of sense experience and their projective relation to regions of the subject's environment. So, for the projective theorist, there is no need to invoke special sensory objects to bear sensible qualities in giving an account of the content of perception.

The central claim of the projective theory is that it is through the inherent projection of the subjective onto a real external framework that sense experience achieves its own intentionality. It will be clear that this is a strongly externalist conception of the spatial features of sensory content. In one way, what makes this possible is that it is not clear how a region of space can fail to exist; as Evans put it,

> Places, however, being – how shall we say? – so much thicker on the ground than objects, a subject cannot fail to have a single place as the target of his 'here'-dispositions at an instant.[7]

Yet this may seem too quick; for can we not make sense of entirely illusory spaces? Of course, typical hallucinations do not involve such an illusion: when Macbeth asks

> Is this a dagger, which I see before me,
> The handle toward my hand? Come, let me clutch thee -
> I have thee not, and yet I see thee still

it is clear that the reference is to a real region of space. But what of dreams, or the experiences of a Cartesian victim?

Dreams are not, I think, a problem; for they are not sense experiences (the dreamer is, after all, fast asleep – 'dead to the world', as we say). So the fact that the spatial content of dreams does not embody reference to the dreamer's actual physical surroundings is no objection to an externalist account of the spatial content of sense experience. I think that one should regard dreams as a kind of fictive, or 'as if' perception, of the same type as conscious visualisation. In both cases the spatial content of the experience will be parasitic upon that of the fictive perception, and although this content would, in a real perception, require reference to the real world, in a mere fiction of it, there is only fictional, or dream, reference. Hence one should not expect here an externalist conception of spatial content. There can also be episodes of madness in which the boundary for the subject between imagination and perception becomes blurred (think of Macbeth and Banquo's ghost); but the madness precisely arises from the fact that the spatial content of the imaginative act somehow loses its 'as if' brackets and becomes incorporated in the projective intentionality of perception.

---

[7]Evans 1982, p. 169. Some of Evans' writings suggest a projective theory; see especially Evans 1985b.

The Cartesian fantasy, however, cannot be handled in this way; for here the thought (though arrived at by a characteristic philosophical fiction) is not of a fictive, 'as if' experience, but of an experience of the normal type caused in an extraordinary fashion. An easy case is one in which, unknown to myself, I am re-wired so that part of my sensory input (e.g. my auditory input) comes from a distant region of space; in such a case we feel no qualms about saying that the sounds are heard by me as in my immediate environment; this is just an auditory illusion, produced in an unusual way. My other sensory input can be assumed to keep me in contact in the normal way with my environment. But what if that assumption is undermined – i.e. where the re-wiring is total? The hypothesis will be that my brain, though actually located in a laboratory in California, is wired up to receive the sensory input (visual, auditory etc.) as of someone giving a paper at King's College London. Is it then absurd to hold that, in the experiences thus caused, I locate in the brain's environment in California the colours of the things in London?

To answer this more needs to be said about the way in which it is determined to which regions of space reference is made in sense experience. This will be different for the different senses, but as usual I will concentrate on the visual system. Our experience of mirror-images and similar tricks shows that the actual location of the distal stimulus does not always determine the apparent location. Instead the visual system computes an apparent location by combining retinal information with information about the body's orientation and movement. This latter information fixes the axes of visual space, and enables the system to separate, as far as it can, the movements of objects from the subject's own changes of position and orientation. The primary third-person evidence of apparent location is, of course, the target of the subject's behavioural dispositions, for the point of the perceptual system is precisely to enable effective behaviour to take place. This evidence is defeasible: in those familiar cases which show that perceptions are not just beliefs, e.g. the situation of one who is familiar with mirror-images, perceived location will not coincide with believed location. Furthermore, it is worth adding that, normally, the target of the behavioural dispositions will be the location of the distal stimulus, the actual cause of the perception. For since the purpose of the senses is to enable us to act effectively within our actual environment, any systematic dislocation of actual cause from behaviour will be highly dysfunctional. Stratton's famous experience of the inversion of his visual field when wearing inverting spectacles brings out this point dramatically – it shows how even within an individual life visual experience seeks to accommodate itself to its actual causes in such a way that behaviour can proceed effectively (see Stratton 1897).

The implications concerning my brain in California of this account of the spatial reference inherent in sensory content are, I think, as follows. If the body's internal senses and the causation of behaviour have not been interfered with, there seems no great problem in having me locate my external sensory input, from London, in what is in fact a region of California. I am just subject to a peculiar, total, illusion about the nature of my actual environment. But what if the brain is just in a vat, and the behavioural output has been shut off? Here intuition begins to lose its grip. The inclination to say that, with the input channels to the brain functioning normally (once 'past' the location of the re-wiring), sense experience retains its full content, including spatial reference, can be countered by observing that in this case there is no significant interaction between the brain and its actual environment – so that it seems absurd to ascribe to the brain's 'subject' illusory perceptions of that environment. We can at best attribute to it a dream-type state, in which it is as if there is reference to an actual environment, but no reference in fact succeeds.

A point that emerges from this is the foundational role of bodily experience in the system of spatial references of sense experience. As long as the body's internal senses remain non-illusory, they provide both a point of origin and egocentric axes within the actual environment upon which the other senses can draw, even if they then project into this space illusory appearances. This role of bodily experience is also, I think, to be invoked in thinking about those familiar, but abnormal, visual experiences when one seems to lose visual contact with one's environment – e.g. when one feels dizzy and faint, or closes one's eyes after looking at the sun and has a vivid after-image. In such cases the visual scene is experienced as just a two-dimensional array of garish colours; and then as normal consciousness is recovered, these colours fade and the whole array merges into the familiar shapes of our normal three-dimensional experience. The projective theorist cannot plausibly deny that in these cases there is experience of essentially the same type as normal visual experience; but it looks as though there is here the material for the representative theorist's account of the visual field as a two-dimensional psychological map. And the threat of this 'argument from illusion' is that if such an account applies in this case, then in principle it should always be applicable, whether or not our experience presents itself as such to us.

In response, the projective theorist must maintain that in cases of this kind spatial articulation of the visual experience is still achieved by the projection of sensory qualities into a visual space that is rooted in the subject's bodily experience. Of course, when the subject actually faints, this grounding is lost and there is no genuine spatial reference. But, the theorist can add, even when consciousness is not lost, the spatial projection is in two ways abnormal: first, the abnormal causes of the experience bring it about that the projection is crude and impoverished, in that the visual space is mapped out only by egocentric relations (left/right, up/down) which suffice to define a two-dimensional space. Thus although the projection is into what is in fact three-dimensional space, it is not articulated as such within the visual system. Secondly, it is usually apparent to such subjects that their experience is completely non-veridical (e.g. because they know that their eyes are closed), and they therefore regard it as altogether different in kind from normal visual experience. Hence it can seem to them as if their visual field is just a two-dimensional screen, and that the spatial articulation is achieved without projection into physical space. According to the projective theorist, however, this appearance is misleading. It is not that a special non-physical visual field is now brought into prominence, it is rather that only a rudimentary method of projection is in play and that the subject dissociates the resulting perceptual content from his actual environment because he is certain in advance that the whole experience will tell him nothing about it. Nonetheless, according to the projective theorist, after-images and the like are seen as located in the subject's visual space; and I think that this position is confirmed by our experience of after-images once we open our eyes. For in this situation we of course readily locate after-images within the three-dimensional visual field that normal visual experience provides us with, and we do so without any sense that we are thereby radically altering their previously perceived location.

So far, in defending the projective theory's externalist account of spatial reference, I have concentrated on the 'existential' implications of this account – that experience includes reference to actual regions of space. But there is also a 'uniqueness' implication that needs comment – for it is implied that the spatial reference of the different sense modalities is always to the one and only environment of the subject. There is here a contrast with classical representative theories which typically assign to each sense modality a distinct space. Is this uniqueness implication problematic? Do we not experience problems in integrating the spatial content of different sensory systems – e.g. hand-eye coordination problems – which, on the projective theory, simply should not arise?

The projective theory includes two responses to this objection. First, and most importantly, there is the intentionality of spatial reference, which here coexists with the existential commitment. So within each sense modality the one and only physical environment is experienced in a different way, in connection with the sensory qualities intrinsic to each sense modality. Hence the theory predicts that there may be difficulties in integrating the different sense fields, in recognising a region of visual space under a tactile description. But, and this is the second point, the theory also provides the basis for our ability to surmount these difficulties – in virtue of its acceptance of the foundational role of bodily experience in providing a point of origin and axes that are common to all sense modalities. Since classical representative theories cannot so readily account for the integration of sensory fields, it turns out that on this issue, the projective theory has a significant advantage. But, as we shall see in the next section, there are further problems connected with this uniqueness implication of the projective theory.

III

The most severe challenge to the projective theory is, I think, posed by a group of pathological cases which are not as well known in the philosophical literature as they deserve to be.[8] These are cases in which some injury to the brain produces a severe visual disorientation, or 'space-blindness', without loss of visual experience or the visual recognition of familiar objects. The brain damage is often the result of warfare – many of the cases described in the literature were caused by injuries sustained during the First World War. The resulting situation is almost the reverse of Weiskrantz's 'blindsight' phenomenon (Weiskrantz et al. 1974): in those cases information is somehow collected by the visual system but without

---

[8]See Riddoch 1917, Holmes 1918 and Holmes and Horrax 1919. There are some similarities between these cases and that of Goldstein's patient Schneider, whose problems are discussed at length in Merleau–Ponty 1962, part 1 chapter 3. For a recent discussion of the phenomenon, with a review of recent psychological literature, see McCarthy and Warrington 1990, chapter 4. I am much indebted to Naomi Eilan and Ros McCarthy for bringing these cases to my attention.

normal visual experience: in these cases there is visual experience, but without the usual spatial information. Here is a description of one case:

> This difficulty in localising correctly in space objects that were accurately seen was greater when the object lay outside his present line of vision; then he always failed to seize it directly, and generally made gross errors in pointing to its direction. When, for instance, the observer's arms were outstretched from his sides, and the patient was asked to point to the moving fingers of one or other hand, he usually only brought his own hand to the observer's face or shoulder. In fact, he stated not infrequently that though he could see the object he was not sure where it was ... Another prominent symptom was his inability to determine, or at least recognise correctly, the relative positions of objects within his field of vision. He was much confused as to which side was right and which left, and even after daily testing he remained uncertain which was his right, and which his left hand ... When he was brought into a large room in which a few chairs had been placed and ordered to walk to any part of it, he almost invariably walked into a chair and then pulled up suddenly as if surprised at its presence, even though he had seen it and pointed to it before he started ... His difficulty in extricating himself and in finding his way round an obstacle in his path was extraordinary; in this respect he was, though he possessed good vision, much inferior to a blind person or a blindfold man. An equally striking phenomenon was his inability, or at least his great difficulty, in finding his way about. When he was taken some distance from his bed he was unable to make his way to it again, even though he could see it and point directly to it. On one occasion he was brought about five yards from his bed, to reach which he had only to take a single right-angle turn, but though he indicated it correctly and recognised the patient in the adjoining bed, he commenced to walk in a wrong direction when told to go to it. (Holmes 1918, pp. 453–455)

The problem here is, clearly enough, that the patient's visual experience seems to have lost most of its usual spatial content; and yet, on the projective theory, visual experience is organised precisely through spatial projection. It will not do just to set these cases aside as abnormal; for such a manoeuvre would imply that the projective theory does not capture a general truth about visual experience. Nor can one just hold that in this case the visual system retains its full spatial content, but somehow fails to transmit all this spatial information to the control of behaviour. For this patient cannot tell his left from his right, and is surprised when he finds himself bumping into a chair he has just seen and pointed to. Instead, visual space seems to have lost its usual axes and dimensions. The loss of the left/right axis is described above; the loss of the third dimension is another common feature of cases of this kind:

> When I was carrying out some of the tests one day he suddenly said: 'Everything seems to be really the same distance away. For example, you appear to be as near to me as my hand' (he was holding his hand one and a half inches from his face and I was sitting about five feet away from him). (Riddoch 1917, p. 47)

It is almost as if these patients literally enjoy (or, rather, suffer from) a view from nowhere. The only egocentric axis within the visual experience of the first patient is provided by central vision:

> Despite the inaccuracy of his movements, he could, however, always succeed in reaching any object which was at the moment in central vision. On one occasion, when he was not aware he was under observation, he wished to get a box of matches from his locker in order to light a cigarette: he sat up in bed, turned his head and eyes towards the locker, stared vacantly at one spot for a moment, then slowly and deliberately moved his eyes into other direction, until, after several seconds, the matchbox, as if by chance, came into his central vision; then he put his hand out to take hold of it, but succeeded in reaching it only after repeated gropings. (Holmes 1918, p. 453)

How, then, if at all, can the projective theory accommodate these cases? Two negative points seem clear enough: first, in the peripheral vision of these patients things are seen, but are not seen as having any definite egocentric location or any definite location in relation to other things: secondly, the extreme paucity of this spatial content does not undermine recognition of shapes, so one should not regard the visual apprehension of shape as dependent upon the apprehension of an appropriate region within a well-defined visual space. The possibility that remains, despite these negative points, is that there should be a kind of visual experience in which colour sensations are projected into regions of space without those regions being identified for the subject as in some egocentric spatial relation to him, or in any clear spatial relationship to regions of space in which other colours are projected. In such a case the subject, say, senses redly with respect to a circular region of space and bluely with respect to another square region; but how these regions are located in relation to each other and to the subject is not thus apparent to him, despite the fact that on the projective theory, there is a fact of the matter about these locations (this follows from the existential commitments of the externalist treatment of space).

This possibility is, indeed, essentially that proposed by Holmes, an early expert on this condition and the author of the paper from which most of the quotations above come; he writes:

> Similarly, the cerebral wounds in these cases affected the local sign function of the retinae, and the patients consequently became unable to project correctly, and arrange in their proper relations in space, the images which excited vision, and to recognise the actual spatial relations of objects seen and their relative sizes and magnitudes. (Holmes 1918, p. 507)

Yet a doubt may remain. One may well wonder how it can make much sense to talk of visual projection without the spatial information that is constitutive of the normal visual field. For the lack here is not to be thought of simply as the absence, so to speak, of labels for the relevant axes; relative locations, as well as egocentric locations, are lacking. Hence the unity of visual space is lost; partial visual scenes are given to the subject, but he lacks any way of integrating them into a single picture of his environment; the unity of visual experience is at best temporal. Central vision provides, not a point of origin around which the visual field is organised, but just a minimal zone of spatial information that makes limited behaviour and movement possible. Things seen (more or less vaguely) in peripheral vision are presented as detached, both from the objects of central vision and from the rest of the field.

The implication of these considerations is that although the projective theorist is committed to holding that visual projection is into the one and only physical environment of the subject, he must avoid any implication of a corresponding subjective unity for the spatial aspects of the subject's visual experience. Instead, he must hold that in these cases the subject's visible environment is presented as a multiplicity of visual spaces, crudely individuated by the visual appearance or not of spatial relations between the things seen. This remains consistent with the basic premises of the projective theory; indeed my previous stress on the foundational role of bodily experience fits with this characterisation of these 'space-blind' patients, for in losing the axes provided by this experience they seem to have lost the unity of visual space. But the puzzling phenomenology of these cases must make any such characterisation of them tentative.

IV

I hope I have now said enough to render the general idea of a spatial projection of sensory qualities intelligible and prima facie defensible. If, as I proposed, this constitutes the primitive intentionality of sense experience, it follows that it constitutes a fundamental stratum in the articulation of perceptual content. I am, however, extremely well aware that it does not constitute a full account of perceptual content. In particular, it does not provide an account of the way in which our experience typically presents itself to us as the appearance of physical substances in space with the qualities of which the intrinsic sensible qualities of experience are the appearance. I am not sure how far this substantive conception of the objects of experience is already implicated in the spatial projection of sensible qualities. At an unreflective level there seem to be differences on this issue among the sense modalities – we are happy to locate smells and sounds in space without any immediate compunction to treat them as properties of physical substances; our normal attitude to colours is that they are colours of physical substances, but familiar phenomena such as rainbows and the sky show that there is no absolute necessity to this; finally, textures and other tactile phenomena do seem unintelligible except as apparent qualities of physical substances. If some of these cases of spatial reference without apparent reference to physical substances can be sustained, then it would seem that the issue of spatial projection can be separated from that of substantive content. This conclusion leaves the topic of this paper unthreatened by the absence of an account of substantive content: but, equally, it implies that a full account of perceptual content requires a good deal more than is offered here.[9]

---

[9]For comments on earlier versions of this paper I am much indebted to Tim Crane, Mike Martin, Bill Brewer, Adrian Cussins and Naomi Eilan.

9 Sight and touch

MICHAEL MARTIN

We can tell what the shape or size of an object is by either sight or touch. These two senses are very different in character, not only in the mechanisms of perception – the physical media, the physiological organs of sense and possibly the psychological processing involved – but also in their phenomenological character, what it is like to see and to feel.

This can lead one to ask how it is that the same properties can be perceived by the two senses, and the issues that surround this question have been discussed by both philosophers and psychologists over the centuries.[1] But a converse question also arises, namely, given that the same properties are perceived, where does the difference between the senses lie? Is this phenomenological difference really a difference in spatial perception between the senses? That is the topic of this paper.

The commonest treatment of these issues fails to offer any satisfactory answer. It suggests that we can look for one in two places: in the different properties of things in the world that are perceptible by each of the senses; or in the different subjective qualities of perceptual experiences.[2] Since we are concerned with the differences between senses with respect to perceiving the same properties, the former approach is not applicable. But the latter approach fails to offer any illuminating answer to the question. For it simply posits some introspectible difference between the senses without saying any more about it. Indeed it is common to suppose that this difference is just ineffable: no more can be said about it than that one can just tell which sense one perceives by.

---

[1] This is the issue surrounding Molyneux's Question, as raised by Locke (1689, II, ix, 8).

[2] See Grice 1962. Grice mentions four criteria for distinguishing the senses. Two come out under what I have called mechanical differences, the other two are as mentioned here. Grice himself argues for the indispensability of an introspectible quality as the criterion of difference.

A way out of this impasse is suggested by Berkeley.[3] This is to find what one might think of as a structural difference between the experiences. Implicit in his discussion of vision and touch is such a structural difference; while he assumes that there is a field of visual sensation internal to the mind, he supposes no such thing for touch. A modern proponent of this approach is Brian O'Shaughnessy. In his striking and suggestive account of touch he writes:

> There is in touch no analogue of the visual field of visual sensations ... in touch a body investigates bodies as one body amongst others. (O'Shaughnessy 1989, p. 38)

These distinctions are ones that are clearly intended to reflect a difference in what the experiences are like, and at the same time they are anything but ineffable. But in making the distinction between the senses in this way, Berkeley and O'Shaughnessy commit one to a particular view of sight, to the idea of a private visual field as posited by a sense-datum theory of perception. So it might appear as if one can only make such a distinction between sight and touch if one endorses this theory. Indeed, such seems to be Gareth Evans' (Evans 1985b) assumption in his discussion of spatial perception where he argues as if the motivation for contrasting visual and tactual spatial perception must depend on an adherence to such a theory.

Following Berkeley and especially O'Shaughnessy,[4] I want to pursue the idea of there being such a structural difference between sight and touch. However I want to argue for this solely in terms of the phenomenological character of these experiences, remaining neutral between different theories of perception. The contrast that I shall argue for is not quite O'Shaughnessy's, that vision has a visual field which touch does not. Instead I shall argue that the visual field plays a role in sight which is not played by any sense field in touch. Touch is dependent on bodily awareness and if, or where, that involves a sense field, it does so in a strikingly different way from that in which visual experience involves the visual field.[5]

---

[3]See Berkeley 1709, pp. 1–59.

[4]In addition to the article mentioned, O'Shaughnessy 1980, volume 1, chapters 5–7 are highly germane to this discussion. Anyone acquainted with O'Shaughnessy's work will recognise the debt this discussion owes.

[5]But this is not to deny that there is some further qualitative difference between the senses. One might, for instance, be inclined to suppose that the TVSS examples of touch-based perception discussed by Bach-y-Rita 1972 involve a sense field akin to the visual field and yet is not vision.

The rest of this paper divides into four parts. In part I, I introduce the idea of a visual field or space which is independent of any sense-datum theory of perception, offering a preliminary contrast with some cases of touch. In part II, I discuss our awareness of our bodies and argue that touch is dependent on this awareness;[6] and in part III, I then draw as a consequence of this the contrast suggested above between sight and touch. In the final part I conclude that these differences between the senses should make us sceptical as to whether there can be a single theory of spatial perception to apply equally to all of the senses.

I

Philosophers often use the term 'visual field' only when discussing sense-datum theories of vision. In such a context the visual field is taken to be some array of colour patches internal to the perceiver's mind; it is a two-dimensional mosaic of which the perceiver is aware and only through which she comes to see objects in the physical world.[7] Its use here is not intended to evoke this theory and picture of perception. Rather the visual field and visual space are taken to be features of the phenomenology of visual experience, aspects which can be identified independent of a commitment to any specific theory of perception. On the view of the visual field presented here, we should think of the colour-mosaic of the sense-datum theory as an attempt to explain this feature of the phenomenology. Rejecting the *explanans* should not be equated with rejecting the *explanandum*.

What features of visual experience do I mean? Normal vision can afford us experience of more than one object simultaneously. Distinct objects are experienced as at distinct locations, and as spatially related to each other. There is also a sense in which the space within which the objects are experienced as located is itself a part of, or the form of, the experience. One is aware of the location of visual objects not only relative to other visually experienced objects, but also to other regions of the spatial array – regions where nothing is experienced, but where something potentially could be.

---

[6]The first two parts overlap with my 'Sense modalities and spatial perception' (forthcoming) which concerns the contrast between the visual field and the spatial aspects of bodily awareness but which offers a more detailed discussion of some of these issues.

[7]See, for instance, Moore 1965, Price 1932, Jackson 1977; and as suggested above, O'Shaughnessy 1980, volume 1, chapter 6. Note that both Price and Jackson deny that the field of sensations is two-dimensional.

Consider the case of looking at a ring-shaped object, a Polo mint, for instance, head on. One is aware of the various white parts of the mint arranged in a circle, and aware of how they are related to each other. One is also aware of the hole in the middle of the mint, and that that hole is there in the middle. If one was not aware of the hole one would not see the mint to be a ring-shape rather than a circle. Nothing need be perceived to be within the hole. One is aware of the hole as a place where something potentially could be seen, not as where something is actually seen to be.

So we can think of normal visual experience as experience not only of objects which are located in some space, but as of a space within which they are located. The space is part of the experience in as much as one is aware of the region as a potential location for objects of vision. This is not to say that one can actually experience all sub-regions of a visual space at one time – the fronts of objects obscure their backs, objects occlude each other. The occluded areas of the visual scene count as part of visual space in the sense that one could come to be aware of something at that location without altering the limits of the visual field provided by the angle of vision at that time. An area can come into view simply by a re-arrangement of things within the field, rather than by changing the field itself.

It is this idea of a visual field or space as part of visual experience itself which is intended. There is no obvious connection between this and some private object of attention such as an internal colour-mosaic. We can think of this visual space as simply a region of public space containing the objects currently seen. So the notion is genuinely independent of such a sense-datum theory. At the same time it should not be thought to be entirely innocuous. Although this picture of a visual space fits well with what normal visual experience is like, it doesn't seem appropriate in the same way for many other examples of spatial perception.

Indeed it seems to fail to fit many examples of touch. Think of the fairly simple case of determining the shape of a glass by running one's fingertip around its rim. In doing this one can tell whether the glass is circular. Nothing like the visual field appears to be involved. At any one time one only has contact with one point on the surface of the glass, so there does not seem to be at any time an awareness of the relations between many points in space. Rather the perception is sequential, essentially involving tracing a path around the rim.[8]

---

[8]Some of the empirical research on these matters suggests that we are in fact very bad at discerning the shape of things by such tracing. See Klatzky et al. 1991.

But I don't mean to imply that the difference here is merely a matter of the one perception being sequential and the other simultaneous. Take a case of simultaneous touch, as when one discovers the shape of the glass by grasping it in one hand. Like the last example, this is a way in which one can tell whether or not the glass is circular. Such perception is spatial perception, but in this case it is not sequential perception. Can we think of this example of touch as akin to the case of seeing the Polo mint to be ring-shaped?

When one grasps the rim one comes into contact with it at only five points, where one's fingertips touch it. Nevertheless one comes to be aware that the glass as a whole is circular. In being tactually aware in this way, is one aware of the parts of the rim in between the points of contact in the same way as one is aware of those points, and is one aware of the region of space lying inside the rim? The answer would appear to be not: one comes to be aware of the glass by being aware of the parts one touches. In this it contrasts with the Polo mint, since one is aware both of the ring-surface and of the hole in the same way.

We noted in the visual case that things could fall within visual space without being experienced, if they were obscured. So one might ask whether points on the rim of the glass with which one has no contact nevertheless fall within a tactual space. If this is to be analogous to the visual case this must mean we are to ask whether these points are themselves potentially points which can be felt as the tactual field stands. For the visual case we could determine this by asking whether if objects were re-arranged within the limits of the angle of vision one could come to experience that point. So in the tactual case we may ask what the limits of the tactual field would be, and why one is aware only of the five points. To this there appears to be no obvious answer.

It is just this which makes the idea of applying the notion of a tactual field to these examples of touch so puzzling. We know in each case that there is definite felt contact with a number of points, one or five, and we know that the perception results in an awareness of the spatial properties of objects in space. But there is no clear sense of what would be the limits to a tactual sense field in which (potentially) objects would be felt to be. If there is one, then we would have to think of it as somehow being boundless. The re-arrangement of objects within it would just be the re-arrangement of objects in space. At the same time there seems to be no possible explanation analogous to occlusion in the visual case to explain why one fails to tactually perceive all of this tactual field. The alternative is to see the lack of any obvious limits to a tactual space as evidence that there is no such analogue in touch to the visual field. This is what we shall go on to argue, once we have seen the dependence of touch on bodily awareness.

II

In talking about bodily awareness, or body sense, I mean to group together some of the various ways in which we are aware of our own bodies. At present I am aware of my posture, orientation in space, the position of my limbs; I have some sense of the shape and size of my body, and within and on it I am aware of various goings on – itches, aches, patches of warmth. What is interesting about these kinds of ways of being aware of oneself as opposed to seeing, hearing or touching oneself is that one is aware of one's body in a way that one is aware of nothing else in the world. One might grandly say that the world of bodily awareness is restricted to one's own body. But there is an important sense for us in which that is false: in our awareness of ourselves we are aware of ourselves as being an object in a world which potentially can contain many other objects. We are aware of ourselves as bounded and limited within a world that extends beyond us.

One's own body is the proper object of such awareness in that anything which one feels in this way is taken to be part of one's body. There is no case, for instance, of feeling someone's legs to be crossed and then determining from how it feels whether the legs are one's own or someone else's. What marks out a felt limb as one's own is not some special quality that it has, but simply that one feels it in this way. Likewise when one feels a bodily sensation to have a location there is no issue over whose body it appears to belong to (see O'Shaughnessy 1980, volume 1, p. 162). Rather in as much as it feels to have a location, it feels to be within one's own body.[9]

Note that neither of these things commits us to saying that in fact one can only feel limbs to be where one's body actually is, or feel sensations to be located within the actual limits of one's body. Both claims are false, as the incidence of phantom limb illusions and cases of projected sensation into prosthetic devices show. The claim is rather that whatever one feels, feels to belong to one's body whether or not it does.[10] This is not because the

---

[9]This is not to deny the possibility of bodily sensations which don't feel to be located at all. For an example of such sensation resulting from damage see Volpe et al. 1979.

[10]There are examples of what are called 'extra-somatic sensations' which may be thought to

feelings have some special quality by which one identifies the felt object as belonging to one, rather a limb or a sensation count as apparently belonging to one's body simply by being felt.[11]

In addition to this there is also in such an awareness some sense of an other, a world which extends beyond this proper object of awareness. One's sensations, for instance, feel to be within one's body. This is not some special quality each one has which it might lack, for then we could imagine the case of a bodily sensation which felt to be completely external to the body. Contrary to that, every sensation which feels to be located feels to be located within the body. For there to be a contrast with being external to the body, there must be a contrast between where it is possible to feel sensation, the apparent limits of the body, and where one could not be feeling a sensation, that which lies outside the body.

A similar point applies to position sense. If one is aware of the position of one's hands relative to each other when one's arms are stretched out ahead of one, the space between the hands is occupied by no part of one's body. But it is not true that one feels one's hands in space only related as through parts of one's body: one feels them to be a certain distance apart in space extending beyond the body. Similarly one feels oneself to have a certain shape and size in a space which contains one and extends beyond one. This space, which extends beyond one's body, cannot be a place where one feels a limb or sensation to be since then it would no longer appear to be somewhere which falls outside of one's body but would come to appear to be a part of it.

In the case of bodily awareness there is a candidate to be an analogue of the visual field with limits analogous to it. We thought of the visual field as a spatial region within which visual awareness was possible. A bodily space would be a region within which bodily awareness was possible. The candidate would then be the apparent body itself, since the apparent limits of the body are the apparent limits of possible sensation. In the visual case

---

contradict the claims here made, see von Békésy 1967, pp. 220–226. However, as von Békésy himself notes, these cases are akin to the phenomenon of projected sensation, and in such cases one's body appears to extend with the projection. For examples of the plasticity of the body schema see Lackner 1988.

[11]Wittgenstein 1958, pp. 49–52, seems to think that it is merely a contingent fact that I can't feel sensations in your body or the position of your limbs as I can my own. This seems wrong, since, where one feels a limb to be, one feels one's own body to be: it would 'add another joint' to our concept of bodily awareness, as Wittgenstein might put it, to make room for a distinction between self and other in such awareness.

one is aware of an object's spatial properties as occupying that visual space, so in the bodily case one might suppose one came to be aware of the spatial properties of something as it occupies bodily space.

However, it is clear that many of the spatial properties of bodily awareness indicated above cannot be thought of as experienced in this way. In order for a sensation to feel to be inner, we need some contrast with outer, so we need to think of it as located relative to a space which extends beyond the limits of possible sensation. If my thumb hurts I am aware of where the sensation is, the place where it hurts, as at a location relative to my mouth. This awareness is reflected in my knowledge of how I would have to move the thumb in order to suck away the pain. But that path between thumb and mouth appears to fall outside the limits of the body, so that the felt spatial relation between thumb and mouth is not one which could be given within the limits of a field of bodily awareness.

That suggests that we cannot think of much of the spatial character of bodily awareness as akin to our visual awareness of the spatial properties of things as located within a visual field. The spatial character of bodily awareness will force on us an alternative conception of spatial experience. Central to it will be this contrast between the sense of that which falls within the limits of experience and things feeling to be within a space which extends beyond those limits.

This feature of bodily awareness, the contrast between inner and outer, provides what we need for a sense of touch. The model of touch here is that of the body as template. We are embodied in a world which contains potentially many other bodies. We can come into contact with other bodies, and they can impede our movement and distort our shape. Such physical impingement on us is reflected in the awareness we have of our bodies. One is aware when one's movement is impeded, and when one's skin is in contact with objects or is distended by them. In being aware of one's body, sensing how it is disposed, where it can and can't move, and where one has sensations, one can attend to the objects in virtue of which these are true. One measures the properties of objects in the world around one against one's body. So in having an awareness of one's body, one has a sense of touch.[12]

The best way of arguing for these claims is just to see how they fit the examples of touch which we mentioned earlier. When contrasted with visual

---

[12]Cf. Sanford 1983, who stresses the role of the boundaries of the body in touch perception.

experience, these common cases of touch appeared strange and puzzling. By contrast, I suggest, when we understand them as deriving from bodily awareness, any such mystery disappears. How exactly is bodily awareness supposed to provide a sense of touch?

Thomas Reid, in his discussion of touch in the *Inquiry*, noted that in tactual perception there were two elements to which a perceiver could attend: a subjective sensation internal to the mind, and an objective perception of the properties of the felt object (Reid 1785). In noting the presence of sensation in touch Reid is undoubtedly correct. Think again of the case of running one's finger around the rim of a glass. When one touches the glass one does feel a sensation in one's finger, something that one does not normally attend to as such, but which is nevertheless present. However, where Reid surely goes wrong is in describing this sensation as nothing more than a subjective sign, internal to the mind, to be contrasted with full-blown perception. For the sensation one feels in one's fingertip has as much claim to be concerned with a feature of the objective world as does one's tactual perception. The sensation itself has a felt location, and that is not some metaphorical location 'internal to the mind' – it is felt to be at some location internal to one's body. The sensation feels to be within one's fingertip, and one's finger is every bit as much a part of the physical world as the glass it touches.

Recognising this feature of the sensation suggests a different description of the phenomena Reid identifies. The sensation one feels in one's fingertip feels to be within one's body and at the limits of one's body, at the skin. One also feels one's fingertip to be pressing against an object, one which resists the further movement of one's finger down through the rim. The place where one feels the sensation to be shares certain spatial properties with the object which impedes one's movement; it is in the same place in space. So the spatial location that the sensation feels to have can provide an awareness of the spatial location of the point on the rim which keeps the fingertip there. We should think of this case not as one in which we have two distinct states of mind, a bodily sensation and a tactual perception, both of which can be attended to; but instead simply one state of mind, which can be attended to in different ways. One can attend to it as a bodily sensation – in which case its spatial character reveals the location of sensation – or attend to it as tactual perception of something lying beyond the body but in contact with it, so that the spatial character is that of the location of whatever it is which connects with and impedes the movement of one's body.

Sensation has a role in touch not, as Reid thought, simply as a subjective precursor to objective perception, but as a form of bodily awareness which provides for the sense of touch. One's awareness of one's body gives one an awareness of it as an inner realm located within a wider world. Where its limits connect with the surfaces of other objects in that world, a sense of one's own limits can also be a sense of those objects' surfaces. A sense of one's own spatial organisation can become a sense of the spatial order of things around one: the body is a template to measure things in the world.

With this in mind we can explain the sequential nature of our original example of touch without introducing any mysteries. Some accounts of tactual perception seem to suggest that such sequential perception comes to have a spatial aspect only as a result of some temporal construction of a perception out of momentary sensations which themselves have no spatial significance.[13] It would indeed be mysterious how non-spatial sensation could generate spatial perception simply on the basis of qualitative variations over time. But the sensations involved in touch do not lack spatial aspects. Rather each sensation is one which feels to have a location, either as bodily sensation a location in the body, or as tactual perception an awareness of the position of a point on the rim in space relative to one's hand. The sequential nature of the perception does not introduce the spatial element as such, rather it introduces a way of determining the spatial relations between points felt.

In feeling a sensation in one's finger one is aware of the position of one's finger relative to the other parts of one's body, other fingers and one's wrist, for instance. In moving the finger, one is aware of it as moving. The finger traces out a circular path, relative to the rest of one's hand, and one is aware of it as doing so. In attending to the rim of the glass, one is aware of the rim as not moving relative to one's finger. So as one's finger moves one can attend to that motion as revealing the shape of the rim. One's movement mirrors that shape; in being aware of the movement one comes to be aware of the shape. This is an example of perception of spatial relations which does not depend on being aware of things as related in a space all experienced at once.

A similar explanation can be given of the second example of touch. When one grasps the glass one has to arrange one's fingers into a shape that mirrors that of the glass. In so arranging one's fingers one is aware of their

---

[13]Cf. here Evans' discussions of theories of touch which involve a successive concept of space versus those which involve a simultaneous: Evans 1985b, pp. 368–369.

positions relative to each other, that they are arranged in a circle. In coming into contact with the glass one is aware that the glass fits the shape of one's grasp. In being aware of the shape of one's grasp one can attend to it as the shape of the rim of the glass, both being coincident. The arrangement of one's body mirrors that of the object touched; in being aware of the former one can attend to the latter.

A sense of one's own body as an object in a space extending beyond it is sufficient for one to have a sense of touch. When one comes into contact with another body one comes to be aware that there is somewhere that one's own body cannot be, and so can attend to the fact that something is there. The two examples of touch which we started with can be explained by just this model, where assimilating them to the model of visual experience would make them mysterious or puzzling.

We noted above that one's awareness of the location of parts of one's body relative to each other can't be a matter of being aware of them as positioned within a sensory field or space. For the notion of a visual field we introduced was that of a region of space within which experience of an object was possible given the current limits of that field. Any such sense field of the body would restrict its limits to the limits that one's body appears to have, but one's awareness of the distance between one's thumb and mouth was an awareness of them as located in a region of space extending beyond the apparent limits of the body. We can only do justice to the spatial character of bodily awareness by denying that spatial experience is necessarily experience of objects in a sensory field.

A consequence of this is that cases of touch which depend on such bodily awareness do not involve a sense field either. We have already noted that we cannot easily model such cases of touch on the idea of a visual field. The above account of touch shows us why we need not do so. When one's finger touches the rim, one is aware of the location of one's fingertip relative to one's wrist. This is an awareness of how they are related in a space which extends beyond the apparent limits of one's body. This is not awareness of them as in a sensory field. It is this very spatial aspect of the bodily sensation which one then attends to as the location of the rim of the glass, when using one's awareness of one's finger and its movements to discern the shape of the glass. Just as feeling one's finger to be in a certain position doesn't require a sense field, feeling the glass in contact with one's finger to be in that position doesn't require a sense field either.[14]

Normal visual experience of the world involves a visual field or space in the neutral sense of simply being aware of objects as within a region of space where one can potentially be experiencing other objects. This is a distinctive feature of the experience in as much as other examples of spatial experience can lack such a sensory field. An example of this was bodily awareness, and now we have seen that at least some examples of touch fit this model as well. We have a contrast between normal visual experience as involving a visual field and common examples of tactual experience which lack such a field.

III

This returns us to the issue of what distinguishes (phenomenologically) visual and tactual spatial perception. Given the examples we have discussed it might be tempting to suppose, with O'Shaughnessy, that the difference lies in whether a sense field is present or absent in experience. Visual experience has a sense field where touch does not.

But the contrast cannot be as simple as that. It cannot be claimed that all vision involves the presence of a visual field. We can imagine very limited kinds of vision, extreme tunnel vision, for instance. Such visual experience would appear to have no intrinsic spatial character, much less a sensory field. Nevertheless it would be possible to exploit such experience in discerning the shape of things in a way analogous to tracing the rim of a glass. One might trace out a pattern of light by moving one's head so as to trace the outline of stimulation: here one's sense of the position and movement of one's head would provide one with an awareness of the spatial organisation of the pattern, just as one's awareness of the position and movement of one's finger does with respect to the rim of the glass.[15]

The claim would have to be that no touch can involve a sense field, and this also seems far from uncontentious. For one's skin offers an extended area of sensitivity, which might suggest that one could be aware of an area of skin as an area of possible locations of stimulation. One could feel things

---

[14]Both of these examples are cases of 'active touch'. Psychologists such as Gibson (1968, chapters 6 & 7) have emphasised the importance of active exploration; but others have questioned whether it is simply the role of kinaesthesia (or position sense) which is distinctive of this kind of touch. In Part III we turn to examples of so-called passive touch.
[15]Cf. the experiments on limited vision through an aperture in Loomis et al. forthcoming.

to be located at positions on it relative to other potential areas of sensation; much as one can be visually aware of something relative to a potential location of a visible object.

For instance, one's fingertips do not just give point sensations; one is sensitive to a pattern as pressed against or brushed by the fingertip. One also has a certain amount of sensitivity in the palm of one's hand, and across regions of skin such as the thigh and back. It is plausible to think of these regions of skin as offering one a two-dimensional field in which one can feel shapes to be located. One might imagine someone who could tell from having a coin pressed against their skin whether it was a 50-pence or 10-pence piece. In learning braille, someone will come to recognise the different arrangements of point stimulation against their fingertip.

It is tempting to think of these as experiences which involve sense fields analogous to the visual field. In being aware of a braille pattern, one is aware not only of points of stimulation and how they are related, but also how they are related to points on the skin where no stimulation is felt but could potentially be felt. So this just suggests that the skin is a sense field for touch analogous to the visual field.

It would be extremely difficult to deny that this is so on the basis of the etiolated notion of a sense field which we have been employing. One might have phenomenological grounds for denying that anyone's tactual experience in fact had this character, that anyone really can distinguish a 10-pence piece from a 50-pence;[16] but this would only be relevant if it could be shown not simply to be a limitation of the acuity of sensation. There seems no phenomenological basis for such a claim.

O'Shaughnessy does deny that there is any such cutaneous sense field. But he does not do so on strictly phenomenological grounds. Rather, he accepts a point which commits him to a sense field in our sense:

> the sensation must in the first place come to consciousness *as* determinately located amidst an actual or merely potential array of sensations that comprise a continuum that is at least akin to a sense field. (O'Shaughnessy 1980, volume 1, p. 207)

He refuses to admit that there is a sense field of the skin only because he understands more by the epithet 'sense field' than we do. According to him a sense field just is the spatial arrangement of sensation within a private,

---

[16]Loomis and Lederman (1986) discusses pattern recognition of tactile displays; this suggests that we are not always as poor at it as this line of objection needs to claim.

psychological space. He is led to deny that there is any such thing present in bodily awareness or touch because this would be to make such awareness mediated where he claims it to be immediate. One can only adopt O'Shaughnessy's position here if like him one adopts a sense-datum theory of vision, and accepts his arguments for the immediacy of one's sense of one's body.

We cannot then simply distinguish the structure of visual experience from that of tactual experience by claiming that the former involves a visual field for which there is no analogue in the latter. But there is still a contrast between them arising from the role of bodily awareness in touch for which there is no analogue in sight, and this I suggest forces a different role on any sensory field in touch from that the visual field occupies.

The putative examples of tactual sense fields are cases of cutaneous sense fields. As such they are further examples of our earlier contention that touch depends on bodily awareness. To feel an object pressing against one's skin is to feel one's skin to be a certain way such that one can feel the object which presses against it. Consider the case of feeling a warmed coin against one's palm. One feels a warm extended area of a sort which one can feel as simply a warm area of skin. Just such a pattern of warmth could be produced simply by the rays of the sun and attended to as such. Since one also feels that there is something pressing against that area one can attend through the patch of warmth to the object which is warm. As before, bodily awareness, this time of an extended area of skin, provides for the attention to that which lies against it, outside the limits of the body.

A consequence of this is that the experience is only experience of tactual objects in as much as it feels to be the limits of the body, such that one can attend to that which lies outside these limits but presses against it. The spatial character of the experience has to be taken as itself located within a space extending beyond what can be given in the sense field. For the sensations can only feel to be internal to the body where one has a sense of a space extending beyond possible locations of sensation and hence beyond any such sensory field. If the sensations cannot feel to be internal then there is no sense of a contrast with that which is outside of what is felt, and there is nothing to attend to as the boundary between inside and outside which can reveal the form of that which presses from outside into the body. The result is that the cutaneous sense field is only a tactual field containing objects of touch in as much as it is embedded within a space which extends beyond any such field.

In contrast to this, our visual experiences are of objects as located within a visual space. There is no sense of these objects being experienced as internal to one's body, nor is one aware of physical objects in space as lying outside the limits of this visual space. Indeed this may be made vivid by imagining what visual experience would have to be like in order to be analogous to tactual experience.

For instance, we might imagine visual experiences as being sensations of stimulation to the retina. When one shuts one's eyes and faces the sun, one has a sensation of warmth on one's eyelids. One also often has a visual experience of an indeterminately extending red wash, which appears to have no determinate location. If one had sensations of the retina, one could imagine such experience being of how one's retina was, that it was currently red. Location of bodily sensation is reflected in our dispositions towards the felt location of a sensation; so we might imagine having such dispositions towards our retinas when having visual experiences.

A more extreme example would be to imagine the retina to be like some extendible membrane which one could press against the surface of objects in one's environs. The membrane would take on the shape of objects it pressed against and their surface colours. In visual experience one would be immediately aware of the surface of the membrane and its colour and shape, and only come to be aware of the physical objects it is in contact with as lying behind it and responsible for its present shape.

These are fanciful stories and very far from what visual experience is phenomenologically like for us. There is no contrast in visual experience when taken as experience of objects in physical space between the experienced objects and objects lying outside of one's body. There is no role in such experience for the limits of the experience; one cannot think of it as a template.

Here we have found an essential phenomenological difference between sight and touch. The former is experience of objects external to one as arranged in physical space. The latter is experience of objects as they come into contact with one's body; one is aware of one's body and its limits and so aware of objects coming into contact with one's body as they discernibly affect those limits. Normal visual experience is essentially experience of objects as they fall within the visual field; tactual experience is essentially experience of objects as they press from the outside onto the limits of a felt sensory field.

IV

We have now articulated differences between sight and touch which are phenomenological in character and independent of a commitment to any specific theory of perception. Anyone struck by these differences might find themselves sceptical as to whether one can give one general theory of what perception is, and in particular what it is to perceive the spatial properties of objects. In this concluding section, we shall pursue just this sceptical line of thought. In the first half I shall give reason for concurring with Berkeley and O'Shaughnessy that a sense-datum theory of vision cannot be extended to the case of touch. In the second half I then express reservations as to whether intentional theories of perception can explain or accommodate the differences between the senses.

A sense-datum theory of vision claims that one's visual experiences are constituted by an awareness of some mosaic of colour patches which are mind-dependent and located within a non-physical, psychological space. According to such theories one perceives physical objects through, and only through, being aware of the mental array of colour.[17]

It cannot be claimed that such an array of mental entities is obvious to one in introspecting one's visual experiences, even though a sense-datum theory claims that this array must be an object of awareness for the perceiver. Rather we can see the motivation for introducing the mosaic as arising from the problems of perceptual error. A visual hallucination, for instance, may be indistinguishable from a veridical perception; so it is not unnatural to assume that such an hallucination would share the same phenomenological character as the perception. An account of the phenomenological character of visual perception must then also satisfy as an account of visual hallucination.

When one hallucinates, the physical scene before one need not match how things look, and even if it does one is not aware of it. The sense-datum theory offers us a surrogate for that physical scene in explaining the phenomenological character of one's visual experience. That is, it claims that there must be some visual array actually experienced, and since there is no appropriate physical scene to match how things look, it offers us a

---

[17] As noted above, a recent proponent of such a view besides O'Shaughnessy is Frank Jackson (1977). Unusually, however, he takes visual sense data to be located in physical space.

mental stand-in. Since the very same type of experience is assumed to occur when one perceives, the conclusion is that the surrogate is present even when there is such an appropriate physical scene.

Two points are worth stressing about this progression. First, the colour mosaic is introduced as a feature of what is experienced, and only as what is experienced; it is not normally taken to extend beyond the limits of the visual field. Second, in being introduced in this way, it is taken to stand in for the physical scene perceived, as the material object of awareness.

Whether or not one is attracted to such a theory of vision, it is at least worthy of note whether a similar theory can be applied to touch, to ask whether there is the same motivation and whether one can make any sense of such a theory. Berkeley appears not to think so, since it offers no analogue to the visual field in his account of touch; while O'Shaughnessy, as we have seen, denies that there can be any such thing as a tactual field.

The justification for such conclusions lies in the phenomenological features we outlined in earlier sections, and principally derives from the claimed dependence of touch on bodily awareness. Tactual hallucination must depend at least partly on bodily illusions or hallucinations. Imagine a case in which it feels to you as if there is a coin in your hand when there is none. Is it possible to have such a tactual hallucination, without some element of illusion in body sense? If so, then one should be able to be aware that nothing is pressing against the skin, and there is nothing to prevent one from clasping one's fist as tightly as possible. How can the appearance of the coin survive the awareness of these facts? Or take a case in which it supposedly feels as if there is a flat surface which one is brushing one's fingertips across. As suggested earlier, that involves an element of resistance; it must appear to the subject as if she can't move her fingers straight through the surface. Suppose now that there is no such kinaesthetic misinformation: how can it still feel to one as if there is a surface present, when it also feels as if there is nothing to prevent the movement of one's body through it?

One can have tactual hallucinations deriving simply from illusions about one's body and how it can move: one can set up cases in which it feels as if there is something present, when nothing is there, and all that one needs to explain the appearance are certain elements of the bodily experiences involved. Suppose that you lay your hand flat out in front of you and it feels as if the palm can move no further, there is a feeling of the skin of the palm being flattened and distended and there are corresponding sensations across the palm. There is some sense of resistance to moving the hand forward, and it feels as if one cannot do so. This is a case of tactual hallucination: it feels as if one's palm is resting against a surface. Yet there is no surface present. Neither a physical surface, nor some mental surrogate for one.

Indeed the introduction of such a mental object would be otiose. A physical object comes to be an object of tactual attention through occupying a certain causal role. Were we to suppose that some mental surrogate were present we would have to suppose it to play a similar role to one's apparent body, as if it resisted the movement of one's body. This is close to ascribing to such entities causal powers. In addition, the sense-datum theory of vision only posits entities existing within a visual space in as much as they are experienced by the subject, falling within the limits of a visual field. But the suggested analogue for touch would be positing objects which fall outside any such sense field (since they are felt as that which is outside the body) and which are therefore not directly experienced. As extravagant as the metaphysics of a sense-datum theory of vision may appear to be, the metaphysics of a sense-datum theory of touch would be far greater.

This difference between sight and touch simply derives from the differences as noted above in the structure of visual and tactual experience. Visual experience presents an array of objects, and it is this array which the sense-datum theory claims must be accounted for in terms of some internal surrogate. Tactual experience presents things as through the felt limits of the body. So as long as the body feels as if it is restrained by things in the way it is when touching them, then it will appear as if there are objects felt through touch. The sense-datum theory at best has an argument which requires the seen or felt elements of experience to be explained by some internal aspect of the experience. While the objects of sight are seen, the objects of touch are those things which are not felt in bodily awareness, but are just adjacent to the objects of such awareness.

Since sense-datum theories of perception do not now generally command acceptance, the conclusion that one cannot offer a sense-datum theory of perception for the senses in general might be accepted with equanimity. However, the differences between sight and touch are also likely to cause problems for the most commonly discussed alternatives to a sense-datum theory, intentional theories of perception.[18]

An intentional theory of perception claims that perceptual states are

---

[18]For a robust defence of a purely intentional theory of perception see Harman 1989. Evans (1985b) appears to adopt an intentional theory of the spatial aspects of perception.

states with an intentional content, analogous to propositional attitudes such as belief and desire. When it looks to me as if there is an elephant in front of me, my visual experience has an intentional content which represents that there is an elephant in front of me. Such an approach to perceptual experience has no problems with examples of perceptual error: one can believe things which are false, so too things can appear to one to be a way that they are not.

Such a theory may seem appropriate to the problem example of touch. Believing that something is round hardly requires that there is some spatial field for beliefs, so why should its appearing to one as if there is something round itself require some such spatial field? The fact that such experiences have a spatial content would be reflected in the perceiver's responses to them, that the experiences in question prompt and make appropriate actions directed onto the spatially ordered world around the perceiver. Indeed, in the face of the kind of problems a sense-datum theory of touch engenders, avoiding any reference to sensory fields or spaces will seem to be a positive advantage.

As capable as an intentional theory of perception might be at explaining the spatial aspects of touch, a sense which does not locate its objects within a sense field, one must surely be sceptical whether the theory can explain spatial perception equally involving and spatial perception lacking a sensory field. Consider again the case of holding a glass in one's grasp. One touches five points on the rim, and has some sense of them. One is also aware that the glass is circular. According to an intentional theory of perception, these facts are to be understood as one's experience having an intentional or informational content that the rim is circular.

If we take this as a general theory of spatial perception we must think of a visual experience of such a circular shape as also having an intentional content that the rim is circular. In the tactual case one has an awareness of the five points of contact of a sort one does not have with any other part of the rim. In the visual case one perceives all parts of the rim indifferently; furthermore in the visual case one is aware of the rim as located within a visually perceived space, one is aware of it as positioned relative to many other points which could potentially contain other visually experienced objects. In the tactual case, there is no such analogue of this visual field. One is aware of tactual objects as located in a space beyond any such experienced spatial region; this is what put paid to any sense-datum theory of touch.

Since there are such obvious phenomenological differences between the two kinds of spatial perception, an intentional theory can only hope to be adequate if it has the resources to explain these differences. It is at this point that one must surely be sceptical. The best the theory could hope for is to claim that the presence or absence of a sensory field is to be explained in terms of an experience's being more or less replete with information about the world. This is unlikely to succeed, though, for it does not seem to be essential to the visual field that it should provide more spatial information than touch. A region of visual space could be a potential position of a visually experienced object without one thereby being aware either that something definitely is there or that nothing is: as when a region is occluded by other things or when one is seeing in a thick fog.

There does not as yet appear to be much consensus on what the correct account of perception is, or even what it should look like. The problems discussed above suggest that things are even more complicated in that there is no reason to think that any theory adequate to one sense should be adequate to all. So Reid's objection to a representative theory of perception, that it could not sensibly be applied to touch, is not a good argument against applying it to sight (this is not to say that there are not many other such good reasons); nor can one assume simply because one's theory works well for one sense that there should be no problem generalising it to others.

At the beginning of the paper we noted that a traditional approach to the differences between the senses was unable to offer us any illuminating answer to our questions, the phenomenological difference being reduced simply to some ineffable quality of the experiences. We might now conclude that this is no accident: if one attempts to offer a general theory of perception applicable to all senses, then one has inadequate resources to account for the phenomenological differences between sight and touch. Correspondingly, once one does focus on these differences, one is left with the conclusion that there is no reason to think that we can offer a single theory to account for the different ways in which we perceive the world.[19]

---

[19]Earlier versions of this paper were read at a conference on space and time in Dubrovnik; at the Wolfson Philosophy Society, Oxford; and at the Spatial Representation seminar, King's College Research Centre, Cambridge. I am most grateful to Bill Brewer, Justin Broackes, John Campbell, Naomi Eilan, Julie Jack, Tony Marcel, David Owens, Paul Snowdon and Peter Sullivan for comments on these papers and discussion of these issues.

10   *The diversity and unity of action and perception*

BRIAN O'SHAUGHNESSY

In this paper I investigate some of the most important relations holding between action and perception. There is reason to believe both of these phenomena are essential constituents of the psychological life of animals. The farther we go back in evolutionary history, the more they tend to occupy of the mind. Indeed, extrapolating backwards to the very simplest of animals, it looks as if active executive function and perceptual cognitive function must all but exhaust the psychological repertoire of the creature. While this does not imply that action and perception are primitive phenomena, it ensures that they are fundamental and in all probability essential to animal life. Then it would be interesting to discover how these elemental inhabitants of the mind manage at the same time to be both absolutely antithetical in character, and profoundly co-operative in function. Accordingly, my discussion polarises into a consideration of issues of antitheticality and issues of unity.

Part I – The relation of perception to action

Before I come to grips with specific questions, a word about layout. My intention in this paper is to examine some of the main relations, mostly causal and/or functional in character, that the phenomenon of perception bears to the phenomenon of action – and vice versa. That is, two particular families of relations. Now in carrying out these two distinct inquiries, due recognition must simultaneously be given to the fact that action takes *two* ontological forms: mental (internal) action, and physical (bodily) action. Theoretically therefore I ought to be considering *four* distinct sets of relations, as set out in Figure 1.

However, because perception (seeing, etc.) has little directly to do with *mental action* (thinking, etc.), at least from the causal and/or functional

216

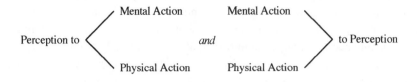

Figure 1

point of view, the first of these four relations can be omitted. The upshot is that Part I could be re-titled: *The relation of perception to physical action.* Then as remarked above, the investigation of the latter family of relations polarises into a consideration of issues of antitheticality and issues of unity.

SECTION A - ANTITHETICALITY (PERCEPTION TO PHYSICAL ACTION)

1 *Introduction*
(1) It is clear that in general action and perception are co-operative phenomena. For example, it is no exaggeration to say that the typical source of our physical actions is the impinging of percepts upon our minds; that physical action is for the most part a special kind of response to the changing environment as given in perception. In short, typically a causal bond links these events. And the relation is close in other ways which will duly emerge. Later in this paper I will try to spell out the extent of the co-operation and, indeed, of mutual dependence, between perception and action. For the moment however I shall follow a different line of inquiry.

Thus, side by side with these co-operative possibilities, one feels at the same time that there must be a limit to their extent, stemming from the gross unlikeness of the two phenomena. Let me at this point try to bring out this unlikeness. It shows in a number of important ways. To begin with action and perception have *opposed functions*, which in turn directly reflects two salient and equally opposed properties: the first is the direction of the line of causation instantiated when they occur; the second is the ontological character of their cause. Thus, the line of causation is from *mind to body* and thereby to environment in the case of action, and the *reverse* in the case of perception; and whereas actions are *internally* triggered, perceptions are caused in the first place by *environmental* and then secondly by optical and ocular events. These important differences condition the very different functions of perception and action. The function of perception is to generate knowledge of the environment, of action to wreak change in the environment that accords with the mind's desires; and such a divergence in function follows directly from the above.

This vitally important opposition in function is a divergence in the typical *effects* of these items. But an even more fundamental difference between these two phenomena appears when we examine an even more basic property: namely, the relation in which the item stands to the subject himself. Thus, actions do not *happen to one* whereas perceptions do and to a *pre-eminent degree*. What exactly does this mean? It could be taken to affirm that actions are *actions*, and perceptions are not (though the factor of degree sorts ill with this reading). However, that is not what I mean. What I am claiming is that in general even if not in particular, and thanks no doubt to the kind of their origin, actions are a phenomenon for which we bear a maximum measure of responsibility; while on this same count perceptions stand at a polar remove from action. The precise nature of this particular unlikeness between action and perception becomes clearer when we consider phenomena situated somewhere between these two opposites: say, the formation of a belief or the occurrence of affect. Now both of these latter events are inactive, and in precisely that sense both events happen to one and are on a par with perception. However, in a different and very important sense of 'happen to one' they are not. For they both differ significantly from perception on the score of *responsibility* – by which I mean: having a hand or say in, or being implicated in some way in their occurrence. Given this reading of the word 'responsibility', it is evident that we bear a measure of responsibility for our beliefs and emotions; indeed, there is even on occasion as a result such a thing as praise or blame in cases of this type. Take the case of belief-formation. Generally one has one's reasons for one's beliefs, which is to say considerations which persuaded one to belief: a self-consciously given persuasion-phenomenon in which one's standards of evidence are openly put on display and responsibly put to use. Matters are a little different with affect; for one is scarcely persuaded to rage, except in the active expressive sense. Nevertheless one is as a rule apprised of the source of one's emotion, for we speak with authority of that on account of which one emotes, and here too attitudes and standards by which one lives are openly exercised. Then this conjunction of self-knowledge with a normative element, which is to be found in cognitive and affective cases alike, constitutes a situation of partial responsibility.

Perception presents a striking contrast, not merely with action, but with both of these intermediate phenomena. Thus, it is not just that perception is essentially inactive – a property it shares with believing and emoting. In addition, one has next to no responsibility for one's perceptions, except in the instrumental sense of active engineering. When I open my eyes and see a roomful of people, indeed when I open my eyes *in order to* have just such a visual experience, there is no such thing as 'my reason for having such an experience': nothing for which I am responsible or even immediately aware, no standards by which I live or any such thing, mediates the parting of the eyelids and the visual experience of seeing people. True, these people have the appearance of people, and in just the sort of setting people might be expected, but I bear no responsibility for the genesis of the experience out of such data – let alone out of the colours and contours that fill my visual field. To repeat, the perception *happens* to one, and to a pre-eminent degree that probably reflects the fact that the origin of the experience is at once: causal, regular, from outside to inside. While my mind is involved in this transaction, I myself am simply not consulted. After all, I know nothing about the nature of that involvement. If action stands at one end of a spectrum of responsibility ranging across the entire mental scene, then perception stands precisely at the other end. Self-determination is at its lowest ebb in this phenomenon.

Now one might be inclined to say that actions do not happen to one simply for the reason that they emerge from within, and that perceptions do simply because they come from without. But this is unsatisfactory. All-important to actions is, not just that they emerge from my own mind, but that they are immediately caused by act-desire and intention: that is, by an impulse to do and a simultaneous superintending commitment-to or endorsement-of such a doing. Perceptions by contrast are essentially inactive, and harbour whatever content the objective environmental facts rather than the mind or preferences of the recipient determine. The contrast is like the opposition between desire and truth. The mind adopts two fundamentally different postures in discharging these two functions: an essentially receptive, and an essentially productive or creative one. They could not be more unlike.

(2) Given this antithetical character, one might expect it to reveal itself in certain ways. If these phenomena are so unlike, certain supposed possibilities in which the phenomena are brought into peculiarly intimate

conjunction may prove on closer study to be strict impossibilities — amounting in effect to a violation of the very identity or being of action and perception. In particular, one might conjecture the two possibilities: active perception, and the perception of action. Then it is the latter that I intend to discuss at this juncture. Thus, I wish to discover whether we can relate perceptually to our own actions. Then there is something about action which suggests it may not be possible. If perceptions impinge on us, if they come upon us from without, whereas actions do the opposite and emerge from within, how can one relate as perceiver to one's own actions? This argument looks at first blush to have force, and yet it must be invalid; for it is obvious we perceive our own actions; indeed, do so and must do so much of the time. I have only to move a finger and look at it to have perceived one of my own actions. And do I not perceptually feel the movements of my own actively moving limbs, and in fact pretty much have to if I am to actively accomplish much? It is true that in one sense of the term I do not relate as *observer* to those movements. Thus, I do not learn of *the existence* of the movements by the standard observational method of perception: the reason being, that I knew it was about to happen anyway and did not need to perceive to know. My knowledge had internal sources which rendered perception epistemologically otiose; for the act and bodily movement were firmly intended and definitively striven for there and then, and that sufficed for me to know. Yet having said that, two important qualifications are necessary. In the first place, without an on-going perception of bodily posture across time, and therefore of any structured bodily movement that I intentionally project, I become less able to execute such a project. This does not mean I cannot know of an intended movement irrespective of perception, but does imply that without perception across time any intended structured act becomes less of a certainty, and in consequence less liable to be an object of knowledge. In the second place, my knowledge of impending body movement depended on my knowledge of my own motor-health; and while the act of arm-moving lies in my power, neither that power itself nor the motor-health upon which it grossly depends are in any sense also within my power. Paradoxically but of necessity powers depend upon non-powers: no power is self-sustaining, limitless, so to say infinite. Then as a result of this inevitable dependence we may say, that when the intended and prognosticated movement actually occurs, and even though I do not learn by seeing that it is occurring, I nonetheless come by a higher degree of certainty than the internal situation alone could confer. So the position is this. There can be no doubt that I can and for the most part must perceive my own physical actions; and that I gain thereby an enhanced measure of certainty concerning their existence. So much for the supposed imperceivability-to-one of one's own physical actions.

Thus, there is nothing to the suggestion that the radically antithetical postures of agent and observer render one's actions imperceivable to one, which is a variant on the idea that one's own actions – rather like the nose on one's face – are epistemologically too close to be perceivable. The failure of this idea derived in part from the hidden dependence of action upon mechanism, whose very existence and state lie outside the scope of the will. In short, something that is internal to action cannot itself be willed, and this fact opens the door to unproblematic perceivability. Not all that constitutes action is so to say as close as the nose on one's face, and as a result events which occur at some kind of a remove from oneself as one wills might enter the realm of the perceivable-to-one. So the theory fails as it stands.

It fails because of the aforesaid gap or remove. But there is one extremely familiar event which occurs when we act which is at no sort of remove from us: namely, the willing itself. What about it? Might the theory hold of the phenomenon of willing? We know that the physical act is perceivable to the agent, but can the same be said of the striving that is contemporaneous with the act? Is this event also perceivable? What one says in reply to this question depends on one's theory of will and action. If you believe in the counter-intuitive 'double-aspect' theory that I endorse, you will have to agree that the act-of-the-will is perceivable to its agent, for on that theory act and act-of-the-will are identical, and we have just seen that the act is perceivable to its own agent. This makes it seem as if the point at issue can only be approached after a large-scale theoretical issue has been settled. But that is a mistake. For there remains an additional question that the above response fails to engage with, and this question puts its finger on the point at issue. The question can be asked, either in an abstract general mode or else in a particular concrete form. Either: do we *psychologically immediately* perceive our own bodily strivings? Or: if a man tries to move an arm, which turns out to be completely paralysed, so that nothing moves or even strains in the least degree, does he *immediately perceive* that event of trying? Either question would suffice, for they are more or less equivalent, but I shall concern myself with the second more manageable question.

2   *Perception*

(1) The subject knows he tried to move his arm. How? Two possible answers come to mind: either immediately and no-how, or else through perception of the event. The question I am asking is: which account is correct? Before I can come to grips with that question, I must say a few words about perception itself. A rough characterisation of this phenomenon goes something like this. Perception is an experience; of the kind of attention or noticing; with an object; which causes the experience; in lawlike manner; such that under given conditions we may legitimately pass inferentially from the occurrence of the experience to the existence of the object (at least under some description); and therefore constitutes a possible basis for knowledge. The objects of perception can be material objects, events, events across time, *qualia*, spatial properties, relations, and so on. It is important to note that perceptions can take direct objects (e.g. the moon) and propositional objects (e.g. that the tree is right of the house). Plainly some seeing-that is non-perceptual: say, the seeing that it rained last night that attends looking out the window onto wet streets; which is instead a cognitive episode grounded upon a visual experience. But some examples of seeing-that are constitutive of visual experience. Thus, I can hardly see a scene without registering or seeing-that certain structural relations obtain, a phenomenon which helps to constitute an internal object for the experience. Clearly all seeing-of must involve some seeing-that. Then whatever seeing-that helps in this structural manner to constitute a perceptual object must on that account be rated perceptual; and whatever goes beyond such a function rates as extra-perceptual. I have singled out the propositional objects of perception for comment, simply for the reason that if it happens to be true that we do immediately perceive our own willings, there is reason to believe that it may have to be of the type of perceiving-that. After all, when we engage in action it seems certain that we are aware *that* we are acting.

Let me at this point provide a possible model for the supposed immediate perception of willing: namely, a case in which perception takes an immediately given psychological object. I am thinking of the example of sensation. For on the above account of the phenomenon of perception, there can be no doubt that we perceive our own sensations. I say so, because any common or garden awareness of a bodily sensation manages to satisfy all of the given tests. Thus, from the existence of an experience of seeming to notice a sensation of pressure on one's left foot, we may in conditions of waking sanity infer to the existence of such a sensation. And the experience and sensation are two and distinct; and one is the cause of the other, and also its object; and since we would not have known of the sensation were it not for the experience, the experience must be our way of knowing. For such reasons this experience seems to be as good a case of perception as the seeing of a house or tree. Then is this particular case a proper model for the situation in which the subject knows he tried to move his completely paralysed arm? Did he immediately perceive his trying? As the subject with the sensation of pressure immediately perceived that sensation, did this particular subject immediately perceive his own trying?

(2) Perhaps the best way to come to grips with this question is by temporarily side-stepping it and considering instead *the knowledge of trying* that accompanies trying. What caused that knowledge? Doubtless trying and/or its causes. But what we want to discover is whether trying causes knowledge of trying through the mediation of a perceptual experience, or instead absolutely without mediation. Now it is true that he was aware of trying; but that sheds little light on the problem. The reason is that the word 'aware' is used in several distinct ways, only one of which is perceptual in character; so that the existence of an awareness of an experience fails to guarantee that the awareness is a perception. Thus, a man who feels amused is aware of his amusement; but this awareness of amusement is not a *perception* of amusement: if it were, an infinite regress of awarenesses of awarenesses would inevitably ensue. Such an awareness is simply a knowledge of amusement that is immediately caused by that amusement. Then here in this example of amusement, or thought or image or intention which are alike in this regard, we have the alternative model for the epistemological situation in the case of a pure bodily trying, i.e. a bodily trying that completely fails and is as a result totally unencumbered with kinaesthetic experience.

Which model is correct? Does trying immediately cause knowledge of itself? Or is there instead a distinct event of attentive awareness which causally mediates trying and knowledge of trying?

Let us restrict the discussion to familiar fully conscious examples of intentional trying – and disregard both sub-intentional tryings (which issue out of no intention and are attentively unconscious) and unconscious intentional tryings (in the Freudian sense or mode). Then to repeat, the question we are considering is the following: whether in the perfectly normal case of a known and conscious intentional trying, let us say a trying that completely fails, we come to know that we are trying through the mediation of a distinct perceptual event of the type of noticing-of or noticing-that. This is the question. Then a compelling reason for doubting the existence of such a perceptual event is that in self-conscious beings intentional trying generally *has to be* accompanied by knowledge of itself, for one who intentionally tries must be assumed to know *why* and therefore *that* he tries. If this is how matters stand, it robs the putative perception of any function; for the function of perception is to generate knowledge of the perceived. This argument finds corroboration in the following significant fact: namely, that the raw materials for the causation of knowledge are in the case of intentional trying already present, independently of any perceptual experience. Thus, intending-now to try, desiring-now to try, indeed one's very reasons for trying and that they are one's reasons, together with now-trying itself, surely constitute enough to ensure and indeed to actually require knowledge. Once again this robs the putative perception of any function.

What I am suggesting is, that it is because the causal source of the event of trying lies within, in a conscious intention and in reasons which are both know-*of* and known-*to-be* reasons, that knowledge of trying must come into being without assistance from perception. For think how the phenomenon of perception arose at all: consider what in evolution must have thrown it up in the first place. The situation in the case of all the rudimentary developing minds of that era was, that if they were to come to know facts concerning the almost limitless array of objects and events that are for us perceptible, then some kind of a linking cognitive device had to come into being. Since almost all perceptibles lie outside the mind, this is hardly surprising. In general perceptibles do not travel in the close company of knowledge of themselves. Therefore if knowledge of such items is to arise, some kind of a mediator must exist which can be a suitable basis for knowledge – in all likelihood a representational experience with matching content. By contrast, when an item is automatically and perhaps even necessarily geared to knowledge of itself, which happens in the case of some internal phenomena (such as intention, or belief, or consciousnesses generally), there can be no functional rationale for the existence of perception, and hence no perception at all. The realm of the in-principle-perceptible ranges across the whole of extra-psychological nature, and includes the one psychological item whose source is of necessity extra-psychological physical: namely, the sensation. It is because the origins of the sensation lie outside the mind, in their entirety and invariably and of necessity, that the psychological raw materials for automatic knowledge of it are inexistent; and hence that the special device of perceptual attention can be turned onto it to bring it into knowledge. Nothing in the mind determines the existence of the sensation, and therefore the distinct device of awareness has scope in its case. Then I am suggesting that it is precisely the opposite in the case of the intentional Will. But if it is so in the case of the intentional Will, it must surely be the same in the case of the sub-intentional Will: in part because it is the identical phenomenon in either situation; but also because the willing of which we become aware, when we actually notice an event of sub-intentional willing, is at that very moment poised on the edge of intentionalness.

I conclude from the above discussion that willing does not lie amongst the class of perceptibles. More precisely, amongst the class of immediate psychological perceptibles. Some of the properties of trying, as it is given to the acting subject in a pure and immediate experience of it alone, seem to confirm this conclusion. Thus, the event of trying of which the subject was aware, in the pure case of total failure in the complete absence of attendant strain or sensation, was not I think experienced as endowed with location, direction, shape, extent, *quale*; indeed, with the solitary exception of intensity, it is not experienced as endowed with any other quality except the identifying property of being a trying with such-and-such a content. In particular, nothing that one could describe as a perceptual modality exists: we see sights, hear sounds, feel sensations and even immediately feel our own limbs and their posture, but we do not feel our own bodily strivings. We are simply aware-of or cognisant-of them. Were we to feel them *qua* psychological entity, they would need to be feelings; were we to feel them *qua* physical entity, they would need to be causally mediated by feeling; and neither obtains. This almost total ineffability of striving *qua* striving doubtless determines resistance to Will-theory.

In sum, bodily willings are not immediately perceived. The reason being that their origin lies within and in such psychological phenomena as to ensure knowledge and as a result an absence of function for perception. This vindicates the original intuition that the antitheticality of the two phenomena has the consequence that, on pain of violation of identity, we cannot immediately perceive our own actions. You cannot relate receptively to productive-function. And roughly for the suggested reason: that the origins of action and perception lie in opposite realms.

SECTION B – CO-OPERATION (PERCEPTION TO PHYSICAL ACTION)

So much for the incompatibilities between action and perception, stemming from their radical unlikeness of character. I turn from now on to the ways in which they work together. Their very primordiality in the animal mind shows they are intended to work together. The mind is a system, and the functional roles of two such basic psychological phenomena must surely be, not schismatic, not indifferent, but co-operative. And in any case it is so. This is plain enough, even obvious, when we consider the use of perception in generating and informing physical action. But it is obvious also when we think about the reverse situation, in which action puts its resources at the disposal of perception. For co-operation takes these two forms. We shall see that it runs pretty deep in either case. I begin with an examination of the first mode of co-operation: that in which perception assists physical action.

1   How perception assists physical action

The respects in which action is in debt to perception are various. The first and most obvious respect is causal. Typically our physical manipulative deeds owe their very existence to perceptions. If I had not caught sight of a moving tennis ball, I would not be engaged in the act of hitting it. But of course the debt is more extensive, and the connection closer, than that indicates. It is not just that I see a moving tennis ball, and find myself as a result engaged in an act of hitting a tennis ball that happens to be the very one that precipitated me into action. Typically perception provides action, not just with its existence, but with its *objects* as well. Thus, action is concerned to wreak change in the world, and in consequence one must be aware of its objects, firstly to know where the Will is to strike, secondly to monitor its effects.

When we speak of 'where the Will is to strike', we could be referring either to its immediate or else to a mediate instrumental object: for example, to a hand or to a piano. I shall not say much about the uses of bodily perception in bodily action, though those uses are real enough. The bodily Will depends on awareness of the presence and posture of a limb in acts of movement. If your left arm seems either absent or flexed, then it is impossible to try to and *a fortiori* impossible to succeed in flexing it. Seeming present or flexed must one supposes be a perceptual seeming, because it is caused by the facts, because in conditions of neurological health it correlates with the facts, because it is a way of knowing these facts. Nonetheless, there is something odd about this example of perception, if only because the contents of the stream of consciousness scarcely make mention of it. Such steady recessiveness seems at variance with the normal function of the attention, which is somehow to bring things before the mind. And yet how could it be otherwise? If our limbs fought for our attention in the way our surrounds and target objects do; if, in trying to move a limb in some determinate manner in attempting to catch a ball, one had to train one's attention onto its position and posture in the way we do on the path of the ball we are trying to catch; we would stand in our own path and accomplish nothing! Yet having said this, I cannot see how we can avoid describing it as perceptual and as engaging the attention in some way or another. In all probability there is something special in the way it relates to the attention in this recessive manner (which I shall not here try to dig out).

Matters look very different when we come to consider the role played by perception when the Will reaches beyond the body and is applied to instrumental targets. Most of the subsequent discussion in Section B will be concerned with such instrumental deeds, and in particular with the contribution made by the sense of sight to these manipulations. Now it is true that instrumental action does not in the binding way of bodily moving depend upon an actual perceptual awareness of the object. I can set a telephone ringing in your flat without myself actually hearing it. On the other hand, I will presumably have to perceive the telephone I manipulate in so doing. And this is, I think, the general rule. One has only to consider what would happen to one's active projects if the world were suddenly plunged into total and unrelieved darkness, silence, intangibility. Instrumental action would grind to a near halt. And the reason for this is that perception discovers for instrumental action both its goals and instrumental means of accomplishment, and then proceeds to acquaint the agent with the course of action and so provides informational feed-back which leads to the formation of the more differential intentions and deeds essential to the completion of the task.

An interesting difference exists on this count between instrumental and mere basic bodily action. It is important to note – and it is a strange fact – that in the case of the presence and posture of our limbs, the perceptual task is already accomplished; or more exactly, there is not and indeed could not be an active enterprise of proprioceptive perception; and *a fortiori* there could not be such an enterprise in aid of intentional bodily action. Contrast the instrumental situation. Instrumental projects which are processive necessitate as a general rule, not merely the assistance of perception and its resultant cognition, but an active intentional perceptual project which effects knowledge in the required manner. Think of a cricketer executing a cut. He does not just suffer a series of glimpses of the ball which happen to be of use to him; he experiences the right kind at the right time, and it is no accident that he does: he engineers it that way. This is because he is *looking*: looking to see where the ball is in relation both to he himself and to his intended stroke; and this is the explanation of his seeing what is needed when it is needed.

So in simple bodily moving we are engaged in activity that is and cannot but be dependent upon inactive already accomplished proprioceptive perception. But in the visual-motor cases that I have chosen to discuss at length, we are for the most part concerned with *two* activities: with the motor activity, and the visual-perceptual activity with which it works in close unison. The problem is to spell out the nature of this relation. Several possibilities must be considered, the most radical of which is that one activity absorbs the other, the next most radical of which is that the two activities fuse to constitute a new complex visual-motor activity. In order to make any progress on this problem, it is at this point necessary to take a look at the phenomenon of act-unification.

2   *Act-unification*

(1) One might at first begin by doubting whether acts can unite to constitute new acts, especially if you believe in acts of the Will. How can two willings unite to make one complex willing? Nevertheless it is obvious that actions can be constituted out of actions: uttering a sentence is one example, and playing the piano another: in one case the act-parts are successive, in the other both simultaneous and successive. Thus, uttering each word is a distinct act-part of the act of uttering the sentence; while playing the left hand of a piano work is an active part of the act of playing that work. So here we have examples in which actions come together and form new actions. Meanwhile there exist pairs of acts, standing in close relation, which refuse nonetheless to unite: whistling and tap-dancing the one tune simultaneously (say) will generally fail to realise a novel act. The principle of act-unity, whatever it is, must leave conceptual space for the following kinds of cases: (A) merely performing two simultaneous acts, (B) merely performing two simultaneous acts with identical content, (C)

intentionally performing simultaneously two acts with identical content, (D) intentionally performing two acts simultaneously with identical content as parts of the one act. Examples are: (A) looking around the room as you tap-dance to a tune, (B) whistling the tune idly to which you are tap-dancing, (C) whistling the tune in strict time with your dancing, (D) whistling and tap-dancing as a way of sounding a somewhat percussive rendition of the tune – being a 'one man band' as one might say. Then whereas (A), (B), and (C) are examples of simultaneous acts which refuse to unite, (D) is a genuine example of act-fusion. This example demonstrates that unification does not find its rationale in the phenomena alone. Origin, and in particular a single unifying act-intention and act-desire origin, is the crucial determining factor in my opinion. Out of such material, and according to some rule or another, unity is forged.

The following principle suggests itself. Suppose I desire and intend to produce event e; and as a result desire, intend, and execute acts a, b, and c, which conjunctively lead to the event-effect e; then acts a, b, and c count as parts of the one act of e-making. Something like this probably governs the unification of actions. However, a principle of this kind has a few difficulties to face: first on the count of re-description, second that of ontological status. A very brief comment on each of these problems, beginning with the problem of re-description. Now it is an inflexible rule in the case of instrumental actions that any act that is instrumental is so only under a particular description; so that it must always be possible to single out under a non-instrumental description the act that finds itself re-described. For example, the act of giving a kick qualifies for the instrumental re-description 'act of door-opening' provided it causes a door-opening; and this same act can be picked out as a kicking. Then what is the act that suffers re-description when actions fuse under an instrumental heading like 'playing a whistle-percussive rendition of a tune'? It is no good saying: the act of blowing through one's lips and moving one's feet – for that is not an act-designation – seeing that these acts constitute one act only when embedded in the right causal framework. I think one has to admit the difficulty, and reply: that the act that gets re-described is an act – *some act or other*, be it noted – that is constituted out of blowing through one's lips and moving one's feet. We thereby accept that the supposedly basic-act description of the fused act is not after all a basic-act description. And yet it is true that the act made out of those two basic acts falls under an instrumental description only because of its causal properties.

The second difficulty, which concerns the ontological status of the novel complex act, seems to echo this problem. It takes the following form. Let us suppose that one of the fused acts is an internal activity like listening, and the other a physical activity like tap-dancing. In certain causal contexts even these ontologically disparate acts could unite to constitute a single act – but of what ontological status? 'Psycho-physical'? But is there such an order of being? The problem is, whether the novel act has anything that one could describe as 'a nature of its own'. Do artefacts have a nature of their own? If absolutely *anything* that generates and is used for the generation of phenomenon x is an artefact of type x-maker, the nature of the 'anything' drops out of consideration. Then how can one speak of the order of being or ontological status of x-makers as such? And one cannot. But one can in a particular case, when so to say coincidentally the particular entity has whatever status it happens to have. And when no one entity as such is named, then I believe the concept of ontological status or order of being is inapplicable. This is what I should say in the case of two ontologically disparate acts which fuse as parts of one instrumental act. In such a case there simply is no ontological status. So much for the two difficulties facing our account of act-fusion.

(2) I return to the relation between motor activities and attendant or accomplice perceptual activities. For example, between arm-moving and looking in the course of painting a portrait. Might 'painting' be the name of just such a complex novel act as we have been discussing? Is painting a motor-visual activity? There are considerations which seem to favour this claim. Do not looking and arm-moving have the common aim and effect of generating an image on a canvas; and do they not both arise out of the one intent and desire to effect the appearance of just such an image? All this is true, and indicates how closely knit are the motor and visual projects in such an example. But it does not I think constitute sufficient ground for unifying these projects as act-parts of the one act-project: to wit, painting. As the construction of a wall is nothing more than the lugging and positioning of a collection of bricks, so painting is nothing more than the lugging of paint into position on a canvas. A very special example of such, no doubt, at least in the right hands; and owing a very special debt to the fruits of vision, in addition; but an example of matter-moving for all that. A blind man could paint a picture in the strictest sense of the word; and it is in any case the hand alone that is responsible for the movement of paint onto canvas in the act of painting; for while it is true that visual perception

makes its causal contribution to this process, it does so at a remove and only through informing the mind that moves the hand. Most important of all, the movement of the hand *is* and the perceptual phenomenon *is not* part of the regular quasi-mechanistic link between willing and intended effect whose activation is such as to ensure that the act of the Will is at the same time an act of producing that effect. It is for reasons of this kind that painting as we at present know it must be accounted a purely motor activity. But, of course, it is sheer contingency that it take the form it does: paint might in principle be manipulated into position on canvas in a limitless number of ways. Painting might take any form.

And so the position we have reached is this. There is no reason in principle why certain motor and visual activities should not in suitable causal contexts fuse as parts of a single visual-motor activity. But they do not in the centrally important and vastly familiar type of case under consideration wherein sight guides an instrumental act to its target: a type exemplified in phenomena like painting, car-driving, tennis-playing, etc. In all these cases the role of the active perceptual project is something other than that of act-part. It is because I believe that this role is the pre-eminent role for vision in animal life, that I have chosen to concentrate the discussion upon this familiar type of case. Then we have seen that it is a co-operative role; more, that sight acts as precipitating cause of motor activity; more again, that it discovers object or target for motor action. Clearly, a role such as to intimately bond the visual project with the motor project. However, as we have just seen, not sufficiently intimate to effect fusion; for the motor project does not assimilate the visual; nor vice versa; nor do they in this particular case fuse to constitute a complex unitary motor-visual activity.

3 *Characterising the motor-perceptual relation in the central case*
(1) The residual problem is to spell out the precise nature of the co-operation that obtains between motor and visual projects in these centrally important cases. Light is shed on this problem through inspecting the *causal situation*. I have claimed that sight causes the motor activity – but this is inexact. What goes on is something like the following. Let us suppose that I am playing tennis, and am as a result continuously watching the ball. Suppose at a certain instant that I see that the ball is going to my right. This sight causes me to act, to embark upon whatever stroke the occasion demands. Then this motor action in turn causes a novel development within the on-going active perceptual project of looking,

whose findings in turn cause, not a novel motor action, but a novel development within the already embarked upon motor action. Therefore even though sight here causes motor action, the desire to engage in that resultant motor action causes the accomplice novel development within the continuing visual project. That is, as the two activities unfold – say, playing a forehand volley and watching the ball onto the racquet – the former is the cause of the latter; and the cognitive findings of this latter cause *developments* within the former. It is because in the first place I had actively embarked upon tennis that I was continuously watching the ball; and it is because I saw the ball going to my right that I tried to play a forehand volley; and it is because I was trying to play a forehand volley that I was actively watching the ball onto the racquet; and it is because of what I saw that I played the shot as I did. Now the causally interactive nature of the two projects should not be allowed to obscure the fact that in cases of this kind sight is subordinated to motor action. Whereas I am playing a volley only because of what I saw, I am nonetheless looking only because I am playing a volley, and indeed only because I am playing tennis. While at each instant sight informs me of something which modifies my motor project, such modifications are not to be confused with novel motor projects. Thus, in these familiar examples where motor action puts perception to active use, that precisely is the situation. Namely: motor action puts perceptual action to use. We express this fact causally by asserting that motor activity causes its accomplice perceptual activity.

(2) The above mix wherein one activity (viz. motor) causally sustains the other (viz. perceptual) which in turn causally fuels the sustainer, is a further element in the characterisation of the intimate relation holding between motor and perceptual projects in this central type of case. At this point I would like to bring out an interesting additional feature of this relation, which comes astonishingly close to unifying the related activities; indeed, may be said to inextricably bind them at the intentional level. The feature emerges when we address ourselves to the question: just exactly *in what way* does sight provide the motor activity with its object? It will help at this juncture to turn to a different and extremely simple example: that in which I intentionally bring my right index finger down onto a cross on a page in front of me: **X**. What precisely is the motor project here? Certainly it is to touch the cross in front of me. But it is, I think, more. It is, I suggest, in addition to bring cross and finger together *in my visual field*. Some may deny this. They may agree that I intend doing what I know will unite cross and finger in my visual field; but they would say that

the latter description of my intention applies merely in consequence of the fact that I am trying to touch the cross and continually using visual data in doing so. In this way they would manage to deny the claim that the motor project is intentional under an irreducibly cross-modal heading. Now it is certainly true that I am using visual data as I act, and at every point in the process. But what would remain of that data at any instant if sight were suddenly to give out? Something less than itself, surely. For is not the data not merely acquired through sight, but actually *cast in visual terms*? Thus, how would one specify the visually disclosed position of finger and target at any point during the act? One might turn to language in an attempt to do so: for example, 'about 2" N.N.E., and at an elevation of about 45°'. But *the very best* linguistic specification one can come up with always lags behind the given (and received) data; that is, lags behind *what one knows*. At no stage is the verbally-available-to-one specification sufficient for this task and therefore for the motor project: after all, one keeps *looking* as one guides the finger, and does so right up until the moment in which the finger contacts the cross, and the reason surely is that sight is continually informing one as to where in one's visual field one is to move one's visible physical finger. It is not that the function of sight is anything more than informational: for example, it is not to keep you to the task or to steady the nerves or anything other than that of purveyor of the kinds of truths that sight is qualified to purvey. What seems to be the case, however, is that what it purveys exceeds what conceptually it purveys, which is to say what conceptually is at one's fingertips. This is not to say that there is not a truth of the matter at any moment, and that concepts are not equal to expressing it; but that we ourselves are not in possession of such a conceptualised specification. At any instant the information that one puts to active use is visually-indexically given: namely, that the finger is 'here' in the visual field and the cross 'there', and that one has to move the finger 'thus'.

Now it is because of this fact that I endorse the aforementioned theory concerning the double or cross-modal intentional character of motor enterprises of this familiar kind. That theory claims that, even though the motor activity is no more than an act of touching a cross on a page, it is nonetheless intentional under both that description *and* a description that makes reference to the sense of sight: say, 'bringing finger and cross together in my visual field'. And the argument is, that it is not just *known* at any instant that this latter description is true of one's activity: at any moment the specification of the intentional object of action makes ineradicable reference to the sense of sight. For as we have just noted, the intentional object is 'to move the right index finger from "here" to "there" in the visual field'. Thus, the intention under which one acts makes simultaneous reference to public physical entities *and* to the deliverances of sight; for it refers to cross and finger *and also* to how spatially they look to one to relate. The contribution of sight to action is therefore not just causal, object-conferring, and informational. Because that information is irreducibly cast in visual-indexical terms, and is in that sense a-conceptually given, it cannot but enter the intentional heading in that concrete unverbalisable form and thereby import an ineradicable reference to sight into the intentional motor enterprise.

Thus, in such situations the motor action is intentional under both a physical specification *and* a specification that refers to the sense of sight. This does not make the action into anything more than a motor action; and in particular does not make it into a motor-visual act, if by that we are to understand an activity that is in part motor, in part visual. Moving a finger just *is* moving a finger, even if it is also moving a finger I am looking at *and* is intentional under both descriptions; that is, even if this particular example of finger-moving could not even in principle have occurred without the co-operation of sight. Then how about the visual activity that is in this secondary sense fed into the very being of the motor activity? Is it likewise fused at the intentional level? I think it is (but will not explore the question). Here, too, it seems to me that the activity is intentional, not merely under 'looking to see where the cross is', but also under 'looking to see where I am to touch'.

It seems therefore that in the central case of visually assisted motor activity, of the kind encountered pretty much all the time, we are in the presence of a peculiarly intimate bond that falls only a little short of fusion. Perceptions elicit actions, providing them with their object; and the resulting actions generate and subordinate accomplice perceptual projects; which in turn present the object irreducibly cast in terms that are partly visual, and at the same time elicit subordinate differential intentions and part-actions. All this goes on when one does something as humdrum as reaching for a cup of tea. It goes on all the time. The relation is intimate and mutual, and attests to their natural functional unity; and it can hardly be an accident that the physical finesse of which actively we are capable, and the perceptual finesse which the sense of sight exhibits, are pretty much of comparable extent. Since in a good sense we live through our eyes epistemologically speaking for much of the time, and since the ultimate function of mentation is the production of physical action, we seem to be in the presence of a core phenomenon of the psychological life of animals generally.

Part II – The relation of action to perception

Once again, a word about layout. We have so far examined the relations, both of an antithetical and of a co-operative variety, holding between perception and action. I now reverse the coin and address myself to the relations in which action stands to perception. Here, too, a measure of simplification is permissible. Theoretically I ought to be considering the relation of mental action to perception, and of physical action to perception; and ought in addition to be examining issues of an antithetical and of a co-operative kind. But in fact only two issues of real substance arise: that of the possible antitheticality of mental action to perception; and that of the co-operation of both mental and physical action with the processes of perception. Considerations of space restrict me to the first of these enterprises.

SECTION C – ANTITHETICALITY (MENTAL ACTION TO PERCEPTION)

1 *Two distinct mental-act schemas*

(1) We began this whole discussion by noting that action and perception are what one might call *original* mental phenomena. Doubtless these phenomena were to be found in the very first minds that appeared on our planet. This is a reason for assuming that they have highly diverse yet closely knit natural functions. My present concern is with their diversity; indeed, their essentially antithetical character. After all, in action we change the World, in perception the World changes us. Such a polarity in nature suggests that it might in effect amount to a violation of the very being of action and perception, to suppose that we could perceive our own 'doings', or 'do' our own perceivings. We have already investigated the first of these two intuitions in Section A, and vindicated it – provided the perception in question is restricted to the immediate variety. I turn at this point to the second intuition, that the very idea of 'doing' one's perceivings is somehow problematic. Now it is clearly possible to actively bring about perception in oneself: one has only to open one's eyes. But is it possible, even in principle, to actively effect perception in oneself non-instrumentally or *immediately*? If it is, that possibility must be realised in

listening and looking. When are we more immediately responsible for our own perceivings than on those occasions? Accordingly, my topic becomes the analysis of listening and looking: a question of some moment in its own right in any case. For the most part I shall concentrate on the phenomenon of listening, on the grounds that it is the simpler of the two activities yet such as to preserve the essentials of the problem under consideration. That problem being: is listening the immediate active producing of hearing? More generally: what is the analysis of listening? More precisely – since I wish to discover both its constituent parts and how they interrelate: what is the *structural analysis* of listening? (And let me for the moment brush sand over the word 'immediate'.)

Mental actions divide into attendings and thinkings; that is, provided the concept of thinking is sufficiently elastic to accommodate the active varieties of imagining. (Why should it not?) Then listening, which is a mode of active attending, must be accounted a mental action. And that is to say, an instance of a type that ranges over *structurally disparate phenomena*. This becomes evident when one considers the question: do mental acts consist in the mediate or immediate producing of some desired event? Various answers prove to be in order, depending on the type of the act; and these answers have structural implications. My claim is that at least three distinct structures – call them (α), (β), (γ) – are exemplified by mental actions. I shall consider these three phenomenal kinds in order, beginning with a somewhat surprising variety (α) of mental action. Thus, there exist active mental phenomena which at first glance look to be the absolutely immediate producings of some desired internal event, but which on closer inspection turn out to be the active producing of *nothing*: sheer doings, as one might say. The very best example of this kind that I can think of is the puzzling phenomenon of talking silently to oneself – which does not, I shall argue, consist in the active producing of imaginative phenomena in one's own mind, nor indeed of any kind of mental phenomenon. I shall briefly consider this case in the next section, but would like now structurally to distinguish it from two other kinds of mental action. The exemplars of those other two varieties are, (β) the phenomenon of voluntary recollection, and (γ) the case under discussion: to wit, listening or active attending. It is my contention that these three types, (α), (β), and (γ), instantiate structurally dissimilar act-situations. More exactly, my claim is that the several whole-events that are the necessary conditions of the occurrence of the act-type in question, instantiate three different structures. This formulation permits the structure under consideration to include the act as a whole as one of its event-parts, or else to be the constitutive structure obtaining within the act itself.

(2) I shall begin this structural inquiry with a few words on the kind (α) exemplified by the phenomenon of talking silently to oneself. This kind of phenomenon can take various forms; so that in a permanently deaf person the phenomenon might be signalling motionlessly to oneself. Since the expression 'silent talking' is as much a contradiction as 'motionless running', 'silent talking' must be a mis-description of silent quasi-talking. This perfectly real mental or internal activity is quasi- the public or bodily activity of vocalising. Then the question I wish to ask, which raises issues of structure, is whether the mental activity consists in actively producing some other desired mental phenomenon. For example: does it consist in doing internally what causes a quasi-hearing, or maybe a quasi-sound, or perhaps a quasi-perturbation of the larynx, or else a quasi-act of vocalising? Well, it can scarcely be the producing by active internal means of a quasi-vocalising, since a quasi-vocalising is what precisely it *is*; and neither can it be the producing of a quasi-hearing, since the event of hearing is strictly speaking irrelevant to the event of vocalising. What remain as serious possibilities are, that it consists in the producing of a quasi-sound, or quasi-laryngeal changes. Is silent speech the active generating of such internal items? But upon what principle does this theory rest? Can a mental act be a quasi- or seeming bodily act of producing bodily movement φ, only if it is itself not merely an *attempted*, but an actual *genuine producing* of a mental or quasi-bodily movement φ? Must the man who is silently talking to himself really be trying to produce an imagined suitable perturbation in the vocal apparatus? And must he be *succeeding*, what is more? Or must he instead really be trying to produce, and succeeding again, an imagined or inner voice? But why should success be of any account to him? Why should it matter to the silent speaker that seeming sounds *actually* issue forth in his own mind? They will not enlighten him as to the content of his willings. And is not the entire point of the exercise to bring a string of words before the mind? But that is accomplished from the beginning. Is he not immediately aware of the verbal content of his on-going mental strivings? It is because of considerations of this kind that I believe of this case that it is the active producing of nothing. It is, so to say, Will through and through. Here we have one structural situation (α) in the case of mental actions.

(3) I turn now to the structural variety (β) exemplified by voluntary recollection. The example for consideration is, trying to remember a

name. Unquestionably this phenomenon rates as an action if successful: an act of the type, jogging the memory. What are the constituents of such an act? In particular, is the event of name-appearance part of the act? Now it is important in cases of this kind that just as typically one's endeavours are unsuccessful as successful. It is important also that the event of name-appearance which signals success, frequently occurs some little time after the endeavour itself. What general conclusions may we draw from these few observations? First, that trying to remember has causal power. Second, that the power must be expressible in loose probabilistic terms which will vary from occasion to occasion. Third, that normally one does not know why on any particular occasion one's endeavour was successful when it was. These three conclusions may be summed up in the following general claim. Namely: that trying to recollect causes recollection through implementing means which have power that is expressible in loose probabilistic terms. In short, a highly fallible but nonetheless worthwhile and therefore real mechanism or *way of producing* must automatically be activated by the will to remember. Then does the existence of this mechanistic link between willing and name-appearance suffice to unite these two events under the one event-head, 'jogging the memory'? I very much doubt it. I doubt it because one has managed successfully to jog one's memory even when the event of name-appearance occurs a few moments after one has stopped one's mental exertions; and has one not done all that one is going to do when one has stopped trying to remember? Pretty plainly, such acts do not encompass the event of name-appearance. But they are more or less as typical as instantaneously successful cases. And are we to suppose these two kinds of acts structurally dissimilar? When these considerations are conjoined with facts like the gross fallibility and unreliability of the mechanism – which incidentally helps to condition 'time-lag' when it occurs – we have a strong case for saying that the act of jogging the memory begins and ends with the event of trying to remember, and fails to include the distinct event of name-appearance or recollection. The structure of the act-situation encountered with (β)-type actions like recollection, is closely reminiscent of that realised in 'instrumental act'-situations in Physical Nature – with one important difference: that a mechanism is activated.

2 Comparing listening and bodily action

(1) So far we have laid out two structural schemas available for mental actions – prior to examining the structural situation in the cases that are

our central concern: listening, or more generally active attending. Then it is clear from what emerged concerning those two structures, that the most familiar example of the type Action, namely bodily action, cannot be taken as a guiding model. Each of these three kinds – Soliloquy, Recollection, Physical Action – embody differently structured acts/act-situations. Thus, whatever one's precise views concerning the constituents of bodily action, it is certain that the bodily act encompasses the bodily movement as a whole-event part. Doubtless this is intimately linked with the presence in bodily action of two elements which were noteworthy absences in the case just discussed. Namely: the extreme reliability of the bodily motor-system, and the near-instantaneousness of its operation. These two factors help to unite the events of willing, of mechanism-activation, and of bodily movement, under the one event-heading of bodily action. Now these few comments serve to explicate the structural difference between bodily action and active recollection; and it is evident enough that both of these cases differ structurally in the same respect from the type of act exemplified by silent soliloquy, for the reason that in this latter type of case there simply is no analogue of name-appearance or willed bodily movement.

The question we must now ask is: which, if any, of the above three varieties of action is a satisfactory model for the structural analysis of listening? Is it to be compared to talking silently to oneself? Or to jogging the memory? Or to common or garden examples of bodily moving? I shall argue for the view that it is to be compared to none of them, and constitutes a novel active structural-situation in its own right.

(2) The discussion of listening or active attending is best conducted by reference to the last of the above three model cases: that of bodily action. This central example of the kind provides a valuable reference-point for the basic elements to be met with in act-situations in general. And it has a second important asset. Thus, bodily action is the most clearcut or unambiguous example of the type Action: the reason being that the distinction between active and inactive events is in the case of the body more decisive than in the mind, which by contrast is populated with phenomena which have, and in continually varying degrees, something of a life of their own. Then I would issue a note of warning at this point: namely, that we ought not to assume that bodily action is a correct model for *any* mental phenomenon. As noted already, the mental *status quo* is so markedly dissimilar from the bodily, that it would be intellectually foolhardy to do so. I say this even though bodily action is surely the

central case, almost the defining case, of the type Action. Yet that it cannot actually *be* the unique defining paradigm, is clear from the preceding discussion. While there exist necessary and sufficient conditions for action, and while action may have an essence, what has emerged is that action has *no structural essence*; and *a fortiori* not that exemplified in bodily action. Nonetheless this central example of the type provides a valuable reference-point.

The elements of bodily action that I shall take for granted are: the willed bodily movement ϕ, the activation of the motor-mechanism M, and the phenomenon of willing or trying or striving or attempting; and I shall not really say much more about their structural relations. Can we discover analogues of each of these elements in attending or listening? I shall begin by looking in attentive situations for an analogue of willed movement ϕ. This phenomenon is a continuity, that is in itself inactive, that owes its existence to the Will, and that can in principle occur in the absence of Will. Is there a precise analogue in listening? A few simple entailments help at this point. Thus, listening to sound S entails hearing S, which in turn entails the here-and-now audibility-to-one of S; and neither entailment is reversible: the clock can be ticking unnoticed, the slam of the door heard but not listened-to. These logical relations are pretty much duplicated in bodily action, with arm-raising the analogue of listening, arm-rise that of hearing, and maybe limb-freedom some kind of analogue of audibility-to-one-now. Then the point that matters here is that hearing looks to be an exact analogue of limb movement. But, it may be objected, limb movement is a continuity; yet how can the hearing that is co-present with listening also be a continuity? I can see no reason why it should not be. To be sure it *sounds a little odd* to say that a continuity of hearing is going on as one actively listens; for it seems as if one were introducing something beyond one's control into the very heart of action. This may or may not be; but there can be no doubt that one hears at each instant that one listens, and no doubt that in either case those instants form a continuity.

Thus far the comparison with bodily action seems accurate enough. A continuity of hearing occurs which, give or take a certain leeway, would not have occurred were it not for one's engaging in listening. Later on I shall have more to say about the 'leeway', but let us assume that *such* a hearing with *such* content would almost certainly not have occurred had one not listened. I turn now to the second element of bodily action: the essentially active element of willing or striving. This surely is present: act-desire and act-intention find immediate expression in listening, the intensity of the desire matching the urgency of the enterprise, and in general when one listens one tries to listen. Despite the fact that the possibility of failure is, in a few stark simple cases, more or less inconceivable, so that the element of striving-*towards* is perhaps absent, all listening is and I think essentially is something that we engage in and *do* – in the special 'will'- and not just 'cause'- sense of the word 'do'. To repeat: while some simple listenings may not be cases of striving-towards, they remain attempts or assays or willings – howsoever certain one may be of success. Just as 'believe' has the core sense 'hold to be true', which is consistent with unshakeable certainty, so I submit 'try' has the core sense 'attempt', which is consistent with the inconceivability of failure. Thus, despite a few misgivings on its exact productive function, the element of Will that we encounter in bodily action we encounter here too. In short, the comparison between the two cases is more or less sustained thus far.

(3) I come now to the third element of bodily action: the activation of a motor-mechanism; indeed, of a motor-mechanism that for the most part works with a sort of flawless ease. We noted the presence of the mechanistic element, though highly flawed and expressible in no more than statistical terms, in Recollecting; and its absence, for want of any putative mechanistically-effected product, in Soliloquy. Then what is the situation with listening or active attending generally? At this point I would like temporarily to change the example under discussion. Since listening, looking, and attending generally, is the phenomenon under scrutiny, considerations of simplicity lead me to substitute the directing of the attention onto a sensation: let us say, onto a naturally recessive sensation such as the sensation of contact. We shall suppose that the intentional project is the directing of the attention onto a medium-intensity sensation of contact, for the relatively brief span of four or five seconds. And so one turns one's attention onto this psychological object; and, of course, succeeds; and instantaneously. Might a mechanism link these two events: namely, the event of turning the attention onto, and the event of noticing or making attentive contact? If so, it must be a mechanism that works with the flawless ease and certainty of bodily mechanisms. Had it been the case that a mechanism linked talking to oneself with some inner 'sound' or 'quasi-movement', we would I think have had to say the same of it; bearing in mind that one embarks upon inner speech with the same certainty and success as outer. Then in either case one would have grounds for suspecting that the situation had been misrepresented: for the mind's mechanisms seem invariably to be flawed (perhaps because the mental

status quo is as mobile as flowing water). So to repeat: might mechanism link directing one's attention onto and noticing a particular sensation? Now it is worth remembering what in general the factor of mechanism accomplishes for a theoretical account: it bridges an explanatory gap, interposing a linked sequence of pellucid enough explanations as a means of explaining what otherwise stands unexplained. Then how can this concept find application when one turns one's attention onto a mere sensation? Is it not *explanation enough* of one's awareness of the sensation, that one voluntarily turned one's attention precisely in its direction? What better explanation could one come by? What explanatory gap is there to bridge? What bridges that are an improvement on what already we have? Are we not in danger of regress in asking for more?

Let me express the matter in slightly different terms. A mechanism is a regular mediating device, a way of producing, a 'how'; and its presence is attested by three distinct factors: the first is the existence of a regular connection between input phenomenon and output product; the second is the occasional breakdown of regularity; and the third is the existence of an explanatory hiatus that is to be bridged. Is not this precisely the situation in the case of the bodily Will? Thus, regularity obtains; and failure exceptionally occurs; and interposing between act of the Will and bodily output lies nothing less than the whole mysterious divide of mind and body (as Hume remarked in the *Enquiries* (1777), section vii, part 1). Then of these three elements, I discover only the first in the simple case of attending under discussion. We have remarked already on the absence of explanatory hiatus. What about failure? When do we try to attend to a bodily sensation and fail? Here we should note a simple ambiguity in the word 'fail': in the central sense of this term we conceive of failure as an unsuccessful attempt, but we should not overlook the existence of a subsidiary sense which merely means an omission to do, let us say in a situation where doing is either the norm or expected. In the first sense I failed to start the car one snowy morning, in the second sense I failed to keep a rather important appointment last week. Can one try and fail, in both these senses, in the simple case of trying to attend to a sensation? I do not think so: I do not think it is possible in the first sense. The only cases of trying and failing that I can come upon are of the second kind, viz. changes or abandonment of project, whether through fascination at the hands of another object, or through boredom, or sheer forgetfulness. Each of these causal influences lead, not to the unsuccessfulness of the project, but to its termination. It is true that we sometimes mean by 'trying to listen', trying to keep my mind on the task of trying to listen, trying for example to fight off the deflecting power of these alien influences, and here of course one can fail; but that is irrelevant, seeing that this is a different variety of failure.

I should like to emphasise four points. (1) The substitution of sensation for sound is irrelevant to the question at issue. Thus, the auditory mechanism, which in regular fashion automatically generates here-and-now audibility-to-one, *precedes* the operation of the supposed mechanism under discussion; and it is the latter I reject (for there is no mechanistic 'how' whereby an attempt to listen to a ticking clock succeeds). (2) I am restricting the discussion to simple cases like single sounds and sensations: the reason being, if we do not understand active attending in these situations, we will certainly not understand it when the object of attending waxes in complexity. The operative policy is: first things first. (3) By 'try' I mean, not 'try to get myself to try' (e.g. take a stiff whisky) or 'try to keep myself trying' (e.g. think of the money), not (for example) 'try to stand over myself and prevent myself from trying instead to listen in to that juicy piece of gossip over there' – but (purely and simply) 'try' (which cannot be better described). Whereas the former tryings are all of them second-order phenomena, the latter trying is first-order. (4) The issue is not, '*What does one do* to succeed in the enterprise?', but '*What mechanism* makes the enterprise successful?' My suggestion is: *no mechanism* makes a genuine trying to attend to a sensation, a genuine attending to that sensation. Regress is the nemesis lying in wait for those who keep insisting that we 'go on'.

It is for reasons of this kind that I believe we are dealing here, not with a flawless or perfect mechanism, but with no mechanism at all. This constitutes a breakdown of the model of bodily action, since mechanism-activation is of its essence; and a breakdown incidentally of the model of voluntary recollection, for the same reason; which we must set beside breakdown again of the model provided by Soliloquy, in this case on the count of the inexistence of an analogue of hearing. We have here a demonstration of the earlier claim, that active attending instantiates a novel fourth act-structure. An act-structure, I should add, of which we are as yet wholly ignorant.

3 *The structure of attending*

(a) *The Identity Theory*

(1) The investigation of the structure of attending must be pursued beyond this point. We have just seen that the comparison with bodily action holds

both in respect of will, and willed event, but breaks down on the count of mechanism. This seems to simplify the picture: we are apparently concerned with nothing more than the relations between active attending, awareness, and the will to attend – with only a few structural relations possible: the problem of structure boils down to that. However, the very factor which led to the deletion of the element of mechanism, raises a new difficulty: to wit, the spectre of necessary causation, from cause to effect, between distinct existents! Namely: between the attempt to direct the attention onto, and the event of awareness. To be sure, the mind, almost like phenomena at quantum level, has the habit of savaging Principles which at a macroscopic and/or merely physical level seem sacrosanct; nonetheless one understandably quails a little before endorsing the reality of such a state of affairs. And yet if failure, if only in the simple cases under consideration, is in the central sense of 'failure' downright inconceivable, it is difficult to see how it can be avoided. But now a desperate expedient comes to mind. Thus, it frequently enough has turned out, when necessary causation seemed on the face of it a reality, that what in fact was happening was that we were merely juggling with necessarily linked descriptions of the one phenomenal item. Could that be how matters stand in the present case?

What are the two elements that are supposedly linked by this improbable bond? They are: the attempt to direct the attention onto a sensation; and the event of awareness of that sensation. But why should we believe that these phenomena are *two and distinct*? Why should we not endorse the view that in actual fact they are one and the same event travelling under different descriptions? This view I shall dub the 'Identity Theory'. It is in effect a theory of act-structure, and its examination advances the overall project of uncovering the true structure of active attending. Then let me at this point spell out precisely what the Identity Theory involves. Now one might at first be inclined to think that, when (say) listening occurs, three particular events are taking place: trying to listen, listening itself, and hearing: maybe distinct from one another, maybe overlapping in places, but enumerable as three. The Identity Theory disagrees: where some may see three such events, and some perhaps no more than two, it sees but one: a solitary event travelling under three descriptions. What is said to justify the multiplicity of characters available to this phenomenon is the complex character of its immediate origins.

When a hearing occurs that is the immediate effect of certain act-progenitors which are expressly dedicated to its occurrence, which is to say phenomena like act-desire and intention with hearing as content, the resultant hearing qualifies for the additional descriptions, 'trying to hear' and 'listening'. Thus, listening is on this account the active occurrence of hearing, not in the sense in which arm-raising is the active occurrence of arm-rise, but in the strict and simple sense of sheer identity. *This* hearing, on this particular occasion, *is* this listening. That is the claim. Accordingly, the activeness of this example of hearing/listening will be a derivative and therefore inessential property: the phenomenon must be essentially a hearing, inessentially a listening, and inessentially active. That is, provided any psychological properties are essential.

(2) This theory has distinct theoretical assets, over and above the virtue of eschewing necessary causation, from cause to effect, between distinct existents. Thus, it identifies the successful attempt and the deed, and this is in accord with a general principle which, for reasons I shall not rehearse here, strikes me as extremely sound. And the offending element of mechanism is, on this theory, banished from the scene. And a precedent exists for the act-structure envisaged by the theory: namely, the strangely simple structure exemplified by the aforementioned phenomenon of silent speech. In addition, the theory has the merit of keeping listening and hearing together – which is surely a virtue: thus, it does not postulate them as two and distinct, and in the strongest possible sense listening on this account involves hearing. Finally, it has the virtue of vindicating the intuition that listening is active through and through; for on this theory no alien inactive element is introduced into listening, which is to say a supposedly inactive hearing-part. And, of course, the theory has economy and simplicity.

(3) Nevertheless, these advantages do not constitute a demonstration. And in fact there exists a more or less decisive disproof of the Identity Theory. A first indication of its falsity is given merely by the oddity of some of the things that would be true or that we should have to say were the theory correct. There should be such a thing as rational hearing; we should be able to say that we were 'engaged in' or 'occupied in' hearing; and we would have our own reasons for hearing, which would exhaustively constitute its cause. A more significant argument against the theory is to be found in the following indubitable fact: that absolutely *all* listenings are active, and that some hearings *at the very least* are inactive. Now this constitutes a convincing reason for believing that hearing is as

such an inactive phenomenon. I say so because the mind is full of phenomena whose will-status is fixed merely by their kind: for example, belief, emotion, desire, and for that matter trying or willing itself. It seems like a general rule that, while some inactive phenomena can actively be engineered with varying degrees of immediacy, no phenomenon that is sometimes inactive ever occurs as active – and vice versa. When is a willing inactive? Accordingly the fact that *some* hearings are indubitably inactive is a strong reason for believing that hearing *as such* and therefore the hearings *contemporaneous with listening* are also inactive.

We encounter an even stronger argument against the Identity Theory when we consider the question of origins. It goes without saying that listening is an activity, and it therefore also goes without saying that it has its immediate source in phenomena of the type of act-desire, intention, choice. Now there is no room amongst these immediate progenitor-phenomena for the sensation that is the immediate material object of attending, or for the sound that is the material object of listening. If I choose to attend to a sensation, that sensation is a cause of my attending only in so far as it appears as incentive or goal in the intention and desire which generated the process of attending. It does not, and cannot, function as immediate cause, in the way that is open to act-desire, snap-decision, and suchlike appointed act-sources. But the Causal Theory of Perception requires, and in any case the facts of the matter demand, that absolutely any event of perception have its source, at least in part, in the perceived object. If it did not, how would perception be a way of knowing about the World? Then when the object of perception is an immediate object of the kind of sensation, the causation is and has to be at once immediate and unrationalised. And the perception that occurs when we actively or voluntarily attend to a sensation, can be no exception to this rule. While the Will is implicated in its origin, so too of absolute necessity is the sensation itself, acting directly and without the mediating assistance of desire, intention, decision, and the like. This after all is the rationale underlying the impropriety of the aforementioned speech-form: 'my reason for hearing'. In sum, if listening were active hearing, the sound must be an immediate unrationalised cause of hearing. But it cannot be. How could listening ever be rational if it were?

Accordingly, I reject the Identity Theory. And in fact I do not see how one could fail to reject it. If the theory were true, a particular example of perception would have to be identical with a particular trying, striving, act

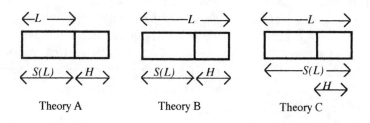

Figure 2

of the Will! But can *any* perceiving ever *be* a striving to do? Surely not. Surely perception is, of its nature and therefore universally, a responding-to or suffering-of at the hands of its object, howsoever much this may be intentionally engineered by the being who suffers such self-engineered experience.

(b) *The structural analysis of Attending*
(1) The situation is as follows. I am attempting to provide a structural analysis of the phenomenon of listening, or more generally of voluntarily attending. I began by comparing it to what I take to be the most ancient, unambiguous, and best understood instance of the act-genus: namely, bodily action. I uncovered in listening two precise structural analogues of the latter: first the act of the Will, second the event that the Will is bent upon producing, in this case the continuing awareness-of or hearing-of the actively attended-to or listened-to. Meanwhile it emerged that a third and vitally important element of bodily action, that of the mechanism whereby the Will achieves its goal, was nowhere to be found in the phenomenon of attending. In the light of the breakdown of this model, and the abandonment of the Identity Theory, what structural theories of active attention remain as viable options? Three theories suggest themselves – call them (A), (B) and (C) – which I now represent diagrammatically (*L* stands for Listening, *S(L)* for Striving-to-listen, *H* for Hearing). I shall discuss these theories in the order given by the diagrams in Figure 2.

First, a comparison or image as a possible model for listening. Namely: that of reaching out a hand and touching something. Thus, noticing is in certain ways like the mind being touched by a psychic thing. Then why should we not actively produce this inactive event? Why should we not conceive of active attending as akin to the active extending of a mental hand in order to generate the inactive event of psychic contact? Alas, persuasive as this picture may be, it must be rejected forthwith. If it were true, that which is active when we attend would lead to and fall outside the confines of its goal event: attentive-contact. This is the first (A) of the three structural theories, and it is plainly wrong. What in effect it claims is that listening *causes* the hearing that listening entails. But it is absurd to suppose that listening and hearing are two and distinct. They cannot as we have seen be identical; but just as certainly they cannot be held apart. There can be no doubt that listening *involves*, but is not actually to be identified with, the hearing that is guaranteed by its occurrence.

Only two theories appear to be viable at this point. Let us remember that the structural raw materials consist in three items: listening, trying to listen, and hearing. No more; and in particular no mechanism, no concealed sector, no subterranean unexperienced part. Finally, we have the following decisive constraints upon theory-formation: the falsity of the Identity Theory, and the non-distinctnesss of listening and hearing. All that remains is to decide between the theory (C) that identifies listening and trying to listen, and the theory (B) that would make the latter phenomenon part of the former. That is, if the above three theoretical accounts exhaust the possibilities – which they certainly seem to do.

I will be brief here. The one theoretical asset of Theory (B) is the fact that according to this theory the exercise of the Will is explanatory of hearing. By and large this is true; though with qualification, as we shall shortly see. For the most part, had one not *listened* one would not have experienced *such* a hearing as in fact occurred. Now this is the doctrine that involves grasping the nettle of necessary-or-near causation from cause to effect between distinct existents, since according to it the act of the Will is distinct from and cause-in-part of hearing; and this relation must, at least in the simple cases under consideration, verge upon necessity. No doubt this characteristic does not automatically disqualify the theory, but it is at the very least a disincentive. In any case other considerations render it unacceptable. First it runs counter to the Principle that the successful attempt is the succeeded-in deed, which for a variety of reasons recommends itself.[1] Second it embeds one act as non-distinct part of

---

[1]Notably the fact that the theory is demonstrably true of absolutely all instrumental actions, whether intentional or unintentional, mental or physical. Thus, the attempt to open the door that took the form of giving a kick is identical with the act of door-opening of which it was the means. Such an account exemplifies a completely universal Principle; and holds for completely general reasons. Then to the latter weighty consideration we add the fact, that not to identify successful attempt and succeeded-in deed, would be to 'embed one act as

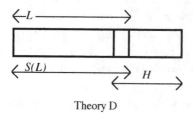

Theory D

Figure 3

another, despite the fact that the supposed 'two' deeds have token-identical act-producer origins. And so on.

(2) The remaining third theory (C) is the doctrine that identifies listening and attempt, and locates hearing as an inactive non-identical part of listening. Let me very briefly run over a few of the theoretical virtues of this account. It eschews mechanism and necessary causation between distinct existents. Identifies act and successful attempt. Disidentifies listening and hearing; yet at the same time holds them together. Thus, it does not suppose listening to be distinct from, and a necessary cause of, hearing: instead it recognises that listening *involves* hearing. Again it does not construe listening as a mere amalgam of an active first half and an inactive resultant second half, offering a sort of oil-and-water account from the point of view of the Will: it does not do so, since on this theory listening itself is an action, and that is that. To be sure listening is said to include the inactive element of hearing; but that no more splits the act into act and non-act than does the presence of arm-rise in arm-raising. In a perfectly good sense, both acts are acts through and through to the end, in despite of encompassing inactive elements. Hearing goes on in its own right in listening, literally overflowed by the Will. What, by contrast, must be avoided in any acceptable account, is the supposition that the event of willing produces a distinct inactive hearing, which would as a result 'come at one' rather like the recoil of a gun. But on the present account hearing no more 'comes at one' than does arm-rise in arm-raising. So much for the virtues of Theory (C). I accept it – qualifiedly. We shall see that it stands

---

non-identical part of another, despite the fact that the supposed "two" deeds have token-identical act-producer origins' (to repeat the above).

in need of precisification or emendation: the emendation that we replace 'hearing is part of listening' by 'part of hearing is part of listening'.[2] I shall call this emendation Theory (D) (see Figure 3). (But, as we shall see, the time for pictures is past.)

Now because the above emendation is a direct consequence of the special explanatory situation that obtains within listening, a proper examination of that emendation must be postponed until Section 5. In the meantime we must deflect the discussion towards the latter explanatory issue.

4   Justifying the existence of active perception

(a) The problem of double causation

Let me at this point review the account of listening that Theory (D) provides. The situation is said to be something like this. A sound exists, or maybe a sensation, of which already we are aware; and for one reason or another this knowledge generates the impulse and intent actively to attend to it. Thus, it produces a Will-to-listen that turns out to *be* a successful listening, with regard to which the sound is at once immediate material object *and* immediate unrationalised part-cause of the hearing-sector of this same listening. This is what is said to occur when we engage in listening. Now how does this account sort with our earlier misgivings that actively and immediately to 'do' one's own perceivings would in effect constitute a violation of the very being of Will and Perception? Has the supposed inconceivable been after all accomplished? What is left of the original intuition which was to the effect that action arises from within, perception arises from without, so never the twain shall immediately meet? Has this been invalidated by the theory of Listening or Attending that we have endorsed?

A vital element in this account (Theory (D)) of listening is the necessity of immediate unrationalised causation of the hearing-sector of listening at the hands of a distinct external sound-object. Just how does this work? I ask, because I detect a difficulty. Well, the sound-object has nothing whatsoever to do with the immediate genesis of willing, but much to do with the immediate genesis of the hearing it encompasses. But surely if it

---

[2] I owe this suggestion to Dr Jeremy Butterfield, who drew my attention to this possibility when I read a version of part of this paper to The Moral Sciences Club at Cambridge in February 1991.

helps to cause part of listening, it helps to cause listening itself? What is the way out of this difficulty? It is to differentiate. The sound is not immediately responsible in the least degree for the occurrence of the event that is a listening, but has much to do with its being a listening. Rather as biceps-contraction has nothing to do with the occurrence of the event that is arm-raising, but much to do with its being an arm-raising – so here. The immediate progenitors of action, which include act-desire and act-intention and suchlike, cannot include sound or sensation – and that is that. It is a universal rule, applicable alike to listening and arm-raising. Rationality in action depends upon it.

(b) *A statement of the problem of justification*

(1) This response may answer the problem of double causation, which is to say the problem of the simultaneous causation from within and without of the phenomenon of listening. But does it constitute an effective response to the intuition that the *self-originating character* of active perceiving is inconsistent with the *elsewhere-originated* character of perception? Can we offer a comparable differential response to this suggestion? Consider the following attempt to do so. Listening arises from within; whereas what determines that it *is* listening, and not just *trying* to listen, arises in part from without. But how does this comment, accurate enough in its own right, bear on the above? The trouble with this statement lies in the account that it offers of the genesis of *the hearing* involved in listening. It shares this out between Will and sound-object. Yet how can a veridical perception owe its existence, in even the least degree, to an immediate will-source? Is it not like supposing that rational belief might derive in part from will or desire? How can a belief be rational and derive in even the least degree immediately from desire?

Before I can attempt to meet this difficulty, I must make a few general comments concerning the structural analysis of listening implicit in the present theory of listening. The first thing to say is that, at least from the point of view of the other three act-models, listening proves to have *a decidedly odd structure*. The theory we have endorsed might at first look like a vindication of the physical-act model – minus the factor of mechanism; for in both cases the successful act of the Will encompasses, so to say as its crown or culmination, the event that was the aim of the whole enterprise: namely, the hearing-sector that would not have occurred were it not for the exercising of the Will. But on closer inspection it can be seen that in fact listening does not duplicate basic bodily action – with or without mechanism. Just how this is so, is directly relevant to the problem raised in the aforementioned intuition. Thus a condition of listening is, not merely as in physical action that the desired goal event owe its existence to Will, but that this very same sector of itself be simultaneously caused by an external event! Nothing like this exists in physical action. And the very oddity of its make-up forbids our construing listening as instrumental action of *any* kind, let us say as a sort of mental touching of its immediate object. For a necessary condition of listening is, not as in instrumentality that it *cause* a distinct external event, but a somewhat mystifying inversion of that requirement, according to which a sector of itself must in part be *caused by* an external! Indeed, the comparison with instrumentality is doubly askew. For an instrumental act *is what it is* irrespective of causing the manipulated event: thus, it might be a turning of a key or a moving of an arm; but listening in the absence of part-causation at the hands of the sound is no more than a failed striving to listen. And that is why I say it has an odd structure. It *completes itself* through external assistance. To be sure, physical action stands in need of causal co-operation from the environment if it is to come to birth, for it is a necessary condition of limb-moving that limb-movement be possible; but surely not in the same way. In a word, listening, and indeed active attending generally, realises an extremely novel act-structure, to be set alongside the three other exemplars: active recollection, silent speech, and physical action. All are, I suggest, 'originals'.

(2) I return to the problem raised by the intuition. The problem is double. It is double because it involves a double paradox concerning action and perception. Thus: how can there so much as *exist* an act-structure in which the actively engineered goal-event owes its existence in part to an external event? And: how can we immediately and willingly produce in ourselves that which of its very nature must be determined *from without*? I believe that the resolution of this problem lies in the differentiation of the modes of causation-of-hearing, open on the one hand to striving-to-listen, and on the other hand to the heard object itself.

We know that in physical action willing leads causally to the desired bodily movement through the regular working of mechanism. Given certain standing conditions, willing is at once a tight sufficient condition-of and an explanation-of willed bodily movement. How does listening compare on this count? What explanatory situation prevails there? Whatever it is, we shall not I think have completed the characterisation of this fourth type of act-schema, until we answer this question. Accordingly, the explanatory situation in listening comes to the fore, in part to help us fill this important gap, in part to resolve the aforementioned puzzle; which is, in effect, to explain the very possibility of such an unusual act-schema.

(c) *The function of listening*

So at this point I raise a simple but fundamental question which until now I have ignored. *Why* do we listen? What is *the function* of listening? More exactly: is the function of trying to listen to *generate hearing*? Does trying to listen *causally explain* hearing? Now to explain why we listen must, one presumes, be to ask for the content of the impelling desire and intention which lead to the movement of the Will. For in listening we aim to take control of our hearings, we seek to remove them from the wilderness of pure chance and to site them firmly in an ordered network of particular purposes. Then is the aim of listening the production of hearing? I think the answer is: yes, and no. A counter-factual question reveals something of the complexities in this issue. Thus: would we have heard the sound we listened to, had we not listened to it? Then in many cases the answer is that we would. And yet, despite the force of this consideration, the content of the impelling act-desire cannot but be to produce hearing. Only it is not just any old hearing that we seek, it is rather a select hearing that is endowed with certain desired properties. Some of those properties are external properties, while some are internal and pertain to content. Thus, one might listen simply in order to hear; but sometimes it will be, not just to hear, but to hear *for certain*; and sometimes it will be, not so much to hear, but to hear *well* or *continuously* or *for all of five seconds*. These are external properties. But one can in addition pursue internal properties of content: for example, a differential perception of timbre, or of pitch, or volume.

Given these several kinds of properties of the internal object of trying to listen, we now re-phrase the earlier explanatory question, taking due account of their existence. Does trying to produce a hearing that is (say) guaranteed, and continuous, and a good example of the type; that is of timbre, or pitch, or whatever-it-be – does a trying with such differential content cause a hearing blessed with such properties? What, in other words, does listening actually *accomplish*? This should tell us what is its causal role or *natural function*. Once again a counter-factual sheds light on the situation. Let us suppose that there exists a soft monotone sound S

which endures for n seconds; and suppose you bring to bear such a listening project upon it; and at the end that you have heard S, continuously, well, and so forth. Can you assert that, in the absence of such action, such a hearing would not have occurred? You can say nothing so simple. The answer must be given both differentially and in probabilistic terms. Thus, you *can* say: in the absence of such a listening project it is *very unlikely* that you would have experienced a hearing endowed with the full battery of desired properties; and you *can* say that it is *unlikely* that you would have experienced a hearing that was (say) both a case of hearing well, and continuous; and you can say finally that it is *quite possible* that you would have heard the sound itself. What you cannot do is *to assert categorically*: 'trying to listen, with such and such an internal object, aided and abetted by the sound itself, was causally responsible for a hearing endowed with such and such properties'. But you are entitled to make a series of probabilistic causal claims. Thus, you are entitled to say: 'very probably, trying to listen, taken in conjunction with the sound-object, was causally responsible for the fact that a hearing occurred that was endowed with the full battery of desired properties'. And you are entitled to say: 'probably, trying to listen was causally responsible for the fact that a hearing occurred that was both continuous and a good example of the kind'. And finally: 'possibly, trying to listen caused the very event of hearing itself'.

Thus, willing is in general a probabilistic causal explanation of the hearing that occurred in listening, an explanation whose probability-value rises with the expansion and development of the content of the hearing involved. But it is never entirely certain, never categorical, always probabilistic: a fact which is doubtless a reflection of sorts of the natural turbulence of the mind, of the fact that there is no stationary *status quo* which is disturbed more or less by Will alone – by contrast with our limbs. So what is the answer to the original question: what does listening actually *accomplish*? There exists a much closer match between what is actually heard and what one sought to hear, than between what is heard and what listening accomplishes. What it accomplishes consists in, what is heard less what would have been heard had listening not occurred: an answer that must be cast in probabilistic terms. So much for the causal role of listening. Then it must at this point be emphasised that all of the above constitutes a decisive break, on the count of explanatory character, with the basic physical model of action. We have already noted a departure, consisting in the absence of mechanism; and a somewhat more radical departure, consisting in the fact that listening stands causally in need of assistance from without if it is to complete itself; but the gross unlikeness of the rationale linking Will and success, in the two cases, takes us far afield from the original model. It serves to emphasise the truth of the claim that we are in the presence of a fourth wholly 'original' schema for action.

(d) *The attractive character of listening*

Now I earlier remarked that the resolution of the puzzle concerning the very existence of this schema lay in the differentiation of the modes of causation-of-hearing, open on the one hand to striving-to-listen, and on the other hand to the heard object itself. We are now I believe in a position to carry this out. We have just noted that the former brand of causation must be expressed in probabilistic terms. Nevertheless, willing-to-listen has a definite causal power, and definitely explains. Not categorically, not on its own, and not through the agency of mechanism, but probabilistically and with the assistance of the distinct external auditory object. How does it manage to do this? Well, we should note that the causal power of the will-to-listen is a function of its own *internal object*. Given a fixed particular external auditory object, one might bring to bear upon it a whole series of different intentional strivings – each with a different causal power – and result. This power is in the nature of an *attractive power*, and it is determined wholly by choice. Thus, selecting whatever feature it is that interests us, let us say the timbre of the sound, we overtly *open the door* to timbre's causal influence upon the Attention. We actively do this. We actively make the Attention open to influence at the hands of timbre, we do what slants any occurrent hearing in this particular direction, and thereby ensure that the Attention lights upon timbre. In this regard the act is not unlike an instrumental act – though strangely in reverse. Thus, we actually *enlist* the timbre of the sound as an external cause of timbre-hearing, through specifically 'grooming' any possible hearing for timbre-affectedness. This trying, that the Attention be thus influenced, is the continuous creation of a causally influential mould; and as the desired effect of this on-going mental work occurs, which is to say a hearing of the desired kind, an act-edifice is completed, namely listening to the heard feature of the sound. Thus, it is not pure mystery that listening has the causal power that it has. It may be a mystery that such things can exist, but it is no mystery that, existing as they do, they have the powers that they have. That, precisely, is their nature. And neither is it a mystery, when that power finds successful expression, that it effects what it effects. It can do no other.

What are we to say then of an act that unites free choice with unchosen external influence? How can such a thing be possible? I think we should reply as follows. That the very nature of the enterprise is the setting-up of an attractive force that draws such responses onto itself; that the creation of that force is almost in the nature of suction, the creation of a vacuum apt specifically to be filled by whatever item the mind of the listener so desires. Then that the completion of this process should occur from without, makes of it neither lucky accident nor chance visitation; for the force that took the form of striving or listening-for took as its object just such an occurrence. Thus, the external influence or sound, while being unquestionably external to both listening and mind, is in no sense an unchosen external influence: its power was conferred upon it from within: it was a chosen external influence. In this sense the external sound, while no part of the listening process, is part of a natural causal system. Perhaps this constitutes explanation enough. Perhaps this resolves the puzzle.

5   *The rationale of Theory (D)*

(1) Theory (C) states that listening is a Will-to-listen that non-mechanistically encompasses the hearing co-present with listening. Then provided we understand 'the hearing' to refer to whatever hearing is entailed by listening, the theory is correct as it stands. But if we take it to refer to the whole-event hearing entailed by listening, then explanatory considerations force one to amend the theory and replace it by Theory (D), according to which listening encompasses only *part of* that hearing. It is time to provide the rationale of this emendation. This requires that I elucidate the closely linked concepts of Structure and Part appealed to in these theories.

The theories in question are *structural* theories. Characterising the structure of an item consists in charting the relations that constitute the item out of a set of its parts. Just what those parts are, depends upon the principle of partitioning. This can take multiple forms: it could be any one out of a number of purely spatial divides, or it might instead be purely temporal in type, or it could divide the item into sets of autonomous individuals, and so on. Some parts will therefore be individuals, such as a car battery; while some contingently will not, such as the first half of a skid; and some could not conceivably be individuals, like the moral part of the mind. Roughly, partitioning an item consists in itemising 'what goes to make it up'. As noted above, the 'what' is protean.

Theories (A)–(C) are structural theories, not merely of *mental actions*, but of *the situation required* if a mental act of a certain type is to be instantiated. Then the Soliloquy proved on investigation to have no event-parts and therefore no event-structure, and this constitutes one significant structural possibility; while the relevant structure of event-parts in the case of the act of Recollection, is the structure of an Act-Situation that encompasses act, mechanism, remembering. But we must recognise that other principles of partitioning would yield different structures of different parts in either of these cases. This option becomes increasingly relevant when explanatory considerations highlight the shortcomings of Theory (C). Thus, the analysis of listening into *event-parts* turns out to be an inadequate instrument for the understanding of the relation between listening and the whole-event hearing that is contemporaneous with listening. This will emerge below.

(2) At this point I need to delineate several related concepts: some of them of actualities, some merely ideal. These concepts are of use in characterising the explanatory situation in listening.

(α) The set of all the audible qualities of a sound: $\{q_s\}$.

(β) Maximal listening: a maximally intense listening to all of $\{q_s\}$: L_{MAX}.

(γ) Maximal hearing: a maximally intense hearing of all of $\{q_s\}$: H_{MAX}.

(δ) Actualised listening: a distributed-intense listening to part of $\{q_s\}$: L_{ACT}.

(ϵ) Actualised hearing: a distributed-intense hearing of part of $\{q_s\}$: H_{ACT}.

Meanwhile, actual and ideal explanatory situations are as follows:

(θ) L_{MAX} & H_{MAX} & (L_{MAX} completely explains H_{MAX}).

(ϕ) L_{ACT} & H_{ACT} & (L_{ACT} completely explains H_{ACT}).

(ψ) L_{ACT} & H_{ACT} & (L_{ACT} partially explains H_{ACT}).

A few comments on these concepts and supposed explanatory situations. The ideal listening (β) and hearing (γ) are doubtless unrealisable; and so too *a fortiori* is the explanatory ideal (θ). The explanatory conjecture that I find interesting is (ϕ). Is it in principle realisable? Now the causal and explanatory power of a Will-to-listen is a function both of the range of its internal object, and the intensity of the Will-to-listen. For of what else? Accordingly, a valid guiding principle must be: the more a listening approaches L_{MAX}, the more it tends both to engender *and* to explain an H_{MAX}. Then how can an L_{ACT} ever *maximally* explain an H_{ACT}? If a particular listening is (say) merely to the qualities *a* and *b* (let us call it L_{ab}), and if it is very far from intense in character, how could it ever *maximally* explain a contemporaneous H_{abcd}? And it could not. This demonstrates the unrealisability of (ϕ) – and the validity of (ψ); which, anyhow, already was evident from the earlier discussion concerning the *accomplishments* of listening. In a word, not all of any hearing that is contemporaneous with listening to that heard, owes its existence to that listening.

(3) It is this fact which pushes us beyond Theory (C) to Theory (D). Now we have just referred to 'all of' a hearing, and thus implicitly to parts. But what principle of partitioning is involved? The partitioning must be such as to help us to answer 'What goes to make up an H_{ACT}?', it cannot be temporal in character since it applies in each instant, and must surely be a qualitative divide. In this particular framework we will assemble (say) an H_{abcd} out of the parts H_a, H_b, H_c, H_d, without supposing that we are referring to actual or potential individual existents. Thus, we might descriptively assemble an H_{ACT} that is an H_{abcd} out of (say): H_a (very well) & H_b (hardly at all) & H_c (marginally) & H_d (well). Then this is the variety of part that we need if we are to state Theory (D), and do justice to the unusual explanatory situation which came to light in the discussion in Section 4(c). But we need in addition a principle of act-constitution.

The principle that we need takes as its point of departure the following question. If a sound is listened-to and one of its qualities heard or noticed; and if that noticing is due in only the smallest degree to the occurrence of the Will-to-listen, so that the audible quality would almost certainly have come to our attention had we not engaged in listening; then what can be the justification for assimilating the hearing of that audible quality inside the boundaries of the phenomenon of listening? It is because I can think of none, that the following principle recommends itself to me. Namely: to the extent that the part of hearing H_x under consideration owes its existence to the Will-to-listen, to that same extent the part of hearing is part of the listening.

This principle governs the H-constitution of L. It enables us to determine the extent of the overlap of L and H. Then as we have already discovered, that extent can only be *probabilistically expressed*! This is because the explanatory justification for citing such an extent is probabilistic in character. And so we shall find that we have to make claims of the following kind: that it is $m\%$ likely that part H_a is part of listening, and $n\%$ likely that H_b is part of listening, etc. And we shall in addition have to accept that listening-hood is never anything more than probabilistically realised: that *absolute listening* is a myth! A strange state of affairs, to be sure; and a direct consequence of the fact that the *status quo* in which listening springs up is a setting of natural turbulence, disturbance of the attention being the norm. And yet it is not really alarming to my way of thinking (though it must surely imply that the utility of diagrammatic representations is at an end). Thus, it does not imply that the event that is listening has only probabilistically-given boundaries, since it is the concept of Will rather than of listening that binds this phenomenon in one piece; and neither does it carry such an implication in the case of the hearing contemporaneous with listening, for the concept of hearing likewise unifies this event. On the other hand it undoubtedly implies that what listening is said to encompass in the way of hearing, has only a certain likelihood of being present; and that in consequence the instantiation of listening-hood itself is only probable (however high the measure of that probability may be). Many a 'listening' is a case of 'not properly listening', as few arm-raisings are malformations of the type. As we have already observed, it is all very strange. But then why not? This unusual structural state of affairs is after all being realised in a unique, highly developed, and ontologically novel sector of Reality: the mind. Why should it take its cue from elsewhere?

Now before I conclude this discussion, I must try to complete the resolution of the difficulty that I have labelled 'The Antitheticality-Puzzle'. This was left in a state of suspension at the end of Section 4(d).

6 *The resolution of the antitheticality-puzzle*
(1) It is significant that the Antitheticality-Problem presents itself in the form of *a puzzle*. A puzzle has the form: certain unexceptionable premises p and q appear to drive one irresistibly towards a contradiction; and finds expression in a question of the form: '*How can it be* that p & q?' The presence of contradiction suggests the possibility of dialectical resolution, the replacement of false antitheses by the appearance of a novel, more

developed, and enlarged concept of the elements involved. Something like this seems to be at work in the present situation. Now the Antitheticality-Puzzle is not, 'How can it be that the hearing involved in listening owes its existence to the Will?', seeing that we continually stage-manage our own perceivings through such active bodily means as head-swivelling, eyelid-opening, sniffing, etc. The puzzle follows upon the expulsion of mechanism from listening. It is expressed in the question: 'How can the veridical hearing that is involved in listening derive in even the least degree *immediately* from the Will?' The difficulty being, that willing in and of itself is entirely without cognitive significance, while perception is of necessity a kind of window opening out onto Reality. How can a Reality-recorder be absolutely-immediately responsive to movements of the Will?

Underlying this puzzlement is a particular conception of the genesis of the hearing that is involved in listening. Thus, the abandonment of mechanism and the rejection of the Identity Theory, taken in conjunction with the truth of the claim that the Will-to-listen explains the occurrence of the hearing involved in listening, demonstrate that the Will-to-listen immediately causally explains the hearing that completes listening. But the Causal Theory of Perception requires that the sound – and in my view its internal sensation-representation – also cause the hearing. Thus, the hearing must have *two* simultaneous causes, one operating from within and the other from without; indeed, if the theory of the sensation is correct, it must have two simultaneous *immediate psychological causes*. More, two simultaneous causes which are *distinct existents*. Accordingly, it looks as if the hearing in question is fathered into existence by two distinct causal agencies, acting in consort simultaneously and from opposite directions. Such a structure of causes seems to be the only operative possibility in the case of the hearing involved in listening; while the only variety of causal power open to the Will-to-listen seems to be of the type, Contributory-Condition.

The Antitheticality-Puzzle shows that there is something wrong with the above account of the genesis of the hearing in listening. It is true that one might try simply to undo the puzzle: for example, by the abandonment of the theoretical position we have adopted on the issue of mechanism; which is to say, by the re-introduction of mechanism into the act of listening. But the arguments against such a move are, I think, too strong: notably, the argument from regress (of explanations). I can see nothing wrong with Theory (D); nor with the idea that the hearing involved in listening is at once caused by sound/auditory-sensation *and* simultaneously and immediately causally explained by the Will-to-listen. What I believe is at fault is the assumption that the causation involved is of the type of multiple determination: that it consists in the operation of distinct causal agencies. More specifically, the fault lies in the supposition that the unquestionably distinct existents Will and sound are distinct causal agencies in the generation of the hearing involved in listening. But precisely how this can be so, remains to be established.

A preliminary indication is given by the singular fact that no matter *how much* the Will-to-listen is causally explanatory of the hearing contemporaneous with listening, there is never any danger that it will become the *sole* explanation, nor even that it will *monopolise* the explanation – to the exclusion of the sound! The object of a perception must in an absolute and non-quantitative sense be a causal agency in *any* perceiving – quite irrespective of the causal efficacy of the Will. Plainly, these two causal agencies cannot act in the manner of 'joint contributors', for if they did one could outstrip the other in the extent of its 'contribution': a fact which strongly suggests that, even though these two phenomena are distinct existents, they cannot in this transaction be distinct causal agencies. Such a theoretical position immediately pushes one towards the instrumentalist re-instatement of mechanism in listening, according to which the Will-to-listen activates a device which ensures that the sound act causally upon the Attention; for this account accords with the non-distinctness of the causal roles of Will and sound. However, I do not follow that course. And yet it has at this point to be acknowledged that the resolution of the problem has something in common with instrumentalism; only it is not instrumentalism. Rather, it is what lies at a dialectical remove from it.

(2) To resume. Let 'H' stand for hearing, 's' for sound, '$S(L)$' for Strive-to-listen-to; and let us assume that we are attempting to discover which, amongst the experienced events at the time of listening, is the final or last determining cause of the hearing involved in listening. Then the question originally posed was: is $H \leftarrow s$ or $S(L) \rightarrow H$ or $S(L) \rightarrow H \leftarrow s$ the correct account of the causal situation? Bearing in mind the strict cognitive significance of perception, one cannot but feel that $H \leftarrow s$ must be correct. And I think it must. Nevertheless, we earlier saw that precisely to the extent to which H is absorbed into L, to that same extent the immediate causal claim $S(L) \rightarrow H$ must also be true. Therefore a certain interpretation

of $S(L) \rightarrow H \leftarrow s$ must be correct; only it is not the interpretation according to which $S(L)$ and s are 'joint contributors', which might as well be depicted as

$$\begin{array}{c} S(L) \rightarrow \\ s \rightarrow \end{array} H;$$

nor the instrumentalist interpretation in which a suppressed or hidden mechanism M appears in the above: viz, $S(L) \rightarrow M \rightarrow (H \leftarrow s)$. Rather, it is the theory that bears a certain resemblance to instrumentalism, lying a dialectical remove beyond it.

The raw materials for that theory, and for a different conception – for a kind of dialectical advance in understanding – of the causation in question, were already noted in Section 4(d), when we drew attention to the specific type of the causal power of the Will-to-listen: namely, attractive. This is the idea that the causal role open to the Will-to-listen is akin to the creation of a kind of vacuum in the Attention, which is apt to be filled uniquely by a particular sound. Now the creation of a vacuum is the doing of some deed x, that generates a vacuum y, which we suppose to be specifically apt for the generation of a unique filler-event z. Then it is clear that this valuable model must be flawed in some fundamental respect; for if it was wholly accurate, instrumentalism would be vindicated and mechanism re-instated within the act of listening. The correct account, as I see the matter, differs from the above precisely on this score. Thus, this theory does not analyse 'Strive-to listen', as 'Willingly generate some y that is specifically apt for generating hearing'. Rather, according to this account the phenomenon striving-to-listen-to-sound-s simply *is* a doing that is specifically apt for generating s's causing hearing-of-s. That is, it is an active event which is directed towards a sound-object, and that is specifically endowed with the following causal power: to cause its sound-object to cause hearing-of-that-sound. Now this latter causal power might well be possessed by a variety of phenomena. For example, a training which repeatedly stressed the importance of hearing some impending single noise, makes it more likely that one notice the noise when it occurs and therefore that the sound cause hearing of itself; and such a training must for these reasons be credited with such a causal power. Then what is special about the phenomenon Will-to-listen is that the means it employs are non-existent and the power it possesses is essential.

(3) The Will-to-listen $S(L)$ is an active event directed towards hearing H, with the power to cause the causing of H by the sound s: a characterisation that is at once essentialist and exhaustive. $S(L)$ is thus an

active power to confer a power – with which it is non-identical and which it takes unto itself; for *S(L)* comes by the power to cause hearing by conferring that power upon the sound. It is therefore a strange situation: *S(L)*'s causing a causing neither instantiates an instrumental causal structure, nor collapses into *S(L)*'s causing *H*, and yet *S(L)* and *s* share a token power to cause *H*. Let me now elucidate these latter three claims in order.

First, even though *S(L)* causes a causing, it does not do so instrumentally. 'Cause a causing' must not be understood in this sense. There are not two causings: *S(L)*'s producing some *y*, which produces *s*→*H*; nor *S(L)*'s producing *s*, which in turn produces *H*. There is *just S(L)* producing *s*→*H*. Yet how does *S(L)* do this? What is its way? *S(L)*'s very being is its 'way': for *S(L) is* a way of getting *s* to cause *H*: it is pure 'way'. That is, *S(L) is* the subject doing what – a 'what' that is never to be unpacked – causes *s* to cause *H*. So much for instrumentalist readings of 'cause a causing'.

I turn now secondly to the reading that collapses 'cause a causing' into 'cause'; that is, renders *S(L)*'s double-headed object as the causing of *H*. This likewise is a misconstrual. The truth of the matter is, that *S(L)*'s causing of *s*'s causing of *H* entails, but does not collapse into *S(L)*'s causing of *H*. If it did, *s* would drop out, and we would be left with the unacceptable *S(L)*→*H*. But in fact *S(L)* can cause *H* only if *s* causes *H* as a result of *S(L)*; and this demonstrates that *s* has an indispensable irreducible causal role in this transaction.

The third thing to say is that even though the causal powers of *S(L)* and *s* are non-identical, they are also non-distinct. *S(L)* and *s* are the one causal agency in *H*-production; for *S(L)*'s producing of *H is* the producing of *H* by an *s* that derives its power from *S(L)*. Thus, the token power to cause *H* is shared by *S(L)* and *s*. But it is not 'shared out' between them. This power is shared, not through division, but in common possession: they both possess the one token power – in entirety. It is the same relation as the 'in virtue of' relation of Perception-Theory. Just as the appearance of the north side of Mt Blanc is shared with Mt Blanc (from the north) without being shared out between them, being instead in common to these two non-identicals; so here.

In short, Will and sound are distinct existents with non-identical causal powers, which are simultaneous token-identical causal agencies in the generation of hearing: not in the mode of 'jointly contributory' agencies, nor that of instrumentally-linked agencies – but in a novel mode which bears a similarity to instrumentality. This novel mode, whereby distinct simultaneous existents can, non-instrumentally and non-distributively, share the one token causal power, is the novel mode of causation pointed towards dialectically by the seeming contradiction visible in the original puzzle.

The correct picture is: not $H \leftarrow s$; not $S(L) \rightarrow H$; not

$$S(L) \underset{s}{\overset{\rightarrow}{\rightarrow}} H;$$

not $S(L) \rightarrow s \rightarrow H$; not $S(L) \rightarrow M \rightarrow (H \leftarrow s)$; but $S(L) \rightarrow (H \leftarrow s)$.

7 Conclusion

(1) I began this paper by asking: Can we immediately perceive our own willings? Can we immediately will our own perceivings? The intuition in either case was that we could not, on the grounds that willing grows out of the mind while perception comes upon the mind from without. Naturally enough both intuitions allowed scope for *mediated* versions of these two transactions, seeing that we must have a measure of informational feedback concerning our interventions in the environment and a measure of control over when and where the environment acts perceptually upon us. The troubles begin when immediate mental causation replaces mediate causation in these situations. At that point these two elemental antithetical mental phenomena begin to look as if they might be too close for their own good.

In Section A I examined the first of the conjectured possibilities: the supposed immediate perception of our own willings. Here the original intuition proved to be correct. Despite the profound co-operativeness of action and perception in animal life generally, their individual characters and natural mental settings are such as to disallow the epistemological gap that is necessary if the putative perception is to have functional space. Because action has its origin in conscious internal phenomena like cognition and desire, the immediate perception of willing lacks a functional rationale and thus a foothold in existence. That is, it is because action comes into being already firmly contained within a cognitive setting, that action cannot be a psychologically immediate object for the attention. Thus far the original intuition is vindicated.

In Section C I addressed myself to the second question. The natural presumption was that the symmetry would hold: the supposition being that the immediately acting Will would prove to be as absolute an obstacle to Reality-confrontation in perception as is immediately expressed desire in the confrontation of knowledge with Truth: 'invented seeing' paralleling 'wishful thinking'. Strangely enough, matters have turned out differently, and the original intuition stands discredited. It is true that perception never *is* an action, any more than any action *is* a perception – but that is not what is at issue; which is instead the supposed immediate willing of perception: a concept that unquestionably poses problems for the understanding. A Spinozist Deity might perhaps be forgiven for finding such a concept unproblematic, but not us. Nevertheless, problematic or not, the concept emerged from the investigation unscathed.

(2) Then what went wrong with the intuition? The trouble almost certainly stemmed from the concept, *the immediate willing of* —. This perfectly legitimate concept inevitably conjures up images of the bodily Will, leading naturally to the assumption that 'the willing of —' designates as such a phenomenon of *pure invention*. Then it can I think be confidently stated that, if this was how matters stood, we would have something like an antinomy on our hands and the active modes of the attention would have to be outlawed. It is of the first importance in understanding the failure of the intuition, that the structure of these active modes (listening, looking, etc.) is significantly different from that of the bodily Will and is in any case *decidedly odd*. Thus, we earlier saw that listening manages to complete itself only with outside assistance: that it becomes something more than a merely failed striving only through the causation of its hearing-component at the hands of its distinct sound-object. And we have subsequently discovered that this causing is precisely to be identified with the causation of that hearing-component by the listening which encompasses it. So the 'willing of hearing' must depend for its success and indeed existence upon the causal action of a distinct objective reality. Such a 'willing of hearing' seems to me to be anything but 'pure inventing'. Then I suggest that the intuition foundered through one's bringing the central or prototypical purely inventive conception of *the willing of* — to bear upon a phenomenon which could not sustain it. An understandable mistake, since the phenomenon incarnates an unusual structure; but a mistake nonetheless.

Let me express the same point in different terms; for the failure of the intuition can be viewed in another revealing light. Thus, we earlier noted that the aforementioned completion of listening from outside is non-instrumental in character, seeing that instrumental acts acquire instrumental status by causing what lies at a remove from their boundaries, whereas listening in a strange reversal of structure acquires its status as listening by inverting the direction of instrumental causation. Nevertheless something *reminiscent* of instrumentality is realised in listening, for the

Will here *uses* its distinct sound-object to cause what it itself seeks to cause. Now we have already remarked that the instrumental mode of 'doing' one's own perceiving presents no particular problem for the understanding. Then it is of some significance that the actually realised possibility, in which we immediately will our own perceiving, should not merely be reminiscent of instrumentality, but should actually lie at a *dialectical remove* from instrumentality. Thus, the only way antinomy can be avoided and causal immediacy preserved in active hearing, is by the arise in Nature of a phenomenon which in the one stroke goes *outside of itself* causally without surrendering its own immediacy of operation; and the Will-to-listen dialectically accomplishes this seeming impossibility. The original intuition was born of the incapacity to imagine such a manner of coming into existence for the hearing component of listening.

(3) In the course of Section C, I have tried to map the several structures realised by the centrally important mental phenomenon: mental action. As it seems to me, I have brought to light a truly surprising structure for an absolutely central example of the type. Mental actions divide into thinkings and attendings. Then it must be of some significance that the form of one half of the active life of the mind should instantiate such an unusual structure.

References

Anscombe, G. E. M. (1962) 'On Sensations of Position', *Analysis* **22**, 55–58.

Armstrong, D. M. (1968) *A Materialist Theory of the Mind*, London: Routledge.

(1988) 'Perception and Belief', in *Perceptual Knowledge*, edited by Jonathan Dancy, Oxford: Oxford University Press, 127–144.

Austin, J. L. (1962) *Sense and Sensibilia*, Oxford: Clarendon Press.

Ayer, A. J. (1956) *The Problem of Knowledge*, Harmondsworth: Penguin.

Bach-y-Rita, P. (1972) *Sensory Substitution*, New York: Academic Press.

Barnes, W. H. F. (1944) 'The Myth of Sense Data', *Proceedings of the Aristotelian Society* **45**, 89–117.

Berkeley, George (1709) *An Essay Towards a New Theory of Vision*, in *Philosophical Works*, edited by M. R. Ayers, London: J. M. Dent, 1975.

Block, Ned (1983) 'Mental Pictures and Cognitive Science', *Philosophical Review* **92**, 399–451.

Boden, Margaret (1988) *Computer Models of Mind*, Cambridge: Cambridge University Press.

Bouwsma, O. K. (1942) 'Moore's Theory of Sense-Data', in *The Philosophy of G. E. Moore*, edited by P. A. Schilpp, Evanston, Ill.: Northwestern University Press, 203–221.

Bower, T. G. R. (1989) *The Rational Infant: Learning in Infancy*, New York: Freeman.

Broad, C. D. (1923) *Scientific Thought*, London: Kegan Paul.

Burge, Tyler (1974) 'Demonstrative Constructions, Reference, and Truth', *Journal of Philosophy* **71**, 205–223.

Campbell, John (1986) 'Conceptual Structure', in *Meaning and Interpretation*, edited by Charles Travis, Oxford: Blackwell, 159–174.

(1989) Review of Gareth Evans, *Collected Papers*, *Journal of Philosophy* **86**, 156–163.

Chisholm, R. (1942) 'The Problem of the Speckled Hen', *Mind* **51**, 368–373.

(1963) 'The Theory of Appearing', in *Philosophical Analysis*, edited by Max Black, Englewood Cliffs, N.J.: Prentice Hall, 97–112.

(1977) *Theory of Knowledge*, Englewood Cliffs, N.J.: Prentice Hall.

Churchland, Paul M. (1984) *Matter and Consciousness*, Cambridge, Mass.: MIT Press.

Clark, Andy (1989) *Microcognition: Philosophy, Cognitive Science and Parallel Distributed Processing*, Cambridge, Mass.: MIT Press.

Craig, Edward (1976) 'Sensory Experience and the Foundations of Knowledge', *Synthese* **33**, 1–24.

Crane, Tim (1988a) 'The Waterfall Illusion', *Analysis* **48**, 142–147.

(1988b) 'Concepts in Perception', *Analysis* **48**, 150–153.

(1990) 'The Language of Thought: no Syntax without Semantics', *Mind and Language* **5**, 187–212.

Cussins, Adrian (1990) 'The Connectionist Construction of Concepts', in *The Philosophy of Artificial Intelligence*, edited by Margaret Boden, Oxford: Oxford University Press, 368–440.

Davidson, Donald (1970) 'Mental Events', in *Experience and Theory*, edited by L. Foster and J. W. Swanson, London: Duckworth, 79–101.

Davies, Martin (1986) 'Tacit Knowledge and the Structure of Thought and Language', in *Meaning and Interpretation*, edited by Charles Travis, Oxford: Blackwell, 127–158.

(1989) 'Tacit Knowledge and Subdoxastic States', in *Reflections on Chomsky*, edited by Alexander George, Oxford: Blackwell, 131–152.

(forthcoming) 'Concepts, Connectionism and the Language of Thought', in *Philosophy and Connectionist Theory*, edited by D. Rumelhart, W. Ramsey and S. Stich, Hillsdale, N.J.: Lawrence Erlbaum Associates.

DeBellis, Mark (forthcoming) *Music and Conceptualisation*, Cambridge: Cambridge University Press.

Dennett, Daniel C. (1988) 'Quining Qualia', in *Consciousness in Contemporary Science*, edited by A. Marcel and E. Bisiach, Oxford: Clarendon Press, 42–77.

(forthcoming) 'Time and the architecture of human consciousness', *Philosophy and Phenomenological Research*.

Dretske, Fred I. (1969) *Seeing and Knowing*, Chicago: University of Chicago Press.

(1981) *Knowledge and the Flow of Information*, Oxford: Blackwell.

Dummett, Michael (1979) 'Common Sense and Physics', in *Perception and Identity*, edited by Graham Macdonald, London: Macmillan, 1–40.

Evans, Gareth (1981) 'Semantic Theory and Tacit Knowledge', in *Wittgenstein: To Follow a Rule*, edited by C. Holtzman and S. Leich, London: Routledge & Kegan Paul, 118–137.

(1982) *The Varieties of Reference*, Oxford: Clarendon Press.

(1985a) *Collected Papers*, Oxford: Clarendon Press.

(1985b) 'Molyneux's Question', in *Collected Papers*, Oxford: Clarendon Press, 364–400.

Fodor, Jerry A. (1981) 'The Present Status of the Innateness Controversy', in *Representations*, Hassocks: Harvester Press, 257–316.

(1983) *The Modularity of Mind*, Cambridge, Mass.: MIT Press.

(1987) *Psychosemantics: The Problem of Meaning in the Philosophy of Mind*, Cambridge, Mass.: MIT Press.

Foster, John (1985) *A. J. Ayer*, London: Routledge & Kegan Paul.

Frege, Gottlob (1980) *The Philosophical and Mathematical Correspondence*, translated by Hans Kall, edited by Brian McGuiness, Oxford: Blackwell.

Frisby, John (1980) *Seeing: Illusion, Brain and Mind*, Oxford: Oxford University Press.

Gibson, J. J. (1950) *The Perception of the Visual World*, Boston, Mass.: Houghton Mifflin.

(1968) *The Senses Considered as Perceptual Systems*, London: George Allen & Unwin.

Godwin-Austen, R. B. (1965) 'A Case of Visual Disorientation', *Journal of Neurology, Neurosurgery and Psychiatry* **28**, 453–458.

Gregory, Richard L. (1970) *The Intelligent Eye*, London: Weidenfeld & Nicolson.

(1972) *Eye and Brain: The Psychology of Seeing*, London: Weidenfeld & Nicolson.

Grice, H. P. (1962) 'Some Remarks about the Senses', in *Analytical Philosophy, First Series*, edited by R. J. Butler, Oxford: Blackwell, 133–153.

Guarniero, G. (1974) 'Experience of Tactile Vision', *Perception* **3**, 101–104.

Hamlyn, D. W. (1957) 'The Visual Field and Perception', *Proceedings of the Aristotelian Society Supplementary Volume* **31**, 107–124.

Hardin, C. L. (1988) *Colour for Philosophers*, Indianapolis: Hackett.

Harman, Gilbert (1989) 'The Intrinsic Quality of Experience', in *Philosophical Perspectives 4: Philosophy of Mind and Action Theory*, edited by James Tomberlin, Atascadero: Ridgeview, 31–52.

Hart, W. D. (1983) 'The Anatomy of Thought', *Mind* **92**, 264–269.

Heidegger, Martin (1968) *What is Called Thinking*, London: Harper & Row.

Hirst, R. J. (1959) *The Problems of Perception*, London: George Allen & Unwin.

Holmes, G. (1918) 'Disturbances of Visual Orientation', *British Journal of Ophthalmology* **2**, 449–468, 506–516.

Holmes, G. and Horrax, G. (1919) 'Disturbances of Spatial Orientation and Visual Attention, with Loss of Stereoscopic Vision', *Archives of Neurology and Psychiatry* **1**, 385–407.

Hume, David (1739) *A Treatise of Human Nature*, edited by L. A. Selby-Bigge, Oxford: Oxford University Press, 1978.

(1777) *Enquiries Concerning the Human Understanding and Concerning the Principles of Morals*, edited by L. A. Selby-Bigge, Oxford: Clarendon Press, 1902.

Humphreys, Glyn and Riddoch, Jane (1987) *To See But Not To See: A Case Study of Visual Agnosia*, London: Lawrence Erlbaum Associates.

Jackson, Frank (1976) 'The Existence of Mental Objects', *American Philosophical Quarterly* **13**, 23–40.

(1977) *Perception: a Representative Theory*, Cambridge: Cambridge University Press.

Julesz, B. (1971) *Foundations of Cyclopean Perception*, Chicago: University of Chicago Press.

Klatzky, R. L., Lederman, S. J. and Balakrishnan, J. D. (1991) 'Task-Driven Extraction of Object Contour by Human Haptics: I', *Robotica* **9**, 43–51.

Kuhn, Thomas (1970) *The Structure of Scientific Revolutions*, Chicago: Chicago University Press.

Lackner, J. R. (1988) 'Some Proprioceptive Influences on the Perceptual Representation of Body Shape and Orientation', *Brain* **111**, 281–291.

Lewis, David (1980) 'Mad Pain and Martian Pain', in *Readings in the Philosophy of Psychology*, edited by Ned Block, London: Methuen, 216–222.

(1983a) 'Individuation by Acquaintance and by Stipulation', *Philosophical Review* **92**, 3–32.

(1983b) 'Postscript to "Mad Pain and Martian Pain"', in *Philosophical Papers Volume I*, Oxford: Oxford University Press, 130–132.

(1990) 'What Experience Teaches', in *Mind and Cognition*, edited by W. G. Lycan, Oxford: Blackwell, 499–519.

Locke, John (1689) *An Essay Concerning Human Understanding*, edited by P. H. Nidditch, Oxford: Oxford University Press, 1975.

Loomis, J., Klatzky, R. L. and Lederman, S. J. (forthcoming) 'Similarity of Tactual and Visual Picture Recognition with Limited Field of View', *Perception*.

Loomis, J. and Lederman, S. J. (1986) 'Tactual Perception', in *Handbook of Perception and Human Performance II*, edited by K. R. Boff, L. Kaufman and J. P. Thomas, New York: John Wiley, 311–314.

Lowe, E. J. (1986a) 'The Topology of Visual Appearance', *Erkenntnis* **25**, 271–274.

(1986b) 'What Do We See Directly?', *American Philosophical Quarterly* **23**, 277–285.

Mach, Ernst (1914) *The Analysis of Sensations*, Chicago: Open Court.

Marr, David (1982) *Vision*, San Francisco: Freeman.

McCarthy, R. and Warrington, E. (1990) *Cognitive Neuropsychology*, London: Academic Press.

McGinn, Colin (1989) *Mental Content*, Oxford: Blackwell.

Mellor, D. H. (1977) 'Conscious Belief', *Proceedings of the Aristotelian Society* **68**, 87–101.

Merleau-Ponty, M. (1962) *The Phenomenology of Perception*, London: Routledge & Kegan Paul.

Millar, Alan (1991) *Reasons and Experience*, Oxford: Clarendon Press.

Moore, G. E. (1905) 'The Nature and Reality of Objects of Perception', *Proceedings of the Aristotelian Society* **6**, 68–127.

(1913) 'The Status of Sense-Data', *Proceedings of the Aristotelian Society* **14**, 355–381.

(1918) 'Some Judgements of Perception', *Proceedings of the Aristotelian Society* **19**, 1–29.

(1922) *Philosophical Studies*, London: Routledge.

(1942) 'A Reply to my Critics', in *The Philosophy of G. E. Moore*, edited by P. A. Schilpp, Evanston, Ill.: Northwestern University Press, 535–677.

(1959) *Philosophical Papers*, London: George Allen & Unwin.

(1962) *Some Main Problems of Philosophy*, London: Collier.

(1965) 'Visual Sense-Data', in *Perceiving, Sensing and Knowing*, edited by R. J. Schwartz, California: University of California Press, 130–137.

Morgan, M. J. (1977) *Molyneux's Question*, Cambridge: Cambridge University Press.

Mundle, C. W. K. (1971) *Perception: Facts and Theories*, Oxford: Oxford University Press.

O'Shaughnessy, Brian (1980) *The Will: a Dual Aspect Theory* (2 volumes), Cambridge: Cambridge University Press.

(1985) 'Seeing the Light', *Proceedings of the Aristotelian Society* **85**, 193–218.

(1989) 'The Sense of Touch', *Australasian Journal of Philosophy* **67**, 37–58.

Palmer, Stephen (1983) 'The Psychology of Perceptual Organization: A Transformational Approach', in *Human and Machine Vision*, edited by J. Beck, New York: Academic Press, 269–339.

Paul, G. A. (1936) 'Is there a Problem about Sense-Data?', *Proceedings of the Aristotelian Society Supplementary Volume* **15**, 61–77.

Peacocke, Christopher (1983) *Sense and Content*, Oxford: Oxford University Press.

(1986a) 'Analogue Content', *Proceedings of the Aristotelian Society Supplementary Volume* **60**, 1–17.

(1986b) *Thoughts*, Oxford: Blackwell.

(1987) 'Understanding Logical Constants: A Realist's Account', *Proceedings of the British Academy* **73**, 153–200.

(1989a) 'Perceptual Content', in *Themes from Kaplan*, edited by J. Almog, J. Perry and H. Wettstein, Oxford: Oxford University Press, 297–329.

(1989b) 'Possession Conditions: a Focal Point for Theories of Concepts', *Mind and Language* **5**, 51–56.

(1989c) *Transcendental Arguments in the Theory of Content*, Oxford: Oxford University Press.

(1989d) 'What Are Concepts?', in *Midwest Studies in Philosophy: Contemporary Perspectives in the Philosophy of Language II* **14**, 1–28.

Penfield, W. and Roberts, L. (1959) *Speech and Brain Mechanisms*, Princeton, N.J.: Princeton University Press.

Perenin, M-T. and Vighetto, A. (1988) 'Optic Ataxia: A Specific Disruption in Visuomotor Mechanisms', *Brain* **111**, 643–674.

Pinker, Steven (1985) 'Visual Cognition: An Introduction', in *Visual Cognition*, edited by Steven Pinker, Cambridge, Mass.: MIT Press, 1–65.

Pitcher, George (1971) *A Theory of Perception*, Princeton N.J.: Princeton University Press

Price, H. H. (1932) *Perception*, London: Methuen.

Putnam, Hilary (1975) 'The Meaning of "Meaning"', in *Mind, Language and Reality*, Cambridge: Cambridge University Press, 215–271.

Pylyshyn, Zenon W. (1984) *Computation and Cognition*, Cambridge, Mass.: MIT Press.

Quine, W. V. O. (1960) 'Variables Explained Away', *Proceedings of the American Philosophical Society* **104**, 343–347.

(1969) 'Propositional Objects', in *Ontological Relativity*, New York: Columbia University Press, 139–160.

Reid, Thomas (1785) *Essays on the Intellectual Powers of Man*, edited by Baruch Brody, Cambridge, Mass.: MIT Press, 1969.

Riddoch, G. (1917) 'Dissociation of Visual Perceptions Due to Occipital Injuries, with Especial Reference to Appreciation of Movement', *Brain* **40**, 15–56.

Rock, Irvin (1975) *An Introduction to Perception*, New York: Macmillan.

(1983) *The Logic of Perception*, Cambridge, Mass.: MIT Press.

Russell, Bertrand (1912) *The Problems of Philosophy*, Oxford: Oxford University Press.

(1918) 'The Relation of Sense-Data to Physics', in *Mysticism and Logic*, London: George Allen & Unwin, 108–131.

(1956) 'The Philosophy of Logical Atomism', in *Logic and Knowledge*, edited by Robert C. Marsh, London: George Allen & Unwin, 175–281.

Ryle, Gilbert (1949) *The Concept of Mind*, London: Hutchinson.

Sanford, David (1983) 'The Perception of Shape', in *Knowledge and Mind*, edited by Carl Ginet and Sydney Shoemaker, Oxford: Oxford University Press, 130–158.

Searle, John (1983) *Intentionality*, Cambridge: Cambridge University Press.

Segal, Gabriel (1989) 'Seeing What is Not There', *Philosophical Review* **98**, 189–214.

Shepard, Roger (1981) 'Psychophysical Complementarity', in *Perceptual Organization*, edited by M. Kubovy and J. Pomerantz, Hillsdale, N.J.: Lawrence Erlbaum Associates, 279–341.

Shoemaker, Sydney (1975) 'Functionalism and Qualia', *Philosophical Studies* **27**, 271–315.

(forthcoming) 'Qualities and Qualia: What's in the Mind?'

Sibley, Frank, ed. (1971) *Perception: a Symposium*, London: Macmillan.

Snowdon, Paul (1990) 'The Objects of Perceptual Experience', *Proceedings of the Aristotelian Society Supplementary Volume* **64**, 121–150.

Stampe, Dennis W. (1977) 'Toward a Causal Theory of Linguistic Representation', in *Midwest Studies in Philosophy*, edited by Peter A. French, Theodore E. Uehling and Howard K. Wettstein, Morris, Minn.: The University of Minnesota Press, 42–63.

Stich, Stephen P. (1983) *From Folk Psychology to Cognitive Science: the Case Against Belief*, Cambridge, Mass.: MIT Press.

Stratton, G. M. (1897) 'Vision Without Inversion of the Retinal Image', *Psychological Review* **4**, 341–360, 463–481.

Strawson, P. F. (1979) 'Perception and its Objects', in *Perception and Identity: Essays Presented to A. J. Ayer*, edited by G. Macdonald, London: Macmillan, 41–60.

Treisman, A. and Gelade, G. (1980) 'A Feature-Integration Theory of Attention', *Cognitive Psychology* **12**, 97–136.

Treisman, A. and Schmidt, H. (1982) 'Illusory Conjunctions in the Perception of Objects', *Cognitive Psychology* **14**, 107–141.

Tye, Michael (1983) 'Functionalism and Type Physicalism', *Philosophical Studies* **44**, 161–174.

(1984) 'The Adverbial Approach to Visual Experience', *Philosophical Review* **93**, 195–226.

(1986) 'The Subjective Quality of Experience', *Mind* **95**, 1–17.

(1988) 'The Picture Theory of Mental Images', *Philosophical Review* **97**, 497–520.

(1989) *The Metaphysics of Mind*, Cambridge: Cambridge University Press.

(1991) *The Imagery Debate*, Cambridge, Mass.: MIT Press.

Valberg, J. J. (forthcoming) *The Puzzle of Experience*, Oxford: Oxford University Press.

Volpe, B. T., Le Doux, J. E. and Gazzaniga, M. (1979) 'Spatially Oriented Movements in the Absence of Proprioception', *Neurology* **29**, 1309–1313.

von Békésy, G. (1967) *Sensory Inhibition*, Princeton, N.J.: Princeton University Press.

Ward, James (1918) *Psychological Principles*, Cambridge: Cambridge University Press.

Weiskrantz, L. (1986) *Blindsight: A Case Study and Implications*, Oxford: Oxford University Press.

(1987) 'Neuropsychology and the Nature of Consciousness', in *Mindwaves*, edited by Colin Blakemore and Susan Greenfield, Oxford: Blackwell, 307–320.

(1988) 'Some Contributions of Neuropsychology of Vision and Memory to the Problem of Consciousness', in *Consciousness in Contemporary Science*, edited by A. J. Marcel and E. Bisiach, Oxford: Clarendon Press, 183–199.

Weiskrantz, L., Warrington, E. K., Saunders, M. D. and Marshall, J. (1974) 'Visual Capacity in the Hemianopic Field Following a Restricted Occipital Ablation', *Brain* **97**, 709–728.

Wittgenstein, Ludwig (1958) *The Blue and Brown Books*, Oxford: Blackwell.

(1980) *Philosophy of Psychology* (2 volumes), Oxford: Blackwell.

Index